WOODROW WILSON

THE MAN, HIS TIMES, AND HIS TASK

Copyright by Harris & Ewing

Woodrow Wilson

WOODROW WILSON

THE MAN, HIS TIMES AND HIS TASK

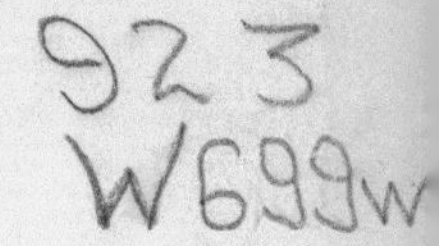

BY

WILLIAM ALLEN WHITE

*Author of "Stratagems and Spoils," "A Certain Rich Man"
"The Martial Adventures of Henry and Me," "In the Heart of a Fool"*

WITH ILLUSTRATIONS

BOSTON AND NEW YORK
HOUGHTON MIFFLIN COMPANY
The Riverside Press Cambridge

SECOND IMPRESSION, OCTOBER, 1924
THIRD IMPRESSION, JANUARY, 1925

The Riverside Press
CAMBRIDGE · MASSACHUSETTS
PRINTED IN THE U.S.A.

CONTENTS

ILLUSTRATIONS

INTRODUCTION

THIS book will try to tell the story, as simply as it may be told, of a man, his time, and his task. The story will disclose no new events nor details nor circumstances in the life of Woodrow Wilson, but perhaps the arrangement of our biographical material may help his contemporaries to a better understanding of him and his work. His partisans have idealized his virtues and so have sought to create a superman — some sort of Heaven-sent Messiah to redeem a wicked world from its iniquity. His enemies — alas, they have seen his weakness through the green and red glasses of envy and hate, and a fine old striped devil they have made of him. He was neither God nor fiend, but in his political career rather a shy, middle-aged gentleman with the hoar frost of the cloister upon his public manner, with an academic respect for facts and with a Calvinistic addiction for digesting the facts into his own God-given truth. On the surface he was half or two thirds Irish, and so turned to his friends a gay and lovely face. But the dour Scot, big and dominant inside him, turned to his adversaries a cold and implacable heart that transformed even the most amiable of his opponents into ardent foes with a lust for torture.

So he went his way through a crisis in the life of our civilization. He took leadership in great days, and put into his leadership all the power outside himself that lay in the hearts of his countrymen yearning for righteousness. Perhaps when the power he wielded is spent, when the forces he released find equilibrium in stable institutions, after the chaos of to-day has settled into to-morrow's order, he may rise from the day of his leadership to heroic stature. No one knows now how the dice of fame will fall. To guess is futile. But to examine the evidence in the story of his life and to try to get at some approximate of reality amid the romance of hero tales and devil myths gathering about the name of Woodrow Wilson may be a worthy exercise for those of us who flatter ourselves with a belief that we see things impartially. For the others, whether they enjoy burning incense or witches, this book will be an offense.

Also it may fail to satisfy scholars who take it up hoping to find historical data in these pages. It is not a source book. It contains only such research as may be achieved by talking with the friends of Wilson's boyhood and youth or occasionally listening to his dear familiar enemies chant an exorcism.

So much for the man. The times in which he

lived and worked probably were just such times as are forever running across the loom of human destiny. But the times in which men live always seem grand and awful times. It is the past which is dull, and perhaps the future seems unimportant. But these present times, the years of the generation now on earth, the period in which Woodrow Wilson worked while we his fellow worldlings lived — how stirring they were and are! The social, economic, and political order all over Europe and America has passed in due form and regular order from the simple to the more complex. In America, this evolutionary change from the reaction of conservatism after the Civil War to the lively struggle for liberalism began with Bryan and the Populists in the last ten years of the nineteenth century, continued under Roosevelt for a decade, and came to a rather substantial victory under President Wilson just before the World War called his country to forget local issues and to fight. He entered politics as an American liberal. He quit politics with the liberal field so widened that for a time he held world leadership.

His task was hard. He worked against terrible odds, many of which were in his own heart. He achieved much; he left much undone. But his sincerity, his honesty, his consecration to the work before him never were questioned. Just how far nobility of purpose will overcome shortcomings of temperament, no one can say. It is not the purpose of this book to answer that query.

If the story that follows reveals the man faithfully going upon his errand — that is enough. Posterity only will know whether he finished the errand or whether he failed before reaching the goal. It is not the purpose of this biography to essay prophecy, to forestall posterity in the joy of crowning its hero, or to trouble posterity if it forgets him. Only this much hope have we about posterity: that if it does crown our hero, it may find here some semblance of his lineaments; the flesh-and-blood faults, the spiritual attributes of striving, if sometimes futile nobility, the parts that make a man.

A word as to the sources of this book. I knew Woodrow Wilson but slightly. I met him casually several times: once while he was Governor of New Jersey, two or three times while he was President, once or twice in the White House, and I saw him once in Paris. I have been in audiences where I have heard him speak. I heard him declare for Preparedness in 1915. I heard him read the covenant of the League of Nations. From these glimpses of his personality, I caught no very dependable impression of the man. All the gayety, affection, and charm to which a crowd of witnesses testify so unanimously, I did not see. He seemed to me hard and repellent. I first met him at Madison, Wisconsin, when he was Governor of New Jersey. I was a fervent believer in his policies, and I came into his presence a hero-worshiper. I had written several editorials supporting his cause which he had seen; which at least he acknowledged. When I met him, he gave me a hand that felt very much like a five-cent mackerel; cold, stiff, moist, unresponsive, extended something as though a clerk desiring a larger sale would casually poke the fish across a counter. He smiled, but I got the wrong side of his face, a side which gave me a certain impression of a reptilian personality — a strong sense of some essential treachery in the man! At the White House, where once I called after coming home from Europe bursting with the feeling that the success of the war demanded that we should declare war on Austria as we had already declared war upon Germany, he met me with some show of grace, some weary attempt at charm, and then cut under my high hopes by explaining why we couldn't declare war on Austria. He began elaborating the theory which maintained that we should drive the Turk out of Europe at all cost.

I had supported him in all of his major policies and he had been kind enough to write to me more than courteous appreciation of my support. Later, in Europe, he appointed me as a delegate to a conference with representatives from exterior and interior Russia which should try to effect a peaceful settlement of the Russian problem rather than the military settlement which the French seemed at that time determined to enforce. The French diplomatically made the conference impossible. A letter or two to me in that period revealed a strong, purposeful gentleman, not too busy to write a kindly line to a follower. My unshaken belief in the sincerity of his purpose and the purity of his motives, together with this slight personal contact, was my only preliminary equipment for this work.

Naturally during the months of preparation, I have traveled far, have talked to many people, and have read many books. Probably those persons to whom I have talked have helped more than the books I have read to realize the inherently sweet and kindly nature of the upper layers of Woodrow Wilson's consciousness. I am under greatest debt to Stockton Axson, brother-in-law of President Wilson; but an obligation nearly as heavy rests upon me when I think of Colonel Edward M. House, his friend for eight years. His friend, Dean Henry Fine, of Princeton, has helped also; and President Wilson's Princeton adversary, Dean West, of the Graduate School, has given me much real assistance. In the South I am indebted to many of his boyhood friends and acquaintances. There are first of all General W. A. Clark, of the Bank of Carolina, Columbia, South Carolina, who knew James Woodrow, the President's uncle; and almost abreast with him is William H. Fleming, of Augusta, Georgia; also Joseph M. Little, of Wilmington, North Carolina; John D. Bellamy and his sister Miss Bellamy, of Wilmington, North Carolina; Mrs. Anna Hardwick, of Augusta, Georgia; Dr. Joseph R. Sevier, of Augusta, Georgia; Major George T. Butler, of Augusta, Georgia; Professor Joseph T. Derry, of Jacksonville, Florida; Mrs. Eugene Vedery, Sr., of Augusta, Georgia; Dr. John M. Wells, of Columbia, South Carolina; the Honorable Pleasant A. Stovall, of Savannah, Georgia; William G. Sutlive, of Savannah, Georgia; E. B. Hood, of Augusta, Georgia; T. A. Cunningham, of Quincy, Florida; Mrs. Thomas E. Winn, of Greensboro, Georgia; David Bryant, of Wilmington, North Carolina, and the MacMasters family, of Columbia, South Carolina.

In Steubenville, Ohio, is a particularly intelligent group of people who are interested in local history. To them I am under deep obligation. They are: the Reverend Burleigh Cruickshank, W. McD. Miller, and Joseph B. Doyle.

Robert Bridges, of New York City; Ray Stannard Baker, of Amherst, Massachusetts; James Kerney, of Trenton, New Jersey; George L. Record, of Jersey City, New Jersey; Mrs. Mary Hulbert, of New York City; Joseph P. Tumulty, of Washington, D.C.; Victor Murdock, of Wichita, Kansas; and Miss Helen Bones, of New York City — all devoted friends at one time or another — showed me the finer, sweeter side of the man with testimony which cannot be shaken.

Others who have substantially helped are: Dr. E. A. Alderman, of Charlottesville, Virginia; Norman Angell, of London, England; George Barr Baker, of New York City; E. G. Conklin, of Princeton, New Jersey; Bennett C. Clark, of St. Louis, Missouri; V. Lansing Collins, of Princeton, New Jersey; W. S. Culbertson, of Washington, D.C.; Cleveland H. Dodge, of New York City; Oscar King Davis, of New York City; Joseph Dixon, of Missoula, Montana; Raymond Fosdick, of New York City; Irving Fisher, of New Haven, Connecticut; Professor Richard T. Ely, of Madison, Wisconsin; Herbert Adams Gibbons, of Princeton, New Jersey; Gilson Gardner, of Washington, D.C.; Christian A. Herter, of Boston, Massachusetts; Herbert Hoover, of Washington, D.C.; Bayard Henry, of Philadelphia, Pennsylvania; Gilbert M. Hitchcock, of Omaha, Nebraska; Dr.

Theodore W. Hunt, of Princeton, New Jersey; George S. Johns, of St. Louis, Missouri; President J. G. Hibben, Princeton, New Jersey; Norman Hapgood, of New York City; H. H. Kohlsaat, of New York City; Vernon L. Kellogg, of Washington, D.C.; U. G. Mitchell, of Lawrence, Kansas; Cyrus H. McCormick, of Chicago, Illinois; Howard W. Odum, of Chapel Hill, North Carolina; C. Wells Reeder, of Columbus, Ohio; William H. Short, of New York City; Henry van Dyke, of Princeton, New Jersey; Huston Thompson, of Washington, D.C.; Miss Margaret Woodrow Wilson, of New York City; W. L. Westerman, New York City; Joseph R. Wilson, of Baltimore, Maryland; Miss Ida M. Tarbell, of New York City; and Mrs. Anna Wilson Maccoy, of El Paso, Texas.

Much of the material from these people has been anecdotal in its form, and one might string out Wilson stories to fill many volumes. I have tried to take only those that were revealing and significant. I have not thought it necessary to set down my sources in footnotes. Perhaps this is a mistake, but as I have said before, this is not a source book nor a documented, official biography. Such a book, of course, will come later and should be widely read.

Many books have been written about Mr. Wilson. I have read and am greatly indebted to the books by

David Lawrence, Josephus Daniels, Ray Stannard Baker, Robert Bender, of the United Press; George D. Herron, Mrs. Borden Harriman, Charles Reed Bacon, Robert Edward Annin, Hester E. Hosford, Marion W. Woodrow, who wrote the life of James Woodrow, the President's uncle; Edward M. House and Charles Seymour; Edgar E. Robinson and Victor J. West, of Stanford University; H. H. Powers, William Bayard Hale, William E. Dodd, and Joseph Tumulty; and the volume of editorials entitled "Cobb of the World."

If these books, these dear friends, and these intimate enemies of Woodrow Wilson have given me a portrait of him that is fairly consistent and upon the whole kind and true, I have tried earnestly and honestly to transform that portrait into this book.

W. A. White

Emporia, Kansas
September 1, 1924

WOODROW WILSON

PART ONE

The Bugle-Call of Youth

WOODROW WILSON

• •
•

CHAPTER I

THE MIRACLE OF HEREDITY

WOODROW WILSON, twenty-eighth President of the United States, had in his veins no blood of our Revolutionary stock. He was a newcomer — Irish for two hundred years and more on his father's side of the family and Scotch back to the Druids on his mother's side. His grandparents left Ireland and Scotland nearly half a century after the Americans had declared their independence. No ancestor fought in any of our American wars — the wars with England, the war with Mexico, or the war between the States. Yet in his spiritual inheritance he held the philosophy that has been remaking the world during the passing four hundred years; the philosophy that more than any other force has directed the course of American institutions and has made the United States the home of the brave and the land of the free. Woodrow Wilson was an inbred Calvinist. His father's father, James Wilson, an Irish emigrant from Londonderry, Ireland, married a Presbyterian Irish girl, a shipmate, the day after their American landing, and their child, Joseph Ruggles Wilson, the father of the President, born in 1822, grew up to be a Presbyterian College professor and preacher who married Janet Woodrow, a Scotch girl nicknamed "Jessie," whose mother died on the Atlantic Ocean. Janet Woodrow, mother of President Wilson, was the daughter and the granddaughter on both sides of her family, of Presbyterian College professors and preachers. It matters little that the Wilson blood was new to the American wilderness of a century ago; spiritually Woodrow Wilson was the inheritor of the race that opened the Bible, and demanded freedom for the conscience of man — as American as Jonathan Edwards or Cotton Mather or John Witherspoon. In his soul echoed the ancient war-cry of the unconquered Celt. The fighting Irish who were his father's people and the rebellious Scots who were his mother's people, welded in him by the non-conforming creed of Calvin and Knox, made Woodrow Wilson what he was. It was foreordained and predestined by the inexorable canons of spiritual biology that a child born in this freehold of Calvin and Knox should serve his God and fight his devil according to his own light, wherever the path of mere circumstances might lead him across a miserable world.

The Irish Wilson, grandfather of the President, was James Wilson, born 1787, who came from a tribe that liked to call themselves Scotch-Irish despite their two hundred and fifty years in Ireland. This Scotch-Irish appellation was presumed to distinguish them from the Roman Catholic Irish of the south of Ireland. His shipmate, Ann Adams, also of the north of Ireland, was from a Presbyterian family.

Naturally this young Irish couple went to the home of the Presbyterian parson of their landing-place, the Reverend George C. Polk, of the Fourth Presbyterian Church of Philadelphia, and were married there November 1, 1808. Thus was the house of Wilson established in America. Ten children were born to this couple, all reared strictly in the faith of Calvin and Knox. James Wilson, the founder of the American family, was evidently a town-bred man. For he was a printer. And he seems to have found a job with a fire-eating editor, William Duane, for whom the first Wilson child was named. William Duane, a local politician, a stormy petrel, one of Thomas Jefferson's friends and enemy of nearly every one else in the young country, left his paper in 1812, when the war with England came, to young James Wilson, who, being Irish, was known as "Jimmie." The young man had the Irish ambition and the enterprise of his race. He had worked up from printer to foreman, from foreman to publisher, and from publisher to editor, all in four years. After the War of 1812, Duane had but small interest in the paper, and a few years later went to South America, where revolutions more fitting to his unfettered style of journalism gave free scope to his talent.

"Jimmie" Wilson and his constantly increasing little tribe of Irish Presbyterians, left Philadelphia soon after the war closed with the Treaty of Ghent. They went West with the great flood of restless Americans to the Ohio Valley. The steamboat had preceded them and the railroad was at their heels. A new civilization was taking root — rank, ugly, vigorous — the civilization that was to bear the terrible, poisonous, beautiful, and appalling flower of American industrialism a century later. Its capital then was Pittsburgh, as it is to-day. Coal had been discovered in the Ohio Valley. Little forges and furnaces were belching smoke in the great woods of the valley and little towns were blistering the clearings. Into this bustling wilderness with his family of four — which in rapid, regular order became ten — "Jimmie" Wilson came, the Irish printer-editor, and Ann Adams, his wife. Passing, we should note Ann Adams, his wife. She was as virile as he. She grew into a rather stern figure. She quarreled with a daughter who left home at marriage never to return,

ANN ADAMS WILSON

and the mother never forgave her. After bearing ten children, she came to wear under her frilled lace bonnet, in her sixties and seventies, a hard, implacable, almost belligerent face. Her husband's face softened as he grew old. He first worked at his trade at Pittsburgh after coming West; then he prospected at Lisbon across the Ohio border. Then he took the plunge into the great adventure of his life and went to Steubenville, Ohio, a new boom river town but a few miles from the Pennsylvania line, and there he bought a paper. It was called the "Western Herald" and was established in 1806.

So "Jimmie" Wilson became a country editor and grew up with the town. He taught every one of his boys the printer's trade, and after they began to grow too big for Steubenville he started a paper in Pittsburgh. He called it the "Pennsylvania Advocate." And though it was printed at first at Steubenville, Ohio, he entered it in the post-office at Pittsburgh and a short time afterward published it there. He finally gave the Pittsburgh paper to his eldest son, William Duane, and the father devoted most of his time to the "Western Herald" at Steubenville.

There, in 1822, Joseph Ruggles Wilson, father of the President, was born. The record of the church at Steubenville, Ohio, where the Wilsons lived for forty years, shows that Ann Adams, his mother, joined the church by examination after profession of her faith. It reads:

38, Ann A. Wilson, E — October 18, 1823.

The initials "C" and "E" are used in the book; "C" indicating entrance by certificate from another church; "E" indicating entrance by examination. The name of her husband, James Wilson, who was an attendant at the church with his family, does not appear on the books. But the Presbyterian mother took no chances with her children. They joined, and the "E's" stand after their names.

Something more must be set down here about the early environment of Joseph Ruggles Wilson. For he was his son's idol, and his son was a President of the United States. Any one who studies the life of Woodrow Wilson finds him time and again paying tribute to his father, who was surely an unusual man. And something of his quality of distinction came out of this country printing office in the noisy, growing river town in Ohio. Editor James Wilson, of the Steubenville "Herald," was true to the professional type of his day. For from the beginning of the nineteenth century until its closing decades, the newspaper business in America was a romantic but precarious trade. It combined polite blackmail and high patriotism with mendacious beggary in such charming proportions that it attracted adventurous youth to whom an effete civilization was punctiliously closing careers in brigandage and piracy in the interests of a stable economic progress. "Jimmie" Wilson, of the Steubenville "Herald," was of that adventurous band. He had a "vitriolic pen," and kept his more intimate enemies vacillating between desires for litigation and assassination. Mr. Samuel Medary of Ohio was one of Editor "Jimmie" Wilson's pet snakes. Mr. Medary was a proslavery Democrat, who afterwards went to Kansas as a Territorial governor appointed by President Buchanan. Medary made a mess of his Kansas job, and hurt the proslavery cause. Naturally Editor Wilson, whose paper had declared against Andrew Jackson and who was to have two sons Union generals in the Civil War, would have none of Samuel Medary and his kind. So he spelled his name "Samedary" and compared him to the Wilson dog, Towser. Editor Wilson went to the legislature while Ann Adams, his wife, got out the paper and boarded the "hands"; later, in life's mellow afternoon, the halo of the judiciary crowned his brow, when he was elected associate justice of the local court in Steubenville. And he who had been "Jimmie," "Uncle Jimmie," "Printer" Wilson, to distinguish him from "Banker" Wilson who was of no kin to him, became "The Judge," thus properly dignifying the latter days of one who was to be grandfather of a President. He was a man of parts and consequence. They will show you at Steubenville the piers of a railroad bridge which he and the Steubenville town boomers built — the first railroad bridge across the Ohio. James Wilson was the first name in the list of incorporators of "the Steubenville and Indiana Railroad" that afterwards became a part of the Pennsylvania Railroad. He was a born hustler, a boomer, a town booster, and when the town and township voted $200,000 to buy the railroad bonds, the "Herald" and its editor urged the people to it with all the fervor of the Irish. When the "Leading Citizens" went out to the mills, got the striking weavers drunk, and voted them on election day, if "Jimmie" Wilson was not of the precious band of patriots who saved the town from the loathed opposition, the "Herald" prints nothing to rebuke the local saviors. The weavers and the Quakers — among whom was the father of William Dean Howells, the novelist — located at Mount Pleasant, a neighboring county town; they and the coal miners and the farmers made the public opinion of the community. It never had a hanging. It established a station for fleeing slaves from the South. The silk weavers wove a silk vest for Henry

Clay, who stopped at Steubenville going to Washington, and the woolen weavers used their bolts of cloth in lieu of currency. Coal oil was in some way extracted from coke. The town had foundries, a glass factory, built steamboats, and maintained a rope walk. It was that kind of a town; boiling with dreams of empire, bubbling with energy, slipshod, slam-bang, and giving lip service to democracy while breeding a plutocracy with all its might. Here "Printer" Wilson cracked his jokes, played politics, hobnobbed with Congressmen — John C. Wright, who later became Judge of the Supreme Court of Ohio, Senator Tom Ewing, Edwin Stanton, afterwards Lincoln's Secretary of War — listened to Emerson, who came to town to lecture, heard Wendell Phillips, who came to agitate, and mingled with the gentle professors in the various seminaries and academies that were set about the county. Here in his latter days he became a bank director and built his grand house, a central edifice planned with two wings like the Carroll house in Maryland. Wilson's house was not completed until after he died. But here Judge Wilson passed his last years in the grand atmosphere of a raw day in our national life; a day of grand vision, grand frauds, and sometimes grand achievement. Here were the roots struck into the heart of his country, from which in the third generation his grandson rose.

James Wilson died of cholera in 1850 — a jovial old soul, if Steubenville tradition preserves him correctly, who dabbled in politics, dealt in real estate, and made money enough to build one of the show houses of the town.

He left his all to his wife by will, and made his youngest son, Joseph, joint executor with his mother.

We may now proceed to consider Joseph Ruggles Wilson, father of the President. The printing office with its lyric position, generating great power out of eternal poverty and eminent respectability, was his boyhood home. In the "Herald" office he printed his own boy's paper. He learned the printer's trade and so earned his board and keep at home attending the schools of the town. He had a head for learning and so the editor, who had put all of his other boys into business, decided to give the youngest a college education. Joseph went to Jefferson College, at Cannonsville, Pennsylvania, one of those little fresh-water colleges that always have thrived in America and have always returned to the country that supports them more than their quota of useful men. Jefferson College afterwards became Washington and Jefferson College. But in those days of the eighteen-forties the school must have taught its simple curriculum rather well. At least it turned out two scholars who were to figure in Woodrow

Wilson's scholarly career, one his father, the other his uncle, Thomas Woodrow. In the midst of his college course, when he was twenty, Joseph Ruggles joined the Presbyterian Church upon a profession of faith. His name stands on page 327 of the church record:

327 Joseph R. Wilson, "E", May 3rd, 1840.

In that day he was a tall, handsome youth who showed his Irish blood by a certain dashing cut of his jib. And while his profession of faith was from a deep and ever-abiding conviction of the righteous order of the universe, he never lost the gayety of his blood in gloomy meditations upon the wickedness of a lost world. To the day of his death the glint of joy twinkled in his eye. He was graduated from Jefferson College in 1844. That he was valedictorian of his class presumes his scholarship and indicates that his gift for writing and speaking was developed in his youth. This talent for language probably was stimulated by the environment of the printing office. He taught a year, taking charge of an academy at Mercer, Pennsylvania, then hurried out of teaching into preparation for preaching by going to the Western Theological Seminary at Allegheny and then on to Princeton. He came home licensed to preach, but not ordained, and waiting for a pulpit taught two years in the "Male Academy" of Steubenville which also supported a "Female Academy."

To this academy came Janet Woodrow, a pretty Scotch girl with curls and a sweet and engaging smile, who first saw through a paling fence the meticulous young theologue, home from college, raking the parental yard in gloves. The gloves caught her eye. Whereat she smiled over the paling fence and produced certain pathological thrills which, unless checked, end in matrimony or the sorrow of a life. They never were checked. Three years later, after her graduation, Joseph R. Wilson and Janet Woodrow, daughter of the Reverend Thomas Woodrow, Presbyterian minister of Chillicothe, Ohio, were married. Her father performed the marriage service for the young couple in the Presbyterian manse. Thus the father and mother of Woodrow Wilson were married in a Presbyterian manse, and all of his grandparents were married in Presbyterian manses — the Wilsons in Philadelphia and the Woodrows in Carlisle, England, just below the Scotch border. President Wilson's father was a Presbyterian preacher, his maternal grandfather and two of his great-grandfathers were Presbyterian preachers. And in his youth Woodrow Wilson, himself, married a Presbyterian minister's daughter in a Presbyterian manse. If ever a man was called and elected, foreordained and predestined to Presbyterianism, he was Woodrow Wilson, for twenty years elder of the Presbyterian Church at Princeton, New Jersey, later communicant at a Presbyterian Church at Washington, whose dust rests uneasily outcast in an Episcopal Cathedral in the District of Columbia; the first of at least ten generations who could not lie down to sleep beside the house of his father's faith.

The marriage of Joseph R. Wilson and Janet Woodrow was celebrated in June, 1849. Joseph Wilson was ordained in July a Presbyterian preacher, and forthwith the young people began looking for a better place than that of teacher in a boy's school. So Joseph Wilson, having early developed a nice ear for language, the heritage of the printing office, became professor of rhetoric at Jefferson College, his alma mater, and later went to Hampden Sidney College in Virginia, where young Wilson pieced out his salary as a teacher of "chemistry and natural sciences" by preaching. He was a thrifty and enterprising man, always climbing up in the world. The ambition of his Irish parents was in him. He was restless and moved often — but always kept an upward trend to his life; never once did it take a downward curve.

The Wilsons went to Staunton, Virginia, in 1855, where the husband had his first pastorate. Preaching, not teaching, was his forte. He adorned the pulpit well — a tall young man with a flashing eye, with a deep resonant bass voice, and with a fine shocky head of hair. He also maintained at the period of his festive young manhood a pious, respectable neck whisker and sideburns which haloed his handsome face. It smiled easily, that gay Irish face, with a charm that its owner could not entirely ignore. He would also have his joke with the people of the street, even in Staunton, Virginia, where the Presbyterian minister was *ex officio* a member of the aristocracy. For no recluse was the Reverend Joseph Wilson nor æsthete. He liked a good Presbyterian Sunday dinner and a good nip of Presbyterian Scotch of a Monday as well as any full-blooded man in the State. And he carried himself and all his contents — his college education, his Princeton theology and the fine Irish way of him — always like the scholar and the gentleman that he was. No gentleman is so courtly as the Irish gentleman. And when the Reverend Joseph Ruggles Wilson, a tall, commanding figure with a college education and a Princeton manner back of him, came to Staunton, Virginia, to shepherd the elect in the Presbyterian Church, he entered the place as a prince into his realm. Steubenville, his birthplace, was new, raw, democratic, boisterous, growing in a boom, after the

REV. JOSEPH R. WILSON

JANET WOODROW WILSON

Western fashion, of course; there the Wilsons led. But they wrested leadership out of Steubenville by their wits, by their energy, by their enterprise and thrift; outhustling the hustlers, outwitting the cunning, outsaving the prudent in a new town intent upon gestating a great civilization in its womb. But Staunton was old as age goes in America — old and static — a finished social product with only such industrial impediments as were necessary to maintain the graceful aristocracy in Augusta County in state and style. Into this painted social minuet stepped Joseph Ruggles Wilson with his pretty wife, with long curls about her face, and with their two girl-babies. There he was an aristocrat by the Divine right of his cloth and the royal grant of his Irish blood. The old Kings of Ireland never begot a more gorgeous prince. Staunton, Virginia, in that day was a town of four thousand, with a dozen churches, a group of female seminaries, an iron foundry or so, and a brickyard; and with the social lines clearly marked — jelly-caked from slave to workman, from workman to the skilled artisan in his own shop, from him to storekeeper, from small merchant to large, from doctor, lawyer, preacher, to landed gentleman, the pink-bedizened frosting on the cake. No uneasy question disturbed the calm of the Virginia community. God — and there was Scripture for it —

had set each man in his place, and it was no part of a young Irish Presbyterian minister to question the conventions of God. So he danced through the figure of the times, ordained in his place, and never questioned the piper nor his tune, nor dreamed of a day when the dancers might pay the piper.

It was three days after Christmas, December, 1856, that Janet Woodrow, his wife, tied up her pretty curls and went down into the shadow and brought him back a son whom they named Thomas Woodrow Wilson, for her father. Much more than the Woodrow name went into that child. In his heart, where his will lay, he was a Woodrow all his life. It will be necessary, therefore, to consider the Woodrows. They, like the Wilsons, were "quality"; but just a little different quality from the Wilsons, the difference between the Irish and the Scotch. The Reverend Thomas Woodrow was from the University of Glasgow; James Wilson from some North Irish school not worth holding in the family tradition; which gives him a preacher or two in the background. The Wilsons in Steubenville were "somebody" in the American country town out on the edge of the wilderness, in a region just beginning to feel the stir of the industrial age that was to make Pittsburgh, seventy miles away, the capital of the world's empire of steel. The Woodrows, children and grandchildren of Presbyterian scholars and ministers, lived in the world of the spirit. From them came "the things of the mind" which so greatly interested our twenty-eighth President. Thomas Woodrow, father of Janet, mother of Thomas Woodrow Wilson, came to Chillicothe, Ohio, in 1837. It was a country just emerging from its pioneer days. The Indians had left but a few decades before and the tradition of bloody battles was in every household. The wilderness was still struggling against the axe and the plough. A few railroads had penetrated into the woods. Canals, rivers, and turnpike roads carried the commerce of the State, and the politicians of Ohio in those days were beginning to question slavery. It would seem to be the last place where a scholar would shine. Yet there the Reverend Thomas Woodrow had his daily exercise in Greek. There in the bald ugliness of pioneership he maintained a library in his home, and amid the odor of sanctity which enveloped his Calvinism, he set up the light of learning. He brought his Glasgow with him. He became a famous preacher in his time, and by 1850 was pastor of the Hoge Presbyterian Church at Columbus, the capital of the State. He had only his intellect to recommend him. But it was enough. It gave him leadership in his community and enough means to educate his family. His daughter, the fifth child in a family of seven, who was born at Carlisle, England, just south of the Scotch border, went to the Female Academy at Steubenville, and one of his sons, James, born also at Carlisle, was graduated at Jefferson College, Pennsylvania, studied in the Lawrence Scientific School at Harvard, went to Heidelberg, Germany, where he received his master's degree and his doctor's "*summa cum laude*," and in the mid-fifties followed the Wilson family South.

The career of this uncle of the President is a prophetic study in the influence of blood upon life. What James Woodrow got from Thomas Woodrow came through Janet Woodrow to her son, Woodrow Wilson. The two men, in different generations, moved along an almost parallel curve. The inner forces impelled both to put them through different circumstances along a common way. James Woodrow in his twenties was head of an academy in Alabama, professor in Oglethorpe University in his early thirties, turned aside from the academic cloister during the Civil War from sixty-one to sixty-five, to be chief of laboratory in the medical department of the Confederacy, and immediately after the war opened a job printing office where he printed books, lawyers' briefs, college catalogues, and church papers; editing and publishing two Presbyterian papers all the time — even during the war — the "Southern Presbyterian Review" and the "Southern Presbyterian" — at the same time teaching in the State College of which he later became President — still running his printing office, bidding for and receiving the State printing of South Carolina. Quite incidental to his secular work he was the executive officer of the Southern Presbyterian General Assembly's Foreign Missions Board, collecting the funds and maintaining the missionaries from sixty-one to seventy-two. Entirely outside his career as editor, teacher, and business man, he was commissioner to the Southern General Assembly eight terms and moderator of the Synod of Georgia once, and of South Carolina once. He was tried for heresy in advocating evolution, twice — once by his church, where he won; and once by the Theological College Trustees, where he lost his teaching job — but was enough of a person to go into a bank as President and to hold that place off and on for fourteen years. All the while he kept up his scholarly interests and was associate of Victoria Institute, London; of Isis at Dresden, Saxony; of the Scientific Association of Germany; of the Scientific Association of Switzerland; fellow of the American Association for the Advancement of Science, and of the International Congress of Geologists. All these things are set forth in "Who's Who" for 1906–07, and in themselves point to a real person. But the man steps out of the record of his achievement in a description of him given in conversation with W. A. Clark, President of the Carolina National Bank of Columbia, South Carolina, a lifelong friend of Dr. James Woodrow. Casting into a narrative form the talk that came from Mr. Clark during several hours, it comes to something like this:

I first knew James Woodrow, a young man in his early thirties, running a job printing office in Columbia, where he edited and published two church papers, taught in the State College, and was doing the State printing under contract, and conducting the financial end of the foreign missions for the Southern Presbyterian General Assembly. I took a law brief to his office. He had a reputation among lawyers all over the State for proof-reading. I found that he did it all himself. He looked up, personally, even the lawyer's citations in his law-books to see that the lawyers had made their citations correctly. When he got the State printing, his competitors gleefully declared that the good Presbyterian would have to do Sunday work to keep up the legislative Record. But every Saturday night at midnight he would go down to the office, put the men out, and lock up. Then at midnight Monday morning, he would go down to the office, unlock, and let the men in and put them to work at a minute past twelve. He delegated nothing. He read his own proof; unlocked his own office; taught his own classes; and kept his own missionary books. In his fights for the evolutionary theory, he fought a lone fight also. His enemies surrounded him, baited him, and finally trapped him into delivering an address on the origin of Adam's body. But he was a scientist — a friend and pupil of Agassiz, a member of many great European scientific societies. He had high scholastic standing in America, and he never compromised. He fought it out and lost his place in the Theological Seminary, but he went into a bank as President, and at about the same time became President of what is now the State University.

And here's an odd thing. He lived here for nearly fifty years, but I doubt if he had a close friend in town. He was too busy for the soft amenities of friendship. He was detached. Not that he was a recluse; he did a full man's part in everything, but he just did not mix with the crowd. He was the most punctual man I ever knew. He never was a minute early or late in keeping an appointment. He lived his life by rule. You never saw such a dauntless fighter in causes which he loved. But he fought straight and scorned to win crookedly. In reconstruction days, when the blacks were in the South Carolina State House piling up taxes on us, we considered for a time defeating them by tampering with the ballots. But Dr. Woodrow said at the meeting: "I am willing to take a gun and help to drive them out, but if you use these tissue ballots I shall make public protest." He was that kind and that way.

In the fight he made for evolution — a famous fight nationally in the eighties — Dr. Woodrow had many opportunities to compromise, to restate his thesis mildly, to win votes in the trial board by personal appeal. He refused either to modify his statement or win over his adversaries by palaver.

In a letter to the writer from a man who worked

with the Reverend James Woodrow in the days of his prime is this description of the spirit of the man under pressure. It might well have been written forty years later of his nephew:

The Woodrow people were very deeply emotional, and while they could contain themselves and not give vent to outbreak of passion, their indignation was deep-seated and rather unyielding in temper. In the discussion of any question, theological or political, while he could use the best of English, his sarcasm cut as keen as a razor, and in the defense of himself he never let up. He carried that principle of the spiritual life very much into practical affairs of life, that is, "forgiveness was in the spiritual life always predicated upon repentance." In everyday life he would insist upon the same principle. His conviction was so deep that he never felt called upon to "forgive" until he saw evidence of "repentance" (see Luke 17: 3-4).

From my knowledge of the Woodrow family I believe that that was the characteristic of them all, and if Woodrow Wilson was subject to any faults of wrathful unforgiveness, then I think it came from the Woodrow side.

The Reverend James Woodrow was a serious, mild-mannered man who rarely joked, never got excited, seldom lifted his soft, mellow voice, nor deigned to put his personality in the balance where a principle was at stake. Also he worked alone, with few friends and no advisers. He failed to win his cause because he respected it too highly to compromise it into victory. That was the way of the Woodrow blood.

Those Virginia days were happy days for the Joseph Ruggles Wilsons with their little brood. Of course they were of the North; from a civilization based upon hustle and bustle; and the civilization of Virginia, founded upon caste and the Divine right of caste, was at war spiritually with the indomitable energy of the Northern and Western democracy. But the Wilsons were not of the rowdy democracy. Four years of teaching laid upon Princeton, and beneath that the Theological Seminary, and underlying that Jefferson College and a youth brought up in the show house of Steubenville, made a fairly firm footing-stone for life in the Virginia aristocracy. And as for Janet Woodrow of the curls, she had three children, a manse, and a handsome Irishman to engage her watchful care and she had no time to speculate upon the variations of American civilization. Virginia was as good as Ohio to her. Wherever she lived, her neighbors tell one story of her — that she was reserved, that she had a certain shy dignity, that she was a musician — a skilled pianist, but diffident about playing for strangers, and that she mingled little with the life about her. But she was no timid shadow of the blithe Irishman whom she married. She was a strong woman in the home; and in Virginia, while the father was occupying himself as a Southern Irish gentleman, Mrs. Wilson was busy with the children; putting the Woodrow in their manners and developing with a mother's ancient art the genius of the Woodrow blood.

It was strong blood, this Woodrow blood, and in the baby born in Staunton, Virginia, the Woodrow blood overcame the Wilson blood. From both sides came the forward urge — the knack for enterprise which we hope is progress; the spirit that moves the pioneer, the crusader, the martyr. From the Woodrows came the capacity for slow, continuous, dogged, undramatic, spiritual struggle. The Woodrows had the brains of scholars and their tradition held a precious inheritance of Calvinist belief that the Right — always capitalized, always of God — will prevail. The word "compromise" makes your true Calvinist froth. From the Wilson heritage came the gay fighting blood of the Irish; contentious, imaginative, often vain, but never cold in pride; restlessly following the call of eerie fairies to lovely and surprising things. What a mix it was, the blood of Woodrow Wilson — pure Scotch, pure Irish, all Celt, with none of the American Revolutionary blend in it; no Dutch, no French, no Swiss, no German, no Norman-Saxon strain that makes us practical men willing to die for what we call righteous causes, but entirely happy living under reasonable compromises. Scotch Calvinism and Irish militancy have poured into the Revolutionary blood in great streams, steadying it and giving it a festive sense of proportion. So because of its Scotch-Irish the American blend takes a Celtic color. But here was bred a man destined one day to come into place and power whose blood was pure Scotch-Irish colored with Calvinism. The modern world for the first time was to come under the dominion of a pure Celt, not as a lieutenant, not as a counsellor, not as an upper servant of any king or commander, but for a year and seven months as the vicegerent of his God. It was all but a prophetic hour when mankind for a moment saw rising John Calvin's millennium.

CHAPTER II

THE INFLUENCE OF ENVIRONMENT

In 1858, when the baby Thomas Woodrow was two years old, the Wilson family moved to Augusta, Georgia. There the Reverend Joseph Ruggles Wilson had a call to preach in the First Presbyterian Church. It was a mark of distinction, that call to Augusta, Georgia. The distinction came somewhat because Augusta was a larger town than Staunton; but chiefly because Augusta held a high place in the South. Augusta was one of the few live industrial towns of the South before the Civil War; a town of commercial promise. But more than its commercial leadership, the town through its First Presbyterian Church held a prestige in that denomination recognized all over the South. It was an old church organized in 1804. Its missionary society lent to Alexander Stephens the money that paid for his education. In the revolt from Episcopacy which naturally followed the American Revolution, the Presbyterians captured the intellectual classes among the revolutionists of the South as the Congregationalists captured intellectual New England. In Virginia Episcopacy held its dominion as it did in New York.

There were the aristocracy, the Tories, the first American Conservatives. So going South to Augusta to take the First Presbyterian Church, a church, as we shall see, destined to lead the Presbyterians of the South into their own revolution, the Reverend Joseph Ruggles Wilson proved his high qualities. He had something back of his regal carriage and demeanor. He could preach. His talent for rhetoric plus the zeal of his spirit gave him eloquence. And those were the days when eloquence counted. The North and the South were coming to war over the question of the extension of slavery. The question rose in every institution of American life; in commerce, splitting old business houses; in politics, shattering parties; in education, disrupting faculties and dividing student bodies; and in the churches, breaking up denominations. What a call for an orator came out of this situation! And how well Joseph Wilson, in his late thirties, responded, we may realize by the fact that he went as a delegate to the National Assembly of the Presbyterians at Philadelphia in 1861, and heard with wrath the Spring resolution read and adopted which expelled slaveholders from the Presbyterian Church. Sumter had been fired on. Sectional passions were aflame. The Presbyterians of the South left the Philadelphia Assembly, reconvened in Atlanta, and, upon the invitation of Dr. Joseph Wilson and his elders, called the first Southern Assembly to meet at Augusta to organize the Southern Presbyterian Church. In that assembly Dr. Wilson was a leader. He became its permanent clerk. Although his brothers were enlisting in the Union Army, Joseph Wilson cast his fortunes with the Southern cause and became one of its religious leaders — a chaplain in the Southern Army acting under the Presbyterian Board of Home Missions of which at the time his brother-in-law, James Woodrow, was a director — and during the whole war Joseph Wilson gave himself to his Church and his State with all the fervor of his Irish heart. For forty years he was stated clerk of the General Assembly of the Southern Presbyterians and once was the moderator of the assembly — always very much of a man among men, as was his father before him.

It was in the family of such a father and of a mother consecrated equally to the Southern cause, though her father and brothers in the North were with the Union, that the boy, Thomas Woodrow Wilson, grew up. His two sisters, four and six years older, of course bossed him and spoiled him, after the primeval fashion of older sisters. For ten years he was the baby of the family until his brother was born in 1866. He might as well have been an "only child" — being a boy with two adoring parents and two older sisters to nag him into various paths of virtue, when by all the inalienable rights of boyhood he should have bruised his dirty little bare feet upon the broad path that leadeth to experience. He was a frail child, and was not sent to school nor even taught his letters at home until he was nine. More than that, he was put into spectacles which kept him out of many of the rougher sports that boys enjoy. The spectacles also limited his gang life, which teaches boys so many vital things that men must know. He did not hunt nor trap. His barn loft, instead of being the site of the neighborhood trapeze and spring board, where the gang congregated to break arms and legs, to produce bruises and sprains, and to give young bodies brawn and young minds a wholesome respect for it, became the home of "the Lightfoots," a juvenile baseball nine. In his forties Woodrow Wilson remembers and tells William Bayard Hale, his biographer, that "the Lightfoots held meetings characterized by much nicety of parliamentary procedure." He emphasized the fact that "every one of the little chaps knew perfectly well just what the previous question was and that only two amendments to a resolution could be offered which should be voted upon in the reverse order." Incidentally "the Lightfoots" practiced and played baseball with the nines of rival gangs. But the hallowed recollection of Robert's Rules of Order is hardly the barn-loft memory of the average American boy.

The great war between the States raged when "Tommy" Wilson was from four to eight years old, and left, as he told his friends, but two pictures in his heart: One is of the lad sitting alone on the gatepost of the Presbyterian manse in Augusta, watching a ragged troop of Confederate soldiers march by and hooting at them in the slang of the day, "Oh, Joe — here's your mule!" The other picture shows the boy of nine standing by an upper window of the manse peering through the blinds at Jefferson Davis, President of the Confederacy, and Alexander Stephens, one of its great leaders, going by in a carriage, prisoners of the Union Army on their way to jail. No passion for the lost cause ever burned in his heart. Whatever his father's rage and sorrow may have been or his mother's — who seems to have been torn between her father's and her husband's loyalties, with a brother and a father on opposite sides — Tommy's soul took no bitterness from the day.

Mr. William H. Fleming of Augusta, recalls Tommy Wilson, as a child, most vividly in church. He has a picture of the lad ten or a dozen years old, flaxen-haired, freckled, with the spectacles on, coming into the family pew, and as he sat there Fleming became fascinated with the unusual size of the back of his schoolmate's head. It seemed a long head and broad; and when he snooped in a phrenology book later, Fleming saw that such a head denoted capacity for great power and so kept his mind's eye upon Wilson as he grew up. The Flemings and the Wilsons visited together, and one memory Mr. Fleming has is of the Wilson tribe all piling out of their buggy after church at the Fleming door; and he and Tommy having to stand around piously all day, dressed up and shod, with no games to divert them while the grown-ups, who had their diversion in talk, had a good time even if it was Sunday.

In the boy's memory also is a Sunday when the Reverend Joseph Wilson rose in his pulpit and said: "A great battle is raging to-day in Virginia and the forces of the Confederacy are suffering from a lack of ammunition. This congregation must do its duty and immediately at the close of these services the ladies will repair to the munition factory to help with the cartridges. You will now rise and sing the Doxology and be dismissed!" Joseph Wilson was no stickler for technicalities when he saw his duty. He went straight to it, never lacking a little dramatic flourish to add the color of an act of God to a necessary procedure. Others in the congregation remember that big moment as of some divinely staged second act when the Doctor in the pulpit invoked the benediction in his deep, rich bass voice, like a high priest with his "Thus saith the Lord," and little Tommy below in the family pew gazing up through his grotesque "specs" with adoring eyes. He never lost the awe of that time and those years for his father. Always the Doctor was Tommy's hero.

The great war of the sixties passed over the boy's head like a cloud. It did not embitter him. He was easily reconstructed. So was his father for that matter. Yet he had his pride. After the war he and Mrs. Wilson hurried back to the North to visit their relatives. "Aren't you glad," Steubenville tradition declares a cousin said to the Southerner, "that you have some Northern connections now that the war is over?"

But Dr. Joseph Wilson's Irish dignity would not let him answer. Nagged further with, "Well, I suppose you are at least a repentant rebel," the humor of it got to him — the folly of trying to get satisfaction out of twisting the knife in his wound, and he came back at the cousins with a merry gleam in his eye, "Oh, no — no, just a whipped rebel," and they all let it go at that. But the Northern visit had its grim side. It was then, for the first time, that Dr.

Wilson learned of the death of his mother. She who was born Ann Adams, of County Down, seems to have been from the Black Irish. Her stern face set in a gloomy lace bonnet shines out in her portrait like a foreboding. She bore ten children, all of whom turned out well. And of the ten there were triplets, and two of the triplets were Union generals, Edwin and Henry Wilson. But their triplet sister was the daughter who left home when she married, after a quarrel with her mother. They never met again. The implacable old lady would not make up. So when she came to die that quarrel rose beside her deathbed and she bemoaned her lot. She shrank from dying, and cried out again and again as her days grew short: "Oh, the iron gates of death — the iron gates of death!" But she did not weaken. She did not send for her daughter. That was the story the Reverend Joseph Wilson heard when he came back to visit his mother's grave in Steubenville, when the war was over.

If hard and cruel things were coming to the elder Wilsons, their little son down in the country near Augusta was having a gay and lovely time. He was visiting with his Aunt Marion out at "Sand Hill" and playing with his cousin, Jessie Bones. The little girl and boy rode on horseback and played in the fields; read the "Leather Stocking Tales" as normal children, stained their faces with pokeberry juice, stuck feathers in their hair, armed themselves with fierce bows-and-arrows, and, hiding upon lonely roads, lay in wait for little darkies going to their homes in the piney woods. When the pickaninnies were scarce, Cousin Jessie had to be the paleface, who was scalped, tomahawked, and burned at the stake.

In town was the grove about the church where the spectacled little boy played alone and dreamed his beautiful dreams. It was when he was in his early teens that he lived as all children long to live — in a dream world. His dream world was a highly virtuous enchanted ship, the Avenger, in which Tommy as Admiral Wilson chased wicked pirates in the South Seas. He kept the ship's log for three gorgeous months, and the record of the raids and bloody battles and glittering treasure which is found in that lusty log proves Tommy Wilson a valiant lad and a good sailor. But here's a significant thing. Always he is "Tommy." No one remembers him as "Tom" or by any other husky nickname. He never really conquered his frail body and his "specs." The pirate ship was his soul's revolt at his body's weakness. A more vigorous boy would have had too much energy to find time to set down his dreams. But in the woods back of the church he sailed his course to the stars and in the manse made an account of it. When the boy was grown to manhood and in the White House, the pastor of the old Church in Augusta called upon him, and the President summoned the dreaming boy out of his heart's past and bade him tell how he used to sail boats in the open ditches that carried the storm water past the manse, and how his first child tragedy came when the hinge of the manse gate crashed upon his finger and ground the little bone all out of shape and made the finger joint stiff for life. That stiff finger also handicapped him in his full fellowship with the gang. So he retired farther into his dream world.

He entered Mr. J. T. Derry's Academy when he was thirteen, and his principal declares that his education at home had prepared him to begin the classical course — as well as the other boys of the town — the classics caught them young and held them hard in the sixties. In Mr. Derry's school when young Wilson entered were the sons of the town's "Best People." They had blood also. J. R. Lamar, afterward associate justice of the Supreme Court, was there; and Pleasant Stovall, afterward President Wilson's Minister to Switzerland, was in the school; and William H. Fleming, later a member of Congress, came to the school.

Dr. Wilson spent his life's passion on the boy. It

was a bookish home in which this great love was founded between the father and son. There was much reading aloud; and there was no ignorant prohibition of good literature because it was fiction. In mid-week when there was no sermon immediately ahead, the family used to sit while the father and mother read Dickens — the Doctor was immoderately fond of "Pickwick"; so forty years later it was a White House favorite. They read Thackeray and Scott and the Lake Poets of England. If the child missed some contact with the boy-herd around him, his loss was replaced in a measure by his early contact with the world of books. None of his boy friends remember Tommy Wilson in a fight. He never gave a boy a licking, and alas, for the history of mankind after 1919, he never had to take one and giggle out of it to the boy-world around him, an experience that makes men gently tolerant as well as brave and wise. But even before he was well into his teens, he had read "The Scottish Chiefs," "Thaddeus of Warsaw," "David Copperfield," "The Arabian Nights," and all the books that boys of his day should come into ten years later. It was a bright and beautiful world in which he walked out of childhood into youth — a world of dreams, a world of unleashed fantasies, but a world without the solid discipline that reality gives one. To know "David

Copperfield" and "Peggotty," and to fight with the Scots upon their border is a splendid spiritual exercise. But for the soul's good it should be offset by an occasional hour at the swimming-hole all alone, untying a wet shirt or pair of drawers tied in hard devil-devised knots by one's dearest and most treacherous friends, who have scampered away down the path through the high horse weeds to wait at the bridge and pelt the poor victim of their gay cruelty with their raucous laughter. There is no such tradition in the Wilson myth. His mother told her friends that Tommy was "a mischievous bundle of nerves," and old men say the boy had a temper. There is an Augusta legend that Tommy Wilson would throw down his bat and leave the field when an injustice was forced upon him. His temper was the natural heritage of a son with two elder sisters and devoted parents who held to ideas of aristocracy, implanted first by their religion and sustained by their contact with life. For the Wilsons were not just called and elected of God; they lived in the big brick manse. They associated only with the gentry. Their dictum was received by a congregation of the prominent citizens of Augusta, of Georgia, of the old South, before the Civil War, during the war, and in the decades that followed. The Wilsons were leaders, people anointed, apart, the Really Best People —

eminently respectable! The son of such a house must needs revere it, and sooner or later must feel a certain satisfaction for his own connection, unless that satisfaction is cooled by "decent respect for the opinions of mankind" as they emerge from the rude contact with the democracy of the boy-world. Certainly "the Lightfoots" with their parliamentary procedure did not supply that cold contact; nor did Professor Derry's select school with its Congressmen, Supreme Court Justices, and foreign Ministers there in the making. The manse library, the mysterious fairy world in the grove around the church, the pirate course down the South Seas upon the Avenger and the healing sympathy of a doting family could poultice any bruise that a boy's vanity might receive from the padded universe enfolding him. If only there could have been in his life some shanty-Irish critic with a penchant for assault and battery, some dear beloved sweetheart to show his notes around the playground, some low-minded friend to fasten upon him the nickname "four eyes," calling brutal attention to his spectacles, or some other nickname in thinly veiled obscenity which would reveal a youthful weakness and so make him truckle to the baser nature of his gang that he might remove the black curse of his sobriquet — what a world we should have to-day!

But no — Tommy Wilson left the enchantment of childhood always walking with the prince, ever the favorite of the good fairy, and beloved of all the genii in the books. And so he came off the isle of dreams into the wide and lovely place of vision where youth first wrestles in the adventure of life. He entered the jousts a knight, without fear and without reproach!

CHAPTER III

THE DEVELOPMENT OF YOUTH

In May, 1870, the big world first touched Tommy Wilson and awakened youth in the child heart. It was when General Lee came to Augusta. The boy was nearly fourteen years old. In the dream world he had been meeting knights and pirates and kings and robbers and other glorious figures. In his real world — if boyhood actually has any real world — of flesh and blood, great men had moved across the scene — phantoms. But General Lee walked out of Tommy Wilson's phantasms of childhood — a man. The day of his coming was a day of triumph in Augusta. The boys from Professor Derry's School and the boys from the Richmond Academy, the flower of the town, were lined up for the festival. And one may be sure that Tommy, with two young lady sisters and a Scotch mother, was dressed for the day. But Will Fleming, from the Richmond Academy, who lived out of town a mile or so, was in his shirt-sleeves. He had in his hand the most beautiful rose from his mother's garden, and as the boys filed past the place where General Lee was standing, Will Fleming darted out of the line in his galluses, too much disturbed by the lump in his throat to care what he wore. He lifted his big Georgia rose toward the place where the General sat and gave the flower to him. "He rose in his seat," wrote Fleming fifty-four years later, "with all the courtesy and dignity of a Chesterfield, took the rose; then, as I thought, with the slightest possible intimation that I had not risen entirely to the chivalry of the occasion, he said: 'I thank you, my son, very much for this rose, and now, with your permission' — gently emphasizing those words — 'with your permission I shall present it to my daughter!' She was sitting behind him. He was the noblest, most God-like man I ever laid my eyes on."

Is it any wonder that Tommy Wilson cheered and that, in cheering, passed from boyhood out of dreams into youth and the big world? Nearly forty years afterward, at the University of North Carolina, Woodrow Wilson, the President of Princeton University, spoke of that day in Georgia when he saw Lee. "I have only the delightful memory of standing, when a lad, for a moment by General Lee's side and looking up into his face. I have nothing but a child's memory of the man." But that memory seems to have made a deep impression upon the boy. For unconsciously he grew to make over his hero into his own likeness. Washington and Lee, the greatest of our Southern heroes, he wrote about in his manhood, and the pictures he made of them were adorned with Wilsonian virtues and shaded with the Wilson weaknesses. Roosevelt treated Lincoln the same way. All men heroize themselves in their heroes. But as Tommy Wilson stood in the street with the boys at Augusta, Georgia, looking up into the face of his great man, the lad touched life with the firm hands of youth. Lee was more than "David Copperfield" or "Thaddeus of Warsaw," or "Sinbad," or "Wallace," or "Captain Kidd." He was a hero out of life — out of the South.

The South was the only civilization Tommy Wilson knew. Up North, where he went in his late teens, he became Woodrow of his own motion. But Tommy Wilson, leaving his boyhood in Augusta, when he was just turning fourteen, went to Columbia, South Carolina, late in 1874. His father became a college professor, teaching "Pastoral Theology" in the Theological Seminary at Columbia, where his Uncle James Woodrow was teaching the sciences — and setting forth the theory of evolution. Columbia knew more of the war than Augusta. In the Georgia town the boy had lived as upon an island in the conflict of the sixties. Sherman going to the sea had curiously let Augusta go unburned. But when Tommy Wilson went to Columbia, he saw a mile of its business district, three blocks wide, standing black ruins, the work of Sherman's men. Naturally hearts were bitter there, and the ruin of the town's business section was but a detail of the damage that the war had done. Columbia was a capital. There the youth saw the legislature, a black horde of field negroes, directed by white scalawags chiefly from the North. They put hundreds of thousands of dollars of foolish taxes upon the State. He saw all the wickedness that follows a vindictive peace, and this picture came to him in Columbia, not as a child, not as a part of the natural order; it burst upon him tragically, suddenly, in his early youth, and made a mark upon his soul. There were no war heroes in his family. His father's brothers fought with the North. His father was a chaplain. His Uncle James Woodrow was in the chemical division of the Confederate service. And so, because his kinsmen were not fighting men, war to Tommy Wilson became to Woodrow the man not a glorious adventure, but a cruel barbarous business that always preceded a wicked peace.

But the South of his youth gave him some things much better than a hateful understanding of war. Youth will not be cramped even by the bars that check social growth around it. So, while the political and economic forces of the South were in the grip of their foes in war and their looting conquerors in peace, the South was still the South. That charm of human association upon a lofty plane, that scorn of sordid things even if they are realities, that calm and gentle assumption that nobility is the natural state of man, all of those fine pretensions that life is a Dresden China universe which motive Southern ladies and gentlemen, Tommy Wilson, child and youth, had before him, as his heart was formed and his mind was trained.

As a youth, he was still apart from the rabble in Columbia as he had been a boy just a shade different from other boys in Augusta.

"What kind of an education did Wilson have in those reconstruction days there in Columbia?" the writer asked Miss Agnes MacMasters, who knew the Wilson family in Columbia and who, being a relative by marriage, often came to the White House — indeed, was invited to Mr. Wilson's first Presidential inauguration. She looked into the eye of her interrogator with all the pride of her race and place as she replied: "Why, a gentleman's education, of course!"

The answer was the truth and enough. But translated into facts, it means that he went to a select school and had some private tutoring in preparation for college. Very likely his Uncle James Woodrow took time from the duties that engaged him at the moment as college professor, State printer, editor of two religious papers, financier of the Southern Presbyterian Missionary Society, and corresponding delegate to churches in Great Britain and on the continent, to instruct young Tommy in the sciences as a Heidelberg doctor knew them. Evidently young Tommy was dull or preoccupied or had no liking for fact-lore. (In all his writings in after years, in the score of books he published and in his hundreds of addresses, we find but scant reference either directly or in figure of speech to chemistry, biology, or geology.) At any rate, family tradition preserves this:

"Tommy," quoth Uncles James, "you can learn if you will. Then, for Heaven's sake, boy, get some of this. At least, if you have no ambition to be a scholar, you might wish to be a gentleman."

It was in those years of the early seventies that Dr. Joseph Wilson, preacher and college professor, was building his new house in Columbia; one of the show places of Columbia in its day, as Joseph Wilson's father's new house in Steubenville, Ohio, had been a show place thirty years before. The Irish love grandeur, and Dr. Wilson used to delight in taking his friends into the new house as it was building. So Tommy Wilson grew from boyhood to callow youth in a grand house. Not so grand as the fine colonial mansions of the old town; still, a grand house for a new house in the hard times of reconstruction in the South; that house added its gentle touch to the youth. One cannot live in a grand house with a handsome Irish father in a circle of most scholarly parts, belonging to the social aristocracy and of the Lord's Calvinized elect, without in some measure developing a sense of personal satisfaction with the way God has ordered the universe. Such circumstances certainly do stimulate one's faith in God's Providence and the immanence of his righteousness in this world. And that old South, stern in its fine devotion to its ideals, with the material evidence of those ideals shattered by the fell circumstance of war, and then looted by the carpetbaggers, the old South, gay even in its ashes and proud as Job among the potsherds, gave the faith of his father to the young man, Tommy Wilson. In his select school and with his tutor preparing him for college, he made that faith his life's armor. But his mother, being wise, knew that he needed something more than he was getting out of life — books, and faith that arises from happiness. She must have seen that the lanky, gawky, flax-topped, bespectacled preacher's son lacked a certain grace of spirit. At least the MacMaster family tradition carries a legend that Mrs. Wilson felt Tommy's need of social polish

HOUSE BUILT BY JOSEPH R. WILSON IN COLUMBIA, SOUTH CAROLINA

One evening in his fifteenth year, she sent Tommy over to the MacMasters' to bring his sisters home. Girls are not supposed to be out alone in the South after dark. The boy stood on the pillared veranda and rattled the blinds, calling to the girls that mother wanted them to come home. He would not come in to see the MacMasters girls, but stood there bashfully and waited for his sisters. It seems to have made a family scandal. For a day or two later, Mrs. Wilson ventured to ask Mrs. MacMasters if she could suggest some way to make Tommy more at home with the girls. It was but a few weeks later that Mrs. MacMasters saw Tommy and her own Ellen strolling along under the trees overhanging the sidewalks, their elbows touching, their voices low, their eyes on the walk, their feet lagging in the idle gait that shows a vain desire to make time lag too. And right there the maternal discussion ended.

A little girl in Augusta, now an old lady with great-grandchildren, has a dear memory in her heart of the little boy Tommy, glasses, freckles, flaxen hair, and all, dancing around her like a puppy, roughing her, teasing her, challenging her to play, with some faint touch of the ineffable mystery in his manner. But life was not ready for the bloom, and so only a vague memory remains to grace her heart. When Tommy was in his later teens in North Carolina — but that is later, eons later, two years, in fact, and the lady lived in another world and another town, and hers is another story which shall be set down duly and in its place. But this we must very well know, that Tommy Wilson and Woodrow, the residuary legatee of Tommy's shy and tender heart, always was a ladies' man. He probably always was in love, yet never a philanderer — never cherished an affair of the heart which hindered him at Saint Peter's gate when Saint Peter looked over the Wilson account in his ledger. In his later youth, he wrote this of another woman: "She had besides beauty, a most lively and stimulating wit; such a mind as we most desire to see in woman — a mind that stirs without irritating you, that rouses yet does not belabor, amuses yet subtly instructs." He just naturally got along with women; liked their gentle ways; delighted in their intuitive cross-cuts to sagacity. To the end of his days he found that satisfaction in the quick brilliant play of their minds that another man enjoys in the profound and awful storms of his body under impulse from those electric currents that feed the torch of life. But the chivalry of the South, the God of Calvin, and the conscience of the Scot probably held the Irish play boy well in the narrow path.

In those Columbia years — only four of them — the Wilsons seem to have impressed themselves upon the community. But one hears much more of the distinction of the father than of the son or the mother. As a college professor, building a house of imposing character for the times, as an orator — and still the South was in a lyric position of oppression where oratory mattered — as a sectional leader in his denomination, a moderator of his national assembly, and withal, as a fine upstanding figure of a man with flashing eyes and a shaggy poll of graying hair, a sturdy, vigorous man in his fifties, bristling with the qualities of leadership and never forgetting how well he really looked, Dr. Joseph Wilson impressed himself upon the town. Trust the simple-hearted to interpret him. Said a colored servant of the MacMasters home when he learned that Woodrow Wilson had been elected President of the United States:

"Yes, of co'se; Mistah Tommy he may have de office — but laws! de old Doctah he certainly had de ways!"

Perhaps the fact that the Doctor had been asked to become President of Davidson College gave a little glossier finish than he needed to his dress-parade form. Washington A. Clark, of Columbia, says of Dr. Joseph Wilson in that day:

Dr. Wilson read his sermons, which were literary, and rhetorically pleasing and convincing. He delivered them well — perfectly, and you got the effect of polished eloquence. He was, I should say, a vain man, but not offensively so, a good mixer in the town. He liked to lead popular causes, but never was a crusader. His pastoral theology was conventional, never advanced, but sane and logical. Yet he defended his brother-in-law, Dr. James Woodrow, with real fervor when he was tried for heresy in teaching evolution. If he had one characteristic more marked than another, it was his love to talk. He liked to let a conversation flow. He would pun and frivol and let his wit play. He never rejected a joke because its point was too blunt. He was a ripe and racy Irish gentleman.

Behold an American expression of the sporting rector in a Calvinized world! The tradition of his love of a merry pun, a wee nip, a grand talk, and the approval of his kind, one finds in the South wherever the old Doctor went. Yet he had his professional pride. His eloquence was never ranting. When it appealed too deeply to the emotions, he was wounded. They say in Wilmington that once, when he was preaching upon the precious Calvinist text, "the pearl of great price," meaning the election unto salvation, a stray from the Methodist fold rose in the congregation and shouted, "Thank God, I've got it! I've got it!" And the good Doctor, aghast and angered that his eloquence should have hit so low a mark, closed his Bible and dismissed the congregation! Emotion is all right in its place; but it had no place in the Doctor's religion. Religion was far too serious a matter, too entirely a matter of the head to let the heart interfere.

Mrs. Wilson had a manner. Every one in Columbia, indeed every one who knew her in the South — in Augusta, in Columbia, in Wilmington, at Davidson College — realized that she had "a manner." But it was a reserve, a dignity, a Woodrow aloofness, an audible aloofness indicated by her sweet and gentle voice. She was an accomplished musician; but her talent she kept chiefly for her family, as she reserved for it her finer graces. This detachment deprived her of close friends, made her a little less cordial than a preacher's wife might be. Of the family exuberance and flare, the Doctor had ninety per cent. But in the family character and ability, the wife, according to all testimony, was more than an equal partner with her husband. So, as we like our antithesis, son Tommy adored his father and was to his mother a most dutiful son.

The Wilsons, Joseph and Janet his wife, lie in the Presbyterian Churchyard at Columbia under two modest stones. The town seems to have been the place of their hearts' desire. Near them rests their daughter, Mrs. George Howe, wife of a local physician. It is a lovely spot, this churchyard, set after the old Southern fashion in the midst of the town where friends who lived in the Lord may rest in the Lord together. If the South was not bred in the bone of these Wilsons, surely it got into their blood.

And here is a curious thing: Even to-day in Columbia, where the Wilson parents lie in the churchyard, in the home of the MacMasters where the Wilsons visited as "in-law" kin through the President's sister, they tell how Theodore Roosevelt's mother, coming back to visit in the South at the close of the Civil War, came and sobbed out her sorrow at her isolation in the North during the war; where her husband, President Roosevelt's father, forbade the boys and girls — young Theodore among them — to discuss the war at home for fear of hurting their mother. And in return for this chivalry she brought up her children loyal Unionists, though her heart was with her father's people and the lost cause. There is an interesting "in-law" relation between the Roosevelts and the Wilsons that hinges in this MacMasters home in Columbia. Mrs. George Howe, whose son married Annie Josephine Wilson, was an aunt of Theodore Roosevelt's mother. The two immortals, Theodore and Woodrow, sitting upon an Elysian cloud trying to figure out the exact nature of their kinship, may be one of the minor sources of delight to the angels. Only in the South would such a remote and delicious blood tradition be happily preserved.

The South must have got into Woodrow Wilson's heart rather deeply. For he returns to it occasionally in his journeyings up and down the earth with a certain wistful delight. In his address before the University of North Carolina in 1909, when he spoke of Lee, he said:

> It is all very well to talk of detachment of view, and of the effort to be national in spirit and in purpose, but a boy never gets over his boyhood, and never can change those subtle influences which have become a part of him, that were bred in him when he was a child. So I am obliged to say, again and again, that the only place in the country, the only place in the world, where nothing has to be explained to me is the South. Sometimes, after long periods of absence, I forget how natural it is to be in the South, and then the moment I come, and see old friends again, and discover a country full of reminiscences which connect me with my parents, and with all the old memories, I know again the region to which I naturally belong.

From Columbia, South Carolina, the Wilsons moved in 1874 to Wilmington, North Carolina, where the First Presbyterian Church called the Reverend Joseph Wilson as pastor at four thousand dollars a year — rather a staggering sum for reconstruction days in a small town. But the Presbyterians in the South are a prosperous sect and they take their religion seriously. Tommy Wilson, at seventeen, came into the town, a frail and callow youth. He had been away to college for a term in his sixteenth year — Davidson College in Mecklenburg County; then and now a sturdy Presbyterian school not unlike the little college at Cannonsburg, Pennsylvania, from which his father was graduated thirty years before. It was primitive in the early seventies. The dormitories were in the building with the classrooms, and the boys brought their own wood to their rooms, filled and trimmed their own lamps, and generally did chores around the place. But it was difficult for a boy with a delicate body. His fellow students remember that he took no great leadership and small interest in games — "shinny" and baseball. "Wilson," said the captain, "if you weren't so damned lazy, you'd make a dandy player!" But the boy wasn't lazy. He had not the physical stamina for the game. So he was exiled in college more or less, as he had been in school — a spectacled child, looking on, eagerly wishing to do all his ambition urged him to do. The boys liked him, but they never really knew him. He did what he could, planted his tree which still stands on the campus, a sheltering elm; and in the literary society he was a shining light. But he could not finish the year and returned to Wilmington, a pale preacher's son, one of three or four youths in the town who were preparing for college.

He spent a year at home studying Greek, and living a rather sedentary though not secluded life. He found the circle limited in which he could move with satisfaction. The South was sending few boys to college in those days of the seventies. Their fathers had perished in the war and many of their elder brothers. Much of their property was gone, and young men in their teens were needed at home. Tommy fell in with young John Bellamy who also was preparing for college. And such a friendship sprang up between the two as inevitably rises when boys of like tastes have leisure to devote themselves to each other. It was their habit to take books and go out in the pine woods and read — sometimes aloud to one another, sometimes sprawling on their backs, flipping the pages, chasing the story. So they read through half a dozen of Scott's novels. They called their excursions "reading raids" — which were really high old intellectual times, and in them the boys went through "The Bride of Lammermoor," "Old Mortality," "Quentin Durward," "The Pirate," and a few others of Scott's stories. The young men boated and swam on the Cape Fear River, roved the woods, tramped over the hills, and talked the tall talk of youth. Together they went girling, after the fashion of sheep-killing dogs, always in pairs — for safety. Mr. Bellamy, recalling those days fifty years after, is sure Tommy was "a raging social lion." They haunted each other's houses and formed that grand passion for each other that only youth may find. With these boys it was "the fellowship of kindred minds," and together they foraged at picnics, church socials, lawn fêtes — there were no dances in the Presbyterian society of those days. But the girls frolicked with the boys and circumspect elders supervised the play. One of the friends of his youth who followed Woodrow Wilson through life was David Bryant, a colored man of Wilmington. David Bryant was the butler and man of all work in the Wilson house. During the later years of his life he was a real estate broker, and a man of intelligence. His recollection of the boy Tommy Wilson is illuminating. Bryant spoke in as good English as the average white man, and in transcribing his views, no attempt will be made to elide his "g's" or make his honest narrative amusing.

When I wanted to find Mr. Tommy in those days [the days of his youth from sixteen to nineteen], I would go to his room, and generally there he would be sitting with his elbows on his knees and his nose in a book. He had just two friends in those days — John Bellamy and the old Doctor. If he wasn't reading a book with one, he was talking about a book with the other. You never saw a father and son tied together as they were. Why, sometimes I had to wait a meal; the old Doctor would not let me serve till Mr. Tommy came down. And how proud the old Doctor was of the boy — and the boy of him, too! They looked alike except his face was longer. He had the same eyes, the same heavy jaw and teeth, and they favored each other about the nose and cheek-bones. But inside — let me put it this way. Outside Mr. Tommy was his father's boy. But inside he was his mother all over. She had English ways — thought she was a little better than other folks — standoffish a little, and folks thought her cold and distant, but it was just that she stuck to her English ways.

She was as gentle and tender-hearted a woman as I ever knew. In those days the land was filled with tramps. She never turned one from the door — black or white — and I have heard her many a time telling the cook to put in a little something extra so if a tramp came there would be plenty for him. Yet she never had many friends. It was her way with people. Tommy inside was like that, good and all that, but he didn't mix up with the other boys — like her, a little standoffish with all the boys but John Bellamy. Sometimes Tommy would work his father so's I could go swimming with him, and the old Doctor would say, "Now, Dave, don't you let Mr. Tommy get into any fights or anything down there." But there was no danger. He wasn't the fighting kind; but his little brother, Mr. Josey — say, there was a real boy!

This aloof attitude of the Woodrows to neighbors and friends, evidenced by Dr. James Woodrow and Mrs. Joseph Wilson, lingers in the memory of all who knew them. The Bellamys remember that one day, when all the town was on some steamer excursion on the Cape Fear River, the Bellamys, who were well-bred Southerners, offered Mrs. Wilson a part of their cake. Every one — except Mrs. Wilson and her family — was eating lunch on the deck. "No," says Mrs. Wilson to Mrs. Bellamy, "no, thank you. I couldn't eat it for anything — not here on the deck!" That dart rankled fifty years.

Mrs. Wilson fell desperately sick of typhoid in Wilmington. It was before the days of trained nurses in small towns, and the church women nursed her. The night of the crisis, Tommy Wilson came over to the Bellamys and asked on behalf of his father that one of the Bellamys "sit up" with his mother. Miss Ellen went. She says she never saw a more devoted son than Tommy. He was in the room every minute. The Doctor went to his study and slept in a chair. The colored mammy snored in her chair at the foot of the bed. The two watchers, Miss Bellamy in her late twenties, Tommy Wilson in his middle teens, watched through the night. The fever broke; the crisis passed. At dawn one of the Wilson daughters came from Columbia. Miss Bellamy went home. She was never invited into the Wilson home again! Tommy was cordial. The Doctor was friendly as usual. But in some way, perhaps by the mere presence of an unmarried woman in the house for the night, or Heaven knows what, some way the Woodrow pride was piqued. Friendship ceased. That Woodrow pride followed Tommy Wilson all his days. How it must have struggled with the affectionate blood of the Wilsons when dear ties were ruthlessly broken in after years!

The picture of those Wilmington days is important enough to draw it in some detail. For in it, during his summer vacation from school, young Wilson moved, and surely it left something in his life. First the exterior of the town as it was in the later seventies — a Front Street lined with two and three-story stores, banks, and commission houses — a port town, one of the important ports of the South. In the harbor stood brigantines and clipper ships from Russia, from Italy, from Holland, from Hamburg, from Liverpool, bringing strange cargoes and taking cotton to Europe. It was to this harbor that John Bellamy went hot-foot when he missed his friend. There he always found him, talking to the sailor men, and Wilson in his later years confessed to his friends that he came within an ace of running away to sea. Back of the wharf, back of Front Street, ran Third Street, the home of the aristocracy — the socially elect. It was one of the wide, elm-shaded streets with a park-way down the center, lined with great houses; the stately pillared homes of the old slave-holding class; the mansard roofs of the newer rich and the towered and gabled homes of the newest rich. On a corner was the church where Cornwallis made his headquarters and, by way of insult, stabled his horses. Near by was the Bellamy home — pillared on three sides, a proud ante-bellum house. Within, on the right side of a broad hallway, running through the house, are two stately salons — parlors, they are called — furnished sumptuously in Victorian mahogany; here are deeply stuccoed coves, sweeping draperies of velvet hanging from gilded Florentine cornices above the windows, cornices that match the gilded mirrors over the spacious fireplaces at the ends of the rooms; rich old-fashioned carpets upon the floors and bric-à-brac of a grand manner properly placed around the grand rooms. Across the hall are the living-room and dining-room, not so sumptuous, but comfortable, elegant, and quite sure of their correctness and adequacy. Above stairs — and the stairs mount with processional dignity — are a dozen bedrooms. The Union soldiers quartered in this house knew no such splendor at home. It was the old South at its apex. Here young Woodrow Wilson chummed with John D. Bellamy, and the Wilsons and the Bellamys neighbored. This home must have influenced the youth, must have given him something of that ornate and festal languor that brocaded the patterns of Irish lace, over his somber and implacable soul.

The streets of Wilmington, the lure of the wharf, the pillared houses, and leisurely life of the town all touched the quick of the youth's being; but the Presbyterian Church, where his father preached and Janet Woodrow his mother worshiped, moulded his life. The old people of Third Street remember the young man walking sedately into church of a Sunday morning with his mother upon his arm; a dutiful son and a proud parent. He was almost but not quite, in that period, an Exemplary Youth. But that church, domiciled in a rectangular edifice with high Gothic ceiling supported by six Gothic pillars of dark oak, with the gallery for the slaves in the rear, with a prosperous, well-dressed congregation that even to this day bows clear to the forward pew rail when the parson prays, with a sort of hard, sour serenity in its secure salvation — that church gave Tommy Wilson, who soon was to become Woodrow, his philosophy of life.

"The only trouble with Woodrow Wilson," said John D. Bellamy, who admired him to the end, "is that he was a confirmed and confounded Calvinist."

There was no doubt of his soul's direction when young Wilson lived in Wilmington. "God, whose I am and whom I serve," was his perennial golden text. In the church of his father, he found his feet upon the rock of his life's path. It was the faith of a spiritual aristocracy. It needed only an intellect and the young man could go into life with his head high and his soul serene. What need he care for man, if he had God and an intellect? He had in his philosophy all the assurance needed for a great life. If propitious events should come — very well; if not, he had forged a strong soul out of his blood and his environment; a strong soul, a clear mind, and a stout heart. Wilmington and the old South had done their work. He could not have come out of the democratic West. He would have smudged himself there — and also maybe burned himself with a base desire to please his fellow men and so forget his God.

But he was no marble statue in those days. The Irish in him asserted itself, and he fell in love. It was a secret love. John Bellamy knew nothing of the love affair, and if Dave Bryant knew, he has forgotten it. It was after all an Irish boy keening at the moon. Yet there were shy notes in it and June roses, and such fleeting meetings and bashful touch of hands as come when the restless tide of life begins to swell in the heart. That was nearly fifty years ago, in the circumspect seventies.

"The parlor," says the simple saga of the prim event, "was made ready for his coming." A modest and somewhat erudite young man was Mr. Wilson. They called him "Mr. Wilson" — not familiar

"Tommy" in that blessed time and place was permitted to the Minister's son who was home upon his vacation from college — from Princeton even. All interferences were removed — they called them interferences by way of polite circumlocution, meaning pa and ma and grandma — and calls were a solemn rite. It was quite out of "Godey's Lady's Book," and when he wrote her notes, it was in the third person, declaring vicariously — and perhaps rather tentatively — a pious adoration. Oh, flaming youth of to-day — !

Nothing came of it but the joy of remembering. No hearts were broken. And to-day in the South, a white-haired lady in her mid-sixties has in an attic a little box with all that remains mortal of that romance, some folded, yellowing notes and the woody stem of a rose — something upon which she wastes the sweet benediction of a smile at odd times in a busy life — a smile, not even wistful, just vagrant and happy. For "Mr. Wilson" in his teens had no time for a grand passion. His father and John Bellamy kept too many books in his life. The long talks in the parson's study were of serious books — philosophies and histories and theories of life.

One fine summer day Dr. Wilson, walking down Front Street with a grin on his face, overhauled Dr. William Bellamy, M.D., elder brother of John, and with the snap of the devils of pride and ribaldry in his eyes said:

"See here, Will — I've something to tell you. Says Tommy to me at breakfast this morning after he had been reading until way after midnight last night:

"'Father,' says he, 'Eureka,' says he.

"And I says, 'Eureka, Tommy, and why?'

"'Eureka,' he repeats, all fine and gay, 'Eureka, I have found it!' says he.

"'Found what?' says I.

"'A mind, sir. I've found I have an intellect and a first-class mind,' says he. He had been reading an abstruse book and the ease with which he mastered it convinced him that he had a mind!"

And the father's mockery did not conceal his pride, says the Bellamy tradition of the episode.

A mind is a dangerous gift for the happiness of a man whose faith tells him that a righteous God is governing the universe. If the man respects his mind, he is liable to confuse his wisdom with God's purpose and so dynamite the world in a holy cause. Little did Dr. Joseph Wilson know, as he sat in his library that day solemnly sucking his long cane-stemmed clay pipe, his great body slouched in his easy-chair, his graying shock of leonine hair merging in gray smoke as he laved the lad with the beaming eyes of paternal pride like an old lion washing his cub — little did he think what that first-class mind in the long Celtic skull set off with serious "specs" would one day do to the white race on this planet.

CHAPTER IV

"WHEN THE EVIL DAYS COME NOT"

TOMMY WILSON at eighteen went to Princeton, the college where his father, Dr. Joseph R. Wilson, took his post-graduate work in theology. A slow bloomer was this tall, fair-haired youth, with a serious mind and a sparkling sense of humor, who unfolded slowly because he had so much to reveal. It is hard to describe precisely this boyhood and youth, handicapped by frailty and "specs," but stimulated with the exceptional mind that comes out of a first-rate inheritance. Immediately comes the impression that here is a young prig. Nothing could be farther from the fact. If ever America bred a normal human animal in trousers, it was this same Tommy Wilson who came to Princeton in 1875 to graduate with "the famous class of '79." He weighed one hundred and sixty-five pounds, stood erect, had a rather bold and searching eye, with the Irish twinkle well set in it, and his strong jaw shows in his student pictures of the period, denoting purpose where his father's jaw upon which the son's was moulded shows rather a certain pride or vanity or courtly consequence. His classmates testify that he had distinction even in his youth. He carried himself with a "go." "No one," said Robert Bridges, his classmate, "ever could put pomp into a college parade like Tommy Wilson. He had a gift for it."

As a freshman he attracted attention by his love of books — not the love of a hungry soul, but the love of a wise youth who knew where to find what he wanted in the library. He fell into the way of reading political essays. As for instance, Bagehot, who was quite the fashion with college professors in the seventies, and Henry W. Lucy, who was "Toby M.P." for "Punch" in his later years, then writing for the "Gentleman's Magazine" gorgeous accounts of the notable parliamentary figures of England. Wilson absorbed political essays avidly. Early in his college career he heroized Burke. First he imitated him; then, even as he transmuted Washington and Lee, made over Burke in the Wilsonian image.

> He learned [writes Woodrow Wilson a decade later of Burke] a vast deal, indeed, but he did not learn much of it from his masters at Trinity. Apparently Master Shackleton at Ballylore had enabled him to find his own mind. His four years at college were years of wide, eager reading, but not years of systematic and disciplinary study. With singular if not exemplary self-confidence, he took his education into his own hands. He got at the heart of books, it would seem, rather than through their grammar. That this boy should have had such an appetite for the world's literature, old and new,

need not surprise us. Other lads before and since have found big libraries all too small for them. What should arrest our attention is, the law of mind disclosed in the habits of such lads: the quick and various curiosity of original minds, and particularly of imaginative minds. They long for matter to expand themselves upon; they will climb any dizzy height from which an exciting prospect is promised: it is their joy by some means to see the world of men and affairs.

Now this may or may not have been true of Burke, but it is exactly true of Woodrow Wilson who wrote it about Burke. The Essay on Burke, "The Interpreter of English Liberty," is an apology for Wilson — a gay, erudite, and often startlingly prophetic apology for the man who was to be.

In Augusta, as a boy, he was barred from some of the gang activities by his frailty. And the fact that he was a preacher's son, of itself, kept any boy, except the devil's own, out of full boy fellowship. In Columbia he was set apart because he was preparing for college. In Wilmington he was in the mooning age and could not make close contact with strange youths. Moreover, he read with his father, played like an overgrown pup with John Bellamy as the two fauns lolled in the piney woods breathing in the romance of Scott with the odor of balsam, or talked to the

> Market girls and fishermen
> The shepherds and the sailors too,

at the wharf on Front Street; he vaguely planned to run away to sea and came back to the library of the manse refreshed — an unwhipped cub who never had quite belonged to the inner society of his kind. That society was in the kingdom of muscle and brawn, the realm where rulers hold sway by brute force. But at Princeton he joined for the first time the aristocracy of youth. At Princeton he came upon a new order. There he found himself master; there the things of the mind — that "first-class mind" which he discovered after a night's orgy with some tough old philosopher — governed his fellows in the aristocracy of books. In the academic world, the unwhipped cub was one of the uncrowned kings. He never left his kingdom. Even when he deserted the cloister, he took with him its serenity, its faith, its bookish ways. Says the senior caricaturist of the class, four years after Wilson entered Princeton, "Tommy Wilson, upon entering college, rushed to the library and grabbed Kant's 'Critique of Pure Reason,'" which phrase indicates that he was a bookish boy rather than a baseball enthusiast. Yet, although he played baseball indifferently, by reason of his capacity for leadership he was at different times Director of the Athletic Association and President of the baseball team. In his life he was manager of three baseball teams beginning with the "Lightfoots," and always managed the teams better than he played the game. He cut loose from anything but the most sketchy adherence to the college curriculum; spent most of his time in the library reading what he liked. To mathematics and the sciences he gave a lick and a promise, and devoted his time with something like passionate interest to history and the study of government. As a collegian he barely squeaked into the honor roll — the first forty-two in a class of one hundred and twenty-six, by being the forty-first to get honors. Which proves that he was no "grind" or "dig" or textbook addict. The thing that he desired to do most of all was to talk. He was a famous debater. Wrangling was his meat and drink. And next he liked to write — the Scotch-Irish of it! The Celt's love of self-expression, the tremendous urge to make their private sentiment public sentiment, to impose themselves upon their fellows, is what makes the Irish the world's divinely appointed rulers and the Scotch the intellectual leaders of their neighbors. And here at Princeton was a ruler by right of spiritual heredity, who also could think, and who by inbreeding was convinced deeply that his God had elected him to a special spiritual privilege appointed and anointed by the covenant, to serve the cause of righteousness in the earth and for service rendered to enter him into a blessed reward hereafter.

So the curriculum did not bind young Wilson as a student. He and the whole Wilson tribe before him had acquired merit from without. They succeeded as he always succeeded in college and out, detached from the regular order — as he educated himself largely outside the curriculum.

For instance, his father and uncle did not have to be born Southerners to take leadership, upon four years' residence, in the Southern Presbyterian Church and head the chemical department of the Southern Army.

The truth is that, although the South impressed itself deeply upon the Wilsonian heart, the externals of the South rested rather easily upon all the Wilsons. Woodrow Wilson, born and reared in the South, never betrayed his Southern training by his speech. In college one of his classmates declares that he never realized Wilson's Southern birth until years after his classmate left school he read Wilson's tribute to Lee in his history of the United States. Yet Wilson remembered a day when the boys in Princeton were discussing reconstruction rather flippantly and he grew white with rage and left the room, calling back, "You don't know what you're talking about." The temper which he discovered in Burke and praised in Washington and Lee, with Wilson was one of the hangovers from his unwhipped cubdom. This temper flared up at odd and unexpected times all his life, producing a queer effect — a kind of imperious puerility.

In college, where we see his Irish jaw filling with Scotch purpose as the years go by, we find the Woodrow blood in him taking more and more control of his life, and that childish temper flashing out where some untoward event falls across his path. Once in college, when his society had made him its debater and staked its fame upon him, he was chosen upon the final team for the great college debate. He went into the contest readily enough. But he refused to take pot luck with his fellows and tore up the slip angrily which he drew from the hat because it appointed him to take the protection side of a tariff debate. And through all the years that followed he justified himself and told his biographers with pride how he had foregone great college honors for a principle; never remotely realizing the obligation to play out the game which was implied when he put his hand in the hat. The feeling of his society, left unprotected by his withdrawal, he did not understand. Nor did the desire of some other boy for a favorite side in the debate ever get to him. If only the gang at Augusta could have larruped the habit of team-work into him, the "Happy Warrior" might not have had so many melancholy hours. Perhaps his Uncle Woodrow, teaching evolution in a Theological Seminary in South Carolina, and refusing to win a fight by using his social blandishments upon the board, was proud of the young man. But his expansive and amiable Irish father must have had his gloomy half-hour when he heard of the episode. Yet these flares of puerility could not have come often in the days of his youth. Princeton remembers Tommy Wilson, the student, as a charming young fellow. He sang in the Glee Club, romped in the Athletic Association, pranked with the other barbarians, was editor of the college weekly newspaper, and through it all made loving friends. If he had charm, he also met the affection that it bred in others. Robert Bridges, editor of "Scribner's Magazine," declares that Wilson the student was an engaging youth "forever playing at the game of being friends — peculiarly adapted to college life." How he must have basked in the warmth and joy of it — he who had held himself restrained through the glowing, growing years of his soul's first great emotional expansion!

The self-education of Woodrow Wilson turned him naturally, indeed inevitably, to a study of the business of his race — the business of government. He went to the study of government both in his classes and in his outside reading as naturally as a pup takes to old shoes. Nothing diverted him. Literature was an incident; if it told him about statesmen, he read good literature. If it told him about love, adventure, beauty, sheer truth — he rejected it and, being what he was, was proud of his rejection. A prize of one hundred and twenty-five dollars was offered for an essay which required him to study Ben Jonson and two plays of Shakespeare. The boys of his society, who knew that his literary skill probably would give him advantage in the contest, urged him to go after the prize, for the society's sake. But he declared he would not waste his time on reading that did not interest him. Modern languages, the sciences, literature as literature — all were outside his realm. He was unconsciously following the urge of his Irish blood, fitting himself for leadership, turning his life to the consideration of government as a science. He read, wrote, and talked throughout his course, of men in public life, of men under various institutions, of men in the evolution of their relations from ancient to modern times. Burke was his hero, then Bagehot, then Disraeli, then Pitt, then Gladstone. He wrote wisely and talked convincingly of these men, their problems and their achievements. His estimate of them and their work, set down in his undergraduate days, will stand up to-day after more than forty years, as solid conscientious

THE EDITORIAL BOARD OF THE "PRINCETONIAN," 1878–1879
WOODROW WILSON, MANAGING EDITOR

Left to right, standing: M. G. Emery, Charles A. Talcott, W. F. Magie, T. D. Warren, G. S. Johns
Seated: R. H. McCarter, E. O. Roessle, Woodrow Wilson, H. B. Fine

work. Many of these essays, collected and published in 1896 under the title, "Mere Literature," were old college orations or essays, or parts of debates, recast in the essay form.

But the chief thing that Tommy Wilson got out of Princeton was an education of the heart, not of the head. He learned there the gentle art of friendship. His life in Columbia and in Wilmington, of the Carolinas, seems more or less detached from association with his kind. He did not join the herd after he left Augusta, a boy of his early teens. But he surely ganged with his class at Princeton. Said his classmate, Robert Bridges:

> To me he has always been so human, so lovable, so much a part of a beautiful friendship beginning on this campus, that I cannot feel his qualities in the cold abstractions of greatness. . . . There is nothing really like it as one looks back on it; several hundred boys fortuitously gathered from the ends of the earth to be thrown into a close relationship that lasts through life. Wilson was a boy like that, peculiarly adapted to college life. We soon found out that he had an eager mind — a rare quality in a youth of eighteen. He was as keen for the life of the college as any of us; but we soon discovered that what he called "the play of the mind" was as exhilarating to him as the play of the body to athletes. To him this "play of the mind" was the staff of existence. He would trail words or phrases hungrily and they would pop out of his conversation at a club table as part of a joke or a noisy dispute. There was always a twinkle in his eye, but he knew and you knew that he

had scored. We realized early that he was interested in government, which sounds dull and abstract. . . . But he soon gathered around him a group of fellows who could play the game of hall or club politics with the skill of practiced parliamentarians. It certainly added to the zest of college life. . . . In all this, good-fellowship was the essential feature. Wilson soon began to use the word "comradeship" as expressing his idea of the best part of college life. This comradeship had a strong hold on him always. It included all kinds of men on the campus and diverse interests. He never lost the joy of it — and I know it often lightened his burdens.

In passing, it should be said that apparently in college and certainly in later years, Woodrow Wilson had no joy in promiscuity in comradeship. He never wallowed in it, as many Americans do. It was his serene boast that in his eight years in the Presidency, he never had a Congressman or Senator as such in to lunch or dinner. He never traded in his joy. Fellowship meant to him, in college and always, the play of the mind. The fatuous, the noisy, the slow-witted he cast aside as viciously as he would kick off dogs. And sometimes the haw-hawing Rabelaisian Pullman washroom type of a good fellow, feeling the *adios* of the Wilsonian boot, would have almost human feelings of resentment, which being translated into political influence played havoc with the noble aspirations of a "first-class mind." He did not learn all there is to learn of politics, in college or from books. But he did learn to give his heart to those whom he regarded as his equals. All his life, the class of '79 was near and dear to him. Six years after graduation, he declared to Robert Bridges: "I believe I love the fellows of that crowd and value the genuine friendships existing amongst us more than I ever did before. I often long for the renewal of old comradeships more than I can tell you. The old love never dies down for a moment, but I can't keep myself from an occasional heartsickness now and again, because of the dispersion of the old crowd and the necessity which keeps us apart."

And when he voiced these doleful sentiments to his friend Bridges, Wilson was a bridegroom of a few months! The full relish of the affection that grew into his heart for the men, his equals, "gentlemen unafraid," of those Princeton undergraduate days, never paled in him. Princeton took the boy who had discovered that he had a first-class mind, and showed him in college life that he had a fine Irish heart. So it made a man of him. No one knew better all the noble emotional qualities of that mind than Robert Bridges, who, speaking of him to the Princeton students, said:

There was a certain integrity in his ideal from boy to man that gave his friends a peculiar confidence in his ultimate destiny as a leader of men. It was a jest of his in college which ended, "when I meet you in the Senate, I'll argue that out with you."

To say that Wilson's political career was an accident at the close of his academic life is a grotesquely cheap assessment of the impulse buried and burning in his heart. He was indeed foreordained for politics. Mr. Bridges continues:

Every step in that great career was like a new chapter in a book that we began long ago and in which we were absorbingly interested. To visualize it, I saw him at his various inaugurations — on this platform, saying of Princeton in the Nation's service: "Who shall show us the way?" — and little dreaming that on his tired shoulders would fall the task in a supreme world crisis. I saw him as he marched on foot at the head of a wartime procession along Fifth Avenue — with head erect — alert and firm and enjoying it as he always did.

I know and you know what tunes were ringing in his head as he marched. No Princeton man forgets them. They speak of life and joy and comradeship — and these he had in full. And at the last scene of all, I could rejoice that I had known such a man — that his was the supreme comradeship that never failed in the right. I could hear the tramp of feet, and boys marching together, and a clear voice singing!

No one can doubt that, with all this success in mind and heart which came to him at Princeton, Tommy Wilson, who was easily winner in all contests, in debate, in oration, in essay writing, and who always took the lives of statesmen as his subjects when he wrangled, orated, or wrote, was himself stung by the bee of a political ambition. The other boys intuitively felt the swelling of the sting upon their classmate. Bridges writes:

> Wilson was just the kind of an undergraduate who was often picked by the men who knew him for distinction in public and literary affairs. He never had any other idea in the back of his mind.

What a curious youth he must have been there in college! No college legend links him with any college joke. He developed nothing to dramatize him except his bad temper in tearing up the slip which he drew from the hat in the drawing for the debate, and yet he took honors for his class — debating honors, athletic honors — despite the fact that he played in no athletic games — and literary honors galore. Yet he was always "Tommy," never "Tom." The difference between an inveterate and unconscionable Tommy and a boy who Toms it is all upon the side of the gentle and insidious approach. "Publicly and privately," said Dean H. B. Fine, his co-editor on the Princeton College paper and later Dean of the College under Woodrow Wilson, its President, "publicly and privately, he was one of the most persuasive talkers I ever heard."

"He had an earnestness that was really intense," declared Theodore Hunt, one of his Princeton teachers, "but we did not follow him outside of the classrooms!" Probably because he created only an academic interest in himself.

Another Princeton friend records this impression: "Tommy seemed to have an uncanny sense that he was a man of destiny. Now that I think back to those days, I feel that he was always preparing himself, always looking forward to the time when he might be called to high service. When he walked alone, it was, as he explained, to have opportunity for calm reflection."

What a marvel it is that he was not called "Thomas"! "Tommy" shows that something sweet, affectionate, and charming in his heart fought and conquered his mind's lust to preen and strut in the shadow of his own intellectual pulchritude. It was the Irishman wrestling with the Scot!

A fine tenor voice helped him like an army with banners. He bayed the moon as a member of a serenading quartet and was a consequential figure in the Glee Club. No Priscilla ever succeeded in singing in a rollicking boy's quartet under the windows of the girls thereunto appertaining. And Tommy Wilson sang. So presumably there was, or were, a girl or girls as the case may have been. And she saved him! But what a conflict, what a complex there was to save! — the Woodrow mind, strong, quick, restless, ruthless, insatiable, and the Wilson heart instinctively directing that imperious mind to the study of politics and government — the education of a ruler, predestined by his blood.

Year by year in Princeton, Tommy Wilson grew in his literary experience of politics, turned his information into essays, and his essays into visions. Hence that "uncanny sense that he was a man of destiny." He was walking in those days on Olympus with the great British and American statesmen — Tommy Wilson, "with an earnestness that was intense," a "most persuasive talker" with a habit of "calm reflection" relieved by a tenor voice! What a lad to walk with his little fingers in the hands of the Olympians! What aspiration must have colored his soul with the gray steel of high resolve! His last triumph at Princeton — one which gave him great acclaim among his fellow seniors — was an article upon "Cabinet Government in the United States" which was accepted by the editor of the "International Review," a magazine of the highest standing in America. The senior class viewed their Tommy with awe. After that he ranked as well as an athlete or a budding young drunkard. He became a man among men — almost, but alas not quite, a "Tom"!

From Princeton, Tommy Wilson went to the University of Virginia to study law. His familiar

Scotch devil would not let him be happy out of books, but his good Irish angel saw to it that they were law-books. For, as he has explained in after years, he had a desire to get into politics and the law was the paved way of Southern tradition. At the University of Virginia he was the same anomalous pair of Scotch-Irish twins that distinguished Princeton so gaudily with solid prose and blithesome song, a bookworm afflicted with social rickets. At the University of Virginia legend carries the two Tommy Wilsons to fame; one, whose light in the southeast corner window of "House F" burned far into the night, as he sat there writing Great Thoughts; the other, Tommy Wilson who organized the Glee Club, sailed out under the moon and sang the ditties of the day, "Over the Banister Leans a Face," "Marguerite," "Speed Away," "The Fox is on the Hill," "Golden Slippers," "Forsaken," or, "Hide Away," and gave a grand concert in the Town Hall. The bookworm left the tracery of his devious way in two biographical and critical essays, one on John Bright and another on Gladstone, work of exceptional quality which in later years appeared in Wilson's collected essays, little changed. Indeed, Woodrow Wilson, the President of Princeton, speaking of his youthful essays upon the lives of the great British statesmen said to Dean Fine, of the Princeton College, "I read them again recently and am chagrined to find that my style hasn't improved since I wrote them!" It never improved. Woodrow Wilson had greater things to say than Tommy, was aglow with nobler passions and saw higher stars to which his wagon might be hitched, but Tommy Wilson wrote as well as Woodrow and probably spoke with more fire. For he recited as orations in his literary society these political essays, and old men who heard him forty-five years ago say he thrilled his world. The gristle of his youth was becoming the bone of his maturity in those Virginia days. Woodrow was hoving in sight. But Tommy kept on singing, roistering, rollicking, playing a little baseball, joining the Phi Kappa Psi fraternity, writing nonsense rhymes for college festivals and cutting gay capers before high Heaven.

That was the last of Tommy Wilson, there at Virginia cavorting through the pillared halls that Jefferson designed after the palaces of Palladio. There, amid the beauty and romance of the hilarious cloister, where youth is eternal, renewing itself every year in happy springs that come bubbling out of childhood, Woodrow Wilson, turning some sudden corner, lost Tommy forever. But always the flaxen-haired boy who kept the log of the avenging South Seas ship, who sailed his boats in the rain-flushed gutters of Augusta, who played Indian and led the "Lightfoots," the long-headed, spectacled lad of the glorious dreams who sat in the Wilson pew or, perched on a gatepost before the manse, jeered the passing soldiers, the unwhipped cub who never chained his temper nor denied his soul's high visions, always this little lost Tommy sat in a secret corner of the man's heart, and sometimes peeked out into life and great affairs with complacent glee or puerile anger as he saw some moving circumstance along the way where the man stalked in the procession of life.

Now, before he goes, we may take one more epitaphic peep at Tommy. We have it recorded by the young Woodrow in an essay on Gladstone written in Virginia. Of his hero, he says:

> He must have been a sober thoughtful boy; full of spirit without being boisterous; eager and impetuous without being imperious; a leader of sport as in study; straightforward in everything — even his hatreds; half-souled in nothing, not even his faults.

So good-bye, Tommy, and God bless you. Father of the man you were — and a real man, too, a big, brave, wise man, "straightforward in everything — even his hatreds; half-souled in nothing, not even his faults." But if the lad who wrote that misread his Gladstone, he surely knew the Wilsons —

Tommy and Woodrow. And being a Celt, the lad was fay before his passing. He was a seventh son of a seventh son of Calvin born with a double caul. He could look back into life and understand how things had been. And also he could look forward into life and see things as they would be. Almost the last thing Tommy ever wrote before Woodrow submerged him was a collegiate oration about Pitt, the Earl of Chatham. Read its climax and see what strange prescience lay in the boy's heart.

With Pitt's acceptance of an earldom not only his official power, but also much of his innate greatness passed away. Disease had unarmed him, and he refused to aid his country at a time of sorest need, thus, in a moment of folly, well-nigh undoing the great work of a memorable lifetime. William Pitt was a noble statesman; the Earl of Chatham was a noble ruin. But in his death we catch a faint glimmer of his manhood. Under the deepening shadow of a gathering storm we obtain a last glimpse of Chatham, as he stands, himself a wreck, holding up before a blind Ministry a picture of the dark ruin which was awaiting them. With some of his old haughtiness the austere old man rises to answer one who had dared to reply to him, and falls, never to rise again.

Ah! Tommy Wilson, Tommy Wilson, frisking with the lads on Princeton campus, singing on the steps of Nassau Hall with the happy seniors, how could you hold your voice from breaking, your eyes always aglow, your hands so steady, with the picture of that broken old man in your heart — an old man leaning upon his cane with his dead hand limp at his side, standing wearily upon his front porch in "S" Street "under the deepening shadow of the gathering storm, himself a wreck holding up before a blind Ministry a picture of the dark ruin which was awaiting them. With some of his old haughtiness the austere old man rises . . . and falls, never to rise again!"

What a broth of boy you were, Tommy Wilson!

CHAPTER V

LAGGING ON THE ACADEMIC STAGE

SOME account of the birth of Woodrow, successor to Tommy Wilson, may be interesting. We have two accounts, differing but not necessarily in conflict. The MacMasters tradition in Columbia, South Carolina, declares that he changed his name from Tommy to Woodrow because "Tommy" lacked dignity. For, said he, "It's Tommy the turkey and Tommy the cat and Tommy the gardener. So I dropped it." But to his friend, Robert Bridges, Woodrow Wilson declared: "I find I need a trade-mark in advertising my literary wares. Thomas W. Wilson lacks something. Woodrow Wilson sticks in the mind. So I have decided publicly to be Woodrow Wilson."

With the acceptance of the essay upon "Congressional Government" by the "International Magazine," Woodrow Wilson seems to have decided rather definitely that he could make his way as a writer. For after that he was continually writing, and writing well, during the twenty years that followed. His bread-and-butter career was in the college. But he depended for his fame upon his pen.

Perhaps the familiar spirit that kept him within the inexorable cycle of his destiny held him more or less of a student in the academic world for nearly six years after his graduation. Certainly his long preparation for serious study and solid writing upon modern governmental problems stood him in good stead. If it was planned, he was wise who planned it. And the purpose and foresight in the Scotch heart of him give every color to the belief that Woodrow Wilson stayed in college, not from any dilettante fear of contact with the world, but from a feeling that he needed more and better preparation for his work than Princeton and the Virginia University gave him.

He never was graduated from the law school of the University of Virginia. The frailty which always was his physical heritage overcame him and in the mid-year he went home to Wilmington. He studied law at home, and in May, 1882, went to Atlanta, the most rapidly growing city in the South at the time and opened a law office with another youth, Edward I. Renick. The best picture of Woodrow Wilson, the lawyer in Atlanta, he has painted himself in his essay upon Burke:

> What he did it is idle to speculate, being confident that he did whatever he pleased. "The law," Burke declared in Parliament twenty years later, "is in my opinion one of the first and noblest of sciences; . . . but it is not apt, except in persons very happily born, to open and

liberalize the mind." And, although himself a person "very happily born" he felt that the life of a lawyer would inevitably confine his roving mind within intolerable limits. He learned the law as he learned everything else, with an eye to discovering points of contact with affairs.

This is Woodrow Wilson describing himself under the title of Edmund Burke. Burke's father, according to the Wilson essay, was "sorely disappointed." According to the Bellamy tradition, Dr. Joseph Wilson one day accosted John Bellamy, a young lawyer in Wilmington, and said: "John, how much are you making?" John knew to a nickel how much he was making, having plenty of time in which to add it up, and some pride. "About eighteen hundred dollars," assured John. "Well," returned the Doctor chewing a bitter cud, "so you are, are you? The boy down in Atlanta isn't making his salt."

The son [continues young Woodrow, writing of young Burke] preferred the life of the town to systematic study in chambers, wrote for the papers instead of devoting himself to the profession he had been sent to master. "Of his leisure time," said the "Annual Register" just after his death, "much was spent in the company of Mrs. Woffington, a celebrated actress."

The parallel in the Wilson case is this. In his Atlanta law office, instead of writing for the papers as Burke did, Wilson began writing a book — to wit, "Congressional Government in the United States," which afterwards was a highly remunerative text-book and became the thesis upon which he got his doctor's degree at Johns Hopkins. As for the Mrs. Woffington of one sort or another usually found in a young man's life, it was a good sort in Wilson's life. And to know about her let us open "A History of Rome and Floyd County," Georgia. On page 290 we read:

The Bones family are related to the Wilson family through Mrs. Bones, who, before her marriage to Mr. James W. Bones, was Miss Marion Woodrow, the sister of Miss Janet Woodrow, who married Mr. Joseph Wilson, the father of President Woodrow Wilson. Hence Mrs. Bones was Woodrow Wilson's aunt. Woodrow Wilson, a young man, visited Mrs. Bones, then living in East Rome, and his cousin, Mrs. A. Thew H. (Jessie Bones) Brower. It was at Mrs. Brower's home that he met Miss Ellen Louise Axson, who later became his wife in Savannah.

The chance circumstance of a slack legal practice for a young lawyer quite possibly explains how Rome was put more prominently in the public eye than in any other chain of circumstances since the city's establishment. Woodrow Wilson was twenty-six years old in 1882, when Judge George Hillyer, of Atlanta, and others signed his license to practice his profession in that city, shortly before he paid a visit to Rome. The Bones family were staunch Presbyterians. Hence, when Sunday rolled around there was no conflict as to whether the young barrister should attend services, and where. With Mr. and Mrs. Bones and his first cousin, Miss Helen Bones, Mr. Wilson went to the Brick Church. The sermon was not so engrossing that the visitor failed to notice the piquant beauty of a girl with brown eyes, and hair that fell in graceful curls upon her forehead, sitting hard by. He looked not once, but several times before the sermon was concluded, and stole a glance or so as the congregation were leaving for their homes. He was so fascinated by this young lady's beauty that he inquired as to who she might be and if by some chance he might not be privileged to meet her. He was told that she was Ellen Louise Axson, daughter of the Reverend Samuel Edward Axson, the pastor.

(Which is all very fine as romantic history. But the cold fact is that the Axson and Wilson families were upon visiting terms in Augusta. And it is family tradition that in the heyday of his youth, say at eight or ten years, young Tommy was fond of the Axson baby who was several years younger than he, and often asked to hold the baby when the Axson family came to visit. Probably this is a big-sister legend, as any self-respecting boy would be ashamed of it and consciously forget it. The legend is a deadly indictment of the family that would repeat it. But they did even worse: the family preserved an awful tale that when the children were little tots, young Tommy swore that he would grow up and marry Ellen Lou! If great men could only have foresight to throttle their big sisters!)

Mrs. Brower found that she could do her Atlanta cousin a good turn, so proposed that they invite Miss Axson and several others to go on a picnic east of Lindale, to a spring which forms part of the headwaters of Silver Creek. The meeting-place was at the Brower home, and when young Woodrow asked if he hadn't better take some lunch, Miss Ellen Lou readily suggested that she had plenty for two, and this offer left no room for argument.

The distance was eight or nine miles, and two rigs were used; the more attractive of the two for the young folks was Colonel Brower's wagon with side seats, in the body of which plenty of wheat straw had been piled; Woodrow and Ellen Lou chose the back of the wagon that they might dangle their feet behind, and away went the future President of the United States and the future First Lady of the Land, caring little whether school kept or law business were remunerative or not. After bumping along country roads for an hour and a half, they arrived at the picnic ground. Lunch-time came and all were summoned to the well-filled baskets. All save two were ravenously hungry after a session of romping and wading. These two were industriously searching for four-leaf clovers on the pasture greensward; playing "Love-me; love me not" with flower petals; blowing the downy tops off dandelion stems.

"I wonder where Ellie Lou and Woodrow can be?" asked Mrs. Brower, as if aware of nothing.

"I know," piped one of the children; "he's over there cutting a heart on a beech tree!"

The preliminaries were all disposed of that day and fervent resolutions made if not promises exacted.

(Wilson was a man of quick decisions and strong purpose — a fast worker.)

The fates which had been cruel to Rome smiled upon the dilemma of the young Atlanta lawyer. A freshet in 1881 swept away the first East Rome bridge (over the

Etowah at Second Avenue). The river separated Woodrow and Ellen Lou, so the former borrowed a batteau and they not only crossed, but paddled up and down. We hear much of President Wilson's famous typewriter, and of how he would put on his old gray sweater of his Princeton days and peck away at it on the George Washington; League of Nations "dope" ground out on the high seas. But again we must go back to Rome. He brought his typewriter with him in 1882 and did some copying for Colonel Brower.

Now possibly this "History of Rome and Floyd County" may be inaccurate in details, but in the main it tells how Woodrow Wilson emulated Burke when the law was an indulgent mistress. Probably Ellen Axson was not, as Wilson describes the immortal Peg Woffington, "sought by men of wit and genius and by men of pleasure." But Ellen Axson could paint and went to New York to study "Art," which was, in the Presbyterian world of Rome, Georgia, and Wilmington, North Carolina, a fair replica of the gay life of the gay old town in Burke's and Goldsmith's day.

This love affair was destined to be the greatest episode that ever came into the life of Woodrow Wilson. From it came twenty-nine years of happiness, three splendid daughters, and the cheerful, wholesome, domestic background of a useful life. So we should consider this affair with Ellen Axson in its early and revealing moments. Let us therefore call upon Stockton Axson, her brother, to testify. He wrote in 1916 when the campaign of that year was a bit heavy with slander, an article for the "New York Times," "The Private Life of Woodrow Wilson," which was later made into a brochure in which we get a picture of the Presbyterian preacher's son, who came to woo the Presbyterian preacher's daughter. Mr. Axson writes:

> But I very distinctly remember the first time that anybody talked to me in detail about Woodrow Wilson; it was my father, in a letter written to me when I was away at school. I think my father went on the theory that his example would do more for my upbringing than wordy precepts, and so the first homily he ever delivered to me was in the form of a long letter written just after Woodrow Wilson had ended a visit to his relatives in Rome. My father made this young man, ten years older than myself, his text, described him, and held him up to me as a pattern of young manhood. I recall one phrase, virtually verbatim: "I can think of nothing that would make me so happy as to have a son like that."
>
> That letter was written thirty-four years ago; but I remember it vividly, both because it was practically the only private sermon my father ever preached to me, and because the wish expressed was fulfilled, not in the way he was hoping, by my transformation, but by Woodrow Wilson himself becoming my father's son by marriage. My father lived to know of the engagement, though he died before the marriage.

Here we confront the danger that seemed always to be hovering like a pall over Woodrow Wilson's

ELLEN LOU AXSON

life. In childhood he came dangerously near the line where the Model Child emerges into the pestilence. In adolescence his enemies would have branded him an Exemplary Youth. And here, by the word of his father-in-law elect, we come to regard him as almost a Worthy Young Man. He was not. College tradition gives him full many a good red damn in his vocabulary. Certainly he set to the task of making love to Ellen Axson, according to the Roman legend, in a business-like way. He might well be called red-blooded in this enterprise. He was a youth of exceptional culture and wise as the canny Scotch blood of him would make him. And with wisdom he had charm; the bite of the Blarney Stone was on his tongue. And to top it all, he was handsome — tall, straight, agile, and flaxen fair; with his father's merry eye and his mother's gentle voice, both speaking in the persuasive fashion of the Celt when he had his say. No wonder parents in Wilmington cleared the parlor decks for action, "removed the interferences," when he called, and that the godly Father Axson clave to the young man as a son.

But we must let the brother-in-law and friend take up the story of the courtship. It differs slightly from the Roman version, but no matter.

It was in 1883 that Woodrow Wilson and Ellen Axson became engaged. She was visiting friends in the North

Carolina mountains when my father fell seriously ill. He had me summon her home by telegram — my mother had died two years before, and my sister was the responsible member of the family. She went to Asheville to catch a train, but as she had to wait several hours for it she went to a hotel and whiled away the time reading by a window. As fate would have it, Woodrow Wilson, who was driving in the mountains, passed the hotel, chanced to look up, and saw her profile at the window. The two had been together in Rome the previous summer, and it needed just the unexpected encounter in the North Carolina mountains to show them what life meant for each and for both of them.

Unforgettable for me is the conversation which my sister and I had on the night of her arrival home. In the earlier part of the evening she had been anxious about my father, but when he had at last been made comfortable and had fallen asleep, she joined me in the little sitting-room, her dear face flushed, her eyes bright. "Can you keep a secret?" she asked, and upon my intimation that I could, she told me that she was engaged to be married, the manner of the meeting, and her joy. "He is the greatest man in the world," she said, "and the best." In that faith she never faltered in all the years that followed.

Of the many mental pictures which I have of my sister three at this moment stand out with peculiar vividness: the way she looked that night when she told me of her engagement, the way she looked when she held their first-born in her arms, waiting for him to come from a distant place for the first sight of his child, and the way she looked in the little cottage at Princeton the night that he was elected President of the United States.

The engagement lasted two years. The young

man quit the law and went to Johns Hopkins to get his doctor's degree; the young woman went to New York to study painting. They met often and were happy. At Johns Hopkins the young Mr. Wilson seems to have lost none of the rollick in his heart. He was the moving spirit in the Glee Club. He stayed there two years holding an historical fellowship and continued writing the book which he had started in his lonely Atlanta law office. He wrote during that Johns Hopkins period a "Sketch of Adam Smith," published later in "Mere Literature," and strengthened the foundation for his career as a public man by studying under Herbert B. Adams, the historian, and Richard T. Ely, the great liberal economist, under whom, through books and in the classroom, so many of the liberals of the first two decades of this century received their inspiration. The Glee Club got into a row with the President of the University. Wilson felt that the Club should charge admission for its concerts at the university in order to pay necessary expenses. President Gilman offered to appropriate the money from the university funds. But, protested Wilson the insurgent, the Glee Club has its dignity to consider as well as the university. So the free and unfettered Glee Club gave its concert and charged admission. The protestant had his way. It was the right way, and he was willing to make a row for it. Calvin felt the same way about his disputes. The Glee Club, the Athletic Association — all the student activities of the university interested the young man. He was what is known as "a friendly cuss" in the American vernacular, and never a grind. Yet he did hard work, important work at Johns Hopkins, work that in his later years gave him the strength and wisdom to be spokesman for the idealism of the world.

He left Johns Hopkins University in 1885 after the university had agreed to accept the book "Congressional Government" as his doctor's thesis. For ten years, at Davidson College, at Princeton, at Virginia University, at Johns Hopkins, he had been living in the academic world. During all that time he had been interested in history and government. He had studied, spoken, and written almost exclusively of his heroes, men in public affairs and leaders of great popular movements. He had in his school and college days met, worked, and played with other boys who were destined to become successful Americans. In his boyhood he played with Justice Lamar, of the United States Supreme Court, Congressman William H. Fleming; Pleasant Stovall, Minister to Switzerland, W. A. Keener, Law Professor at Harvard and later head of Columbia Law School; at Wilmington he chummed and read with

John D. Bellamy, later a Congressman. In his Princeton class were Robert Bridges, editor of "Scribner's Magazine"; Rev. Dr. A. S. Halsey, Secretary of the Presbyterian Mission Board; Congressman Charles A. Talcott; Mahlon Pitney, Justice of the United States Supreme Court; and Robert H. McCarter, Attorney-General of New Jersey. At Johns Hopkins he sang in the Glee Club with Albert Shaw, editor of the "Review of Reviews"; F. M. Warren, Professor of Modern Languages at Yale; Dr. E. L. R. Gould, of New York; Charles H. Levermore, winner of the Bok Peace Prize; Arthur Yager, college president, and Governor of Porto Rico. With these young men, who had in them the fire that circumstance blew upon and gave them distinction, inevitably came a clash of minds, a stimulation of purpose, a mutual development of spiritual earnestness that helped the young academic statesman as he surely helped them. They and his home with books and the talk of things of the mind made his spiritual environment a veritable nursery wherein the heredity of the line of Presbyterian ancestry — Scotch and Irish, mostly preachers, with an editor by way of spice — worked with the miraculous precision which heredity performs when environment encourages. And we have here, stepping out of his decade of hard intellectual training, a man with a hard-fibered brain, an intellectual athlete, morally endowed by his forbears with spiritual brawn — a veritable bridegroom coming forth rejoicing as a strong man to run a race. And what a track lay before him!

But why hinder the bridegroom? Let his brother-in-law, Stockton Axson, unleash him. We read:

It was two years before they were married (he was studying at Johns Hopkins University in Baltimore) in the manse of the Independent Presbyterian Church in Savannah, Georgia, his father and her grandfather officiating. I remember how he and I chatted about the books in my grandfather's bookcases while we waited for the bride to come downstairs. I also remember a less idyllic circumstance, how bliss was jarred and the scent of orange blossoms temporarily annulled while two small boys, the bridegroom's nephew, Wilson Howe, and the bride's brother, Edward Axson, "mixed it up" in a gorgeous fight over some difference in boyish opinions. The bride was much shocked; but I caught a twinkle in the bridegroom's eye, which seemed to say, "Let's separate them; but don't let's be in too desperate haste about it."

That fight was Heaven-sent. It lifts a cloying narrative to an epic plane and must redeem Wilson forever from the white curse of perfection. A man who could rejoice in a kin fight on his wedding day surely has that broad catholic taste in joy which shows the understanding heart. Perhaps civilization had softened him. Three generations up the ancestral tree he would have participated in the fight. But his encouraging twinkle proves that his instincts were good. The little boy in his heart clapped his hands in glee. It was pie for Tommy.

CHAPTER VI

OUR HERO WAITS FOR OPPORTUNITY

WOODROW WILSON had his golden years in his thirties and mid-forties. In those years he was a college professor. They were happy, growing years; years without strife or conflict — indeed, without great responsibility. In the period from 1885, when he became a professor at Bryn Mawr, until he was chosen President of Princeton, life handed Woodrow Wilson most of the good things that come to common men. He quit school as a student, but remained as a teacher in the academic world, which he loved. As a teacher, he kept on intimate terms with books. He read widely in his chosen field of knowledge — a fairly narrow sphere, limited largely by the relation of man to his fellows — history, government, and economics. And because his field was narrow, he filled up and spilled himself in books. He read that he might teach well. And then, having taught what he read, he put it on paper and printed it in books — books made from books. They were creditable books, showing careful and intelligent research. They sold well because they filled a need — chiefly a need in American colleges for honest, interesting texts along the lines which he was following — a consideration of man in his social relations. He never strayed. Poetry, fiction, drama, the natural sciences, mathematics, and the beckoning vista of pure logic never lured him. He had no hobbies, no intellectual diversions. He gloried in what he called his "single-track mind." The purpose of the Woodrows never bent in the Wilson flare for felicity. Yet in his iron purpose, he must have been happy. One gets a picture of him from the beginning of those professorial days, a gay, charming, resolute young man — a picture not unlike that of his country in those days, a gay, charming, resolute young land.

It is odd and noteworthy that the historian and sociologist, who had been reading books about history and social relations for a dozen years and writing books about his country, its history, and its government, should have written nothing and probably had seen little of the miracle of American development growing up beside him. In the seventies and eighties of the last century and well into the nineties, the three decades following the Civil War, the American continent for the first time came under the plough. More land changed from pastoral agriculture to crop-farming than ever underwent that change in any other three decades in the history of the earth. A new civilization was set up. And out of it was coming a new political idea—a revolutionary change in American political institutions. As the farmer of the Middle West began ploughing, he began working out a new government. It voiced its ideals raucously in Greenbackism and in Populism. These "isms" were the farmers' protest against a threatening plutocracy. For, as the farmers hurried westward, they carried their exploiters with them, as happy a band of freebooters as ever boarded an honest ship. They built the railroads, threw the iron and stone and wood and brick together that made the towns; opened the banks, bought the legislatures, owned the sovereign States; ruled with a high and often a noble hand. It was gorgeous, the government established by these dear old pirates of commerce — railroad lords, trust magnates, money kings. It was the temporary feudalism of a transition period. It was not democracy. And the protest of the man at the bottom, the exploited, was a strange note in American politics. The clash between the mushroom lords of the new order and the improvised serfs of the new order made a most picturesque combat. But the young professor of history, busy with his books and his typewriter in the industrial section of his country, did not see it. Or, if he did see it, he never wrote or talked about it. He lived the sheltered life. The protesting clash of the farmer with the capitalist was of the earth earthy; bewhiskered, sockless, noisy, mad, blind, but bitterly sincere. It was something that no son of Dr. Joseph Ruggles Wilson, scion of the old Kings of Ireland, should look upon except in high disdain. Yet out of that wild clamor of the Greenbackers and Populists came the Progressives, and later the Liberals who were to choose Woodrow Wilson for their leader. It was odd that when they were young and he was young, "and lutes were touched and songs were sung," they were strangers to one another!

Woodrow Wilson and Ellen Axson, his bride, came to Bryn Mawr, a college for women, a few miles out of Philadelphia, in the autumn of 1885. That was the year when the young bridegroom was eating his heart out in sorrow for the fellows of the Princeton class of '79 from whom he had been exiled six long dreadful years! Youth does have a sad time with sorrows like that! At Bryn Mawr the bridegroom made small impression on the woman's college. To-day tradition there says: "Bryn Mawr got two things from Princeton: its architecture and Woodrow Wilson." It was a new institution, brand-new when the bridegroom came. Along with him came a lot of other pedagogic fledglings from Johns Hopkins, so many, indeed, that the new college was nicknamed "Johanna Hopkins"! And only two things significant of those first days of his work in the school are embedded in the legend of his life: first, that Miss Thomas, Dean of the school, advised him to offer his new book, "Congressional Government," as a thesis for a doctorate at Johns Hopkins; and second, that Ellen Axson, always his good angel, advised him there to cut off the long drooping silken mustache that he had grown since his Princeton days. It never returned, and Woodrow Wilson went smooth-faced through life. That at least is worth a tablet at Bryn Mawr!

For some good reason the young married couple did not like the situation as they found it at Bryn Mawr. Mr. Wilson told one biographer that "the social advantages were inadequate," which reveals little. His fellow workers on the faculty remember the young doctor as a hard worker. He tried to make his lectures interesting. But politics, American history, and economics were not subjects that appealed greatly to young women of that day. And if Woodrow Wilson did not do a casual thing well enough to succeed and to prove his success by the approval of his kind, he would inevitably quit it. Anything but neglect might be borne with humility by a Wilson. But neglect, indifference, mere tolerance — a classroom of drooping, yawning girls, with here and there a bluestocking rampant — these were not for the son of his father. Those were the days of the dominant Wilson. In unison tradition chants the legend of his charm. He had a way with him — the old Doctor's way, elegant but facile, gracious but dignified, and always decently merry; cracking his erudite professorial jokes, picking with loving care his professorial language, and being young and handsome and never unaware of it, displaying his professorial charm in the hope which proved a vain hope that he would bring into his classroom the fickle goddess of success. But she spurned him. Tommy Wilson, who played with Jessie Bones out at Sandridge, who had his little lonely love affairs in Columbia and Wilmington, who had a few meager fellowships with the youths of the South, might have snapped up the crumbs of comradeship at Bryn Mawr. But Woodrow Wilson had known the tall towers of fellowship at Princeton, in Whig Hall, in the Glee Club at Virginia University, and always in the class of '79. Never could he be a squire of dames. So he left Bryn Mawr and went to Wesleyan University at Middletown, Connecticut.

There were men, and there was a man's job. Women came to Wesleyan in those days, but they were not in the Wilson cosmos. We must never forget, in dealing with the young professor, that we are dealing with a man who had in the back of his head always, as Robert Bridges, his best friend, remembers him, the notion that he was to be some one in the political life of the Nation. When a boy says, even jokingly, "I'll argue that out with you in the Senate," as he meets a tough opponent in debate, and when he goes to Atlanta to practice law before becoming a college professor, it signifies something in his life. The college profession was bread and butter. But public affairs were his meat and drink! So he took leadership among the boys of Wesleyan University naturally, unconsciously, as he taught economics, history, and political affairs — men's affairs in those days.

We may well pause to look at him as he "comes forth from his chamber rejoicing as a strong man," in his first thirties in the first term of Grover Cleveland, when the land is booming, when all that Grandfather "Jimmy" Wilson dreamed of — a great industrial Nation — is coming true in the East; and when all the righteousness that Grandfather Thomas Woodrow preached is rising in protest in the breasts of the bewhiskered political pariahs of the West and South, against the iniquities of a booming land. The grandson, under his academic elms, seems quite oblivious of the tumult in the East and the turmoil in the hinterland. He stands, a tallish, straight-limbed, well-tailored, fashionably haberdashed man of full vigor in the youth of his manhood — almost in its adolescence. For he is still a slow-bloomer, still with much to reveal. His brownish hair is thick, though not a leonine mane as his father's was in Staunton, because barbers' styles have changed. He has long legs and a short body, quick and nimble, but a bit inept, though never gawky. For he has grace in him — the young Irish rascal — and charm. Always from those days comes the story of his charm. He looks much as the old Doctor looked in his early thirties; has that long jaw, the horse face of the North-of-Ireland man, a strong, sensuous mouth — big and resolute with a loose upper lip — and big ears well set below a narrow but ample brain pan. His eyes in those days were the bold, clear, wistful, yet always indomitable eyes of the dreamer. But let a fellow faculty man of Wesleyan, Professor Morris B. Crawford, tell how Wilson and his family came to Wesleyan. Nearly forty years later he writes:

They were cared for for a couple of days in two or three of the faculty homes. So Mrs. Crawford and I had them as guests under our roof. I shall never forget the easy and companionable way in which he fitted into the new fellowship which greeted him in our faculty circle; nor the breadth of information, the humor, the rare gift of expression that made it a delight to hear him talk.

Mrs. Wilson, too, was a person of rare charm, a gifted talker, manifestly devoted in fond admiration to her talented husband. And she had an apparently artless knack of suggestion which from time to time recalled to his memory a happy anecdote or started him on a new line of discussion.

Ellen Axson was a young wife then, barely out of her honeymoon, carrying her first child. She lived with her husband nearly thirty years, knitting into his life deeply and closely, until, as is inevitable in unions where there is close comradeship, their lives became a sort of joint ownership of character, aspiration, and happiness. And while she lived and they loved and together strove for their hearts' desire in the way of worldly or spiritual things, it was one career, one common complex character that they welded out of life and circumstance. Woodrow Wilson was that kind of a married man, entirely domestic! This must be set down early and never be forgotten in this story. James Wilson and Ann Adams were in him and old Thomas Woodrow and his first wife; very much in him, complicating his life, were Joseph Ruggles Wilson and Janet Woodrow, all mixing his blood inheritance and producing his spiritual environment, and so, like relentless fates, weaving the fabric of his life. But into the texture of their spiritual woof came the bright skein that a long line of Presbyterian preachers, one generation out of New England, and preachers' daughters had woven into the life of Ellen Axson. When he stood up in that Wesleyan Chapel to pray, it was not only that the Reverend Thomas Woodrow and his father before him and Ann Adams and her Presbyterian father and the Reverend Joseph Ruggles Wilson and Uncle James Woodrow should all be clamoring in his veins for Presbyterian liberty and power of speech, but also Ellen Axson and her father and her father's father's father all descended upon Woodrow Wilson and gave him grace in prayer. Is it, then, a wonder that Professor Crawford should write:

> I love to recall one occasion when he conducted the morning college chapel service. While Mr. Moody, the revivalist, was conducting a series of meetings in Middletown, Mr. Wilson, who evidently had been touched, as we all had been, by the intense earnestness of the great evangelist, voiced his prayer for us in his own words, which, by their earnestness, their originality and beauty of expression, their precise adaptation to the demands of the moment, were far more effective than any possible prescribed form of prayer could have been. Nobody who heard that prayer could doubt that Woodrow Wilson was a man of profound faith in God.

No intelligent consideration of the life of Woodrow Wilson can omit the influence of Ellen Axson, his wife. So let us set down something of the kind of woman she was in those formative days of the late adolescence of this pair. Of course she was Southern, and had that exterior languor and softness which seemed at the time to be the necessary crust of a well-bred Southern lady. The word "woman" was not used politely in her girlhood days. And always Ellen Axson was a lady. Beautiful she was; with an exquisite sweetness which belied a rather stern and somber soul beneath her gentle manners. She was the exact complement of her husband; serious where he was gay; questioning where he was sure; patient where he often was brusque. Her grandparents, coming out of New England, must have packed in their belongings a New England conscience which came to her. Once, in the golden age of their thirties, when Mrs. Wilson had doubts of her Calvinistic religion, "Woodrow," says the narrator of the incident, "had no doubts!" Grimly she set to work to read philosophy, to delve into history, and so to quell her doubts. No light woman was she who lightly accepted her religion. It was the core of her soul. She kept her interest in painting while the babies came and the family duties widened. Beauty always enthralled her. But it didn't entice her to gayety. The blitheness, the eternal fun-making of her husband never aroused in her a frivolous mood. But she was wise. She surrounded him, whenever she could, with those who would feed her husband's hunger for gayety. So always in the Wilson home she kept young life; her brothers, at times his father, who was Ariel grown gray, and young cousins of various degrees. With these about him in his home Woodrow Wilson frisked into a middle-aged faun still cutting the gay capers of youth. But when he needed counsel, when his purpose needed strengthening, when the iron prods of life lost their velvet paddings, he turned to Ellen Axson for help, for strength, for wisdom.

So, when Professor Crawford tells us "that nobody who heard that prayer could doubt that Woodrow Wilson was a man of profound faith in God," we must remember that also he was Ellen Axson's husband, but that there was a considerable area outside of her sphere wherein he was not a Calvinistic monk. He was far from it.

The ambition in the back of his head was forever pushing him into leadership. He had been in Wesleyan but a few months when he organized among the boys two things: the football team and The House of Commons, a debating society. "Professor Wilson," declares a writer in the "Wesleyan Alumnus," "put new life into the practice of debate. As he put it, 'To argue on any side without the basis of conviction is mental suicide.' On his arrival at Middletown, Professor Wilson was made one of three members of the Wesleyan Football Association, serving throughout the weeks of fall practice as one of the coaches, assisting the captain in devising new plays. He told them there that he was referee and one of the directors of the Princeton team in its championship days, and was kept from being on the victorious team only by a prolonged illness." That illness was part of the frailty that made him teach the "Lightfoots" parliamentary law, handicapped him and sent him home from Davidson, put him in executive places rather than active work in athletics in Princeton, barred him from the team and sent him home from the University of Virginia, and followed him through life in every great crisis. But he made a good coach. "Football tactics underwent a change at that time, and those men mapped out a plan whereby the rush line was so contracted that the men stood side by side about as to-day, while the backs were brought nearer to the rush line. Quick line plunges and double criss-cross plays were also worked out"; and so Wesleyan had a winning team. It whipped everything of its size, and when there was talk of trying to score against the big teams — Yale, for instance — Wilson, who never could bear to admit inferiority, told the team: "That's no ambition at all. Go in and win. You can lick Yale as well as any other team. Go after their scalp. Don't admit that they can beat you." Again the "Alumnus Magazine" tells a football story:

Thanksgiving brought a hard storm, and the day's battle was fought in a sea of mud. The Lehigh team developed an altogether unexpected strength, and the game was going their way. Twice Lehigh scored easy touchdowns, and it seemed as though Wesleyan faced certain defeat. Then suddenly, from the Wesleyan bleachers, a man walked out in front clad in heavy rubber boots and a raincoat. He shouted to the Wesleyan contingent, reproaching them for not cheering for their team, and at once began to lead them in the Wesleyan yell, beating time for them with his umbrella. He continued this violently until the Wesleyan cheers heartened Slayback's men in spite of their handicap, and the tide of the game turned for two touchdowns as Peck, McDonald, Slayback, and Hall crashed into the Brown and White line, and tied the score. After the game, the Lehigh players, inquiring about the magnetic cheer-leader, were informed that he was Wesleyan's professor of history, Dr. Woodrow Wilson. "Well," returned the Lehigh men, "he is all right, for he saved you."

There was the leader developing, organizing men, starting them on new trails, goading their ambitions, spurring them to their best form.

Now let us look at him as a young teacher. The Wilsons lived in a white frame house on High Street — a street which Charles Dickens, visiting Middletown twenty years before, called "the most beautiful avenue in America." The house stood among great elms and maples in a wide lawn, all typical of our American college towns. When he was not teaching, he was writing his "History of the American People."

But in classroom he was a most engaging young person. A member of his classes at Wesleyan writes:

> As the lecture began, there was an air of expectancy — and often we were so interested in the diction and body of his discourse that we forgot to take notes. I can see him now with his hands forward, the tips of his fingers just touching the table, his face earnest and animated, many times illuminating an otherwise dry and tedious subject by beautiful language and apt illustrations. When we came unprepared to his first lecture, the young professor said: "Well — gentlemen, if you want me to lecture on constitutional law, offhand, I suppose I can!" And thrusting his hands deep into his trousers pockets as a bracer, he proceeded to lecture extemporaneously for an hour.

It was that fine free way with him that made the young professor a favorite in the college. When he had been walking the floor with the baby the night before, he said so, and asked his classes to bear with him. He cracked jokes and got on fraternal terms with every one. Those were the Wilsonian days; the Woodrows lay submerged in his being. If he had adversaries, he loved them and forgot them. It was a gala time in the Wilson life. Ellen Axson was young and lovely. The house was full of joy and children, and the world was bringing him rare gifts, fame through his books, success in his classes, the comradeship of friends, and the sweet communion with his beloved: his wife, his father who sometimes came

North to visit him, young Stockton Axson, who all his life was a dear brother to him, and the adoration of his little children. His God, all his life, had showered upon him benevolences which strengthened his faith in the moral government of the universe. He lived in the best houses, with the best people, in the most favored and beautiful places in his land. He had a clear, quick mind and a handsome body, though frail, in those Wesleyan days and in the decade that followed those days. Then, by way of rooting Woodrow Wilson's faith in the goodness of God and the essential nobility of man, destiny gilded and bejeweled all his gifts. His family idolized him. His books brought him money along with his fame. He went out lecturing, and audiences applauded and paid well. Success came in his calling.

Ten years after he left Princeton as a senior, he came back there as a teacher — Professor of Jurisprudence, teaching political science. It was a triumph, a triumph of virtue. For we must never forget what kind of a boy, youth, and man Woodrow Wilson was — a "mischievous bundle of nerves," but good; a studious and devoted son, slanting slightly toward piety; a gay and affectionate man, but powerful in prayer — "a perfect and an upright man" — barring a bad temper. He had every reason that Job had before his affliction for the faith that was in him.

CHAPTER VII

MR. WILSON TAKES HIS PEN IN HAND

All his life Woodrow Wilson's major delusion was that he had a first-class mind. Tommy in the library with the old Doctor, suddenly bursting forth with the confession that he had a first-class mind, seems to have erected one of the stumbling-blocks of Woodrow Wilson's career. What he had was a clear, clean, strong brain that was inadequately supported by a frail body. Always the brain was active. He had "the 'satiable curtiosity" of Kipling's "Elephant's Child." He never was content to loll mentally in the idle luxury of his achievement. He wrote well. He had capacity for research, not an extraordinary capacity as scholarly capacity goes; not the capacity which a first-class German savant would develop, but still the five good talents.

The period, approximately a decade, of his Princeton professorship, was a period devoted to writing. It was profitable. His work in that decade was highly enriching to the American collegiate world, but of no great importance outside that world. Few men of his attainments have exceeded the quantity and quality of his literary achievements. But he was not in the world's first or second class of thinkers or writers. If he had known this later in life, it would have been easier for him to mingle in fellowship with third and fourth raters in their lines of activity and of thought, with a tolerant patience which would have been beneficial to mankind.

His Princeton position as a teacher gave Mr. Wilson much time for writing. During his professorial days at Bryn Mawr, at Wesleyan, and at Princeton, the serious academic writing of his life was done. It is his best literary output. Speaking broadly, this includes his books, "Congressional Government; a Study of American Politics," 1885; "The State: Elements of Historical and Practical Politics," 1889; "Division and Reunion — 1829 to 1889," published in 1893; "Mere Literature," 1893; "An Old Master and Other Political Essays," 1893; "George Washington," 1896; "A History of the American People," 1902; "Constitutional Government," 1908 — but largely written in his early academic years. These books are known mostly as college texts or supplemental reading in college work. They are entirely concerned with politics, chiefly British and American politics. They represent the research which a college professor would make for his daily lectures, and in spirit these books reflect the liberal conservatism of the last two decades of the old century. Wilson, the militant liberal of the second decade of the twentieth century, was unborn when these college books were written. "Congressional Government," the earliest book, is the most advanced of the lot. It advocates a government in which a cabinet is responsible to Congress, which in turn is responsible to the people, holding that government the safest for America. "The State" is an attempt to set forth the evolutionary progress of the institutions of man. It is the only Wilson book in which we find figures of speech drawn largely from the natural sciences. This book is political biology and not important in any way. "Division and Reunion" is the most significant of the Wilson books of this period; for it shows the fine detachment that the young Southerner has in considering the problems of his country. In "Division and Reunion" he covers the great upheaval in American politics, through the Civil War and the reconstruction days. He writes judicially, dispassionately, intelligently of a period in which, as a child and youth, he came to know as a living witness the wickedness and futility of war, as well as the horrors of a vindictive peace. The book is not extraordinary in its research. He used only the known and common sources of historians. It contains no such work, for instance, as Von Holst did nor Rhodes. Yet, because it is so fair and so scrupulously honest, the book became at once a college text in the North and soon was accepted in the more intelligent colleges of the South. The book displays a strong character if it does not reveal "a first-class mind." "Mere Literature" and "An Old Master" are made up of collected essays, undergraduate orations, political papers, the hodge-podge of writing that a professor of political science and history would be doing in the day's work. And "George Washington" shows the seamy side of the man who wrote "Division and Reunion."

The "George Washington" reveals Woodrow Wilson just as the essays on Burke and Gladstone and Lee reveal him. But they give us a peek at only one phase of him. It is as though Narcissus had a mirror for each of his fine features. And in the "Washington" we have Wilson preening before his vision, unsatisfied — the dream of old Doctor Wilson's son — shy, bashful, physically frail and so sometimes a little inept, as a Virginia gentleman, "born a gentleman and a man of honor," all caparisoned in satin breeches, wig, lace, and military hardware. The log of the "Avenger of the South Seas" chasing pirates, which Tommy Wilson wrote to put himself right with himself as a frail and lonely lad, is a childish replica of the "Life of Washington" written by Professor Wilson in his cloister, surrounded by an adoring family — a devoted wife, three amiable daughters, a gentle and loving brother-in-law, and a father worshiping the young god created in his own image — shielded by a decent academic salary, talking daily to respectful and even fervid youths, yet only talking; writing books out of books for other youths in the world of books to read, while outside the big world of deeds was going by making big times. Washington, in Berserker rage; Washington, who "fared forth very bravely caparisoned in proper uniform"; Washington, whose "haughty carriage" went dashing through the world doing a variety of admirable things, was to the yearning Celt in the quiet precincts of the old University a symbol of all that he would have been. No man who wrote that gala story of the wax-work Washington, the story with its paper frills and social furbelows, could honestly be said to have put aside the things of this world. Whatever professorial vows of asceticism are implied by the teacher's job were violated a hundred times over by the lustful wishes for power and glory that shine out in this book. As history, it is rather fourth-rate stuff. As biography, holding a mirror to the biographer, it is perfect. President Wilson touring Europe, bowing to the multitude along the way, throwing kisses at the throng in the Milan opera house of a Sunday night, dining with kings, patronizing premiers, all are in embryo — in the heart of the man who wrote this "gallant" Washington, this "Virginia gentleman of breeding," who resigned from his place in the army rather than submit to some legislative regulation because "it was no part of the tradition of his class to submit to degradation in rank!" Perhaps John Calvin was right in his theory of foreordination. Emerson confirms him when he says we are cramped in the cycle of our destiny.

The campus books written in the eighties and nineties are first-class work of a kind — but not of an important kind. They are sanely conceived, consistently worked out with such diligent preparation and research as a good college library would allow, and they are charmingly written. They are not, however, the work of an original mind, as, for instance, Franklin's work, or Josiah Royce's, or Emerson's was; yet they were written by a greater man than any of the others. And, moreover, in the very writing of these books, Woodrow Wilson acquired a certain element of his greatness. Here his purpose was tested. Here he welded the chains of the habit of tedious, painstaking mental work. Here he took on the studious detachment which in crises gave him power over men and events. And also, here in the study looking at history — particularly at the history of the institutions of the English-speaking races — Woodrow Wilson drained pure springs of faith in the purpose of God in the affairs of men. All these books give out this faith, this faith in men as the instruments of a moving spirit of progress which he learned to know as God.

It was not as a great mind that he was called and elected, but as the exponent, the crusader, the covenanter of a great faith to save the world. In writing these books, hardly above the ordinary, books based somewhat upon the premise of the need of an aristocracy, which he afterward abandoned in humility, he buttressed the faith of his fathers, the Calvinism of the eighteenth century with the wisdom of the nineteenth, and so went to the conflict of the twentieth a knight full-panoplied.

It is difficult to picture those two homes of Professor Wilson in Middletown and Princeton as forges of this spiritual Thor. The fires were there, fires of learning and love — chiefly love. The old Doctor comes into the picture again, sturdy in his seventies, with white soft hair still a shaggy mane, with his long, cane-stemmed, clay-bowl pipe, with his proud, fiery eyes and his love of talk. All his life he had talked for a living, as teacher and preacher. But in his early seventies he quit preaching, and ceased teaching. His wife, Janet Woodrow, was

GROUP OF THE WILSON FAMILY IN THE EARLY NINETIES

TAKEN AT THE HOUSE OF DR. GEORGE HOWE IN COLUMBIA, S.C.

Top row, sitting, left to right: Woodrow Wilson; Mrs. George Howe (Annie Wilson, sister of Woodrow Wilson) with infant daughter; Rev. Joseph R. Wilson; Mrs. Joseph R. Wilson, Jr.; Joseph R. Wilson, Jr.
Bottom row: Dr. George Howe; Wilson Howe; Annie Howe; George Howe, Jr.

resting in the Presbyterian churchyard at Columbia, South Carolina, and the old Doctor, retiring upon his honors, visited around with his children. But he seems happiest at Princeton. Stockton Axson, who came into the Wilson family in the late eighties, was teaching English literature in Princeton in the nineties; and was living with the Wilsons. It was the daily habit of the three, the father, the son, and the brother-in-law, to gather in mid-afternoon to talk in the Wilson library. The old Doctor and young Axson smoked. The son carried his fancy without nicotine. They used to let the talk drift in some sort of a slow Johnsonian current for the sheer joy of talking. So writes Stockton Axson, again describing his brother-in-law:

> In the family circle he gave his affections full reign, and allowed his spirit to move him whither it listeth. He simply cannot live without affection, for this is no superman, but human to the core.
>
> In the long years of his and my sister's life together, they were more completely one than any two people with whom I have been thrown into intimate contact. They took color from each other, as water and sky reflect each other's moods. Their tastes in books, pictures, statues, and architecture coalesced. He taught her to love his prose favorites, Burke and Bagehot and Birrell (the first Birrell book I ever saw was an inscribed gift book from him to her); she taught him to love her poetic favorites, especially Wordsworth and Browning; he had a deep and true instinct for architecture, which

he imparted to her; and she in turn quickened his discrimination for color in landscape painting and in nature — for she had a skill in color that would have made her a distinguished artist had she not made her painting secondary to her greater career as wife and mother.

We often hear it said of a married pair — so often that it has become a sort of "bromide" — "A cross word never passed between that couple." I have been honestly trying to think if I ever heard anything approaching an altercation between Mr. and Mrs. Wilson, and I cannot recall even a shadow of such. And yet these were no weaklings; but two spirited people, each with a power of conviction possible only to very strong characters. They would sometimes differ in their opinions, but their relationship was so rooted in mutual love and loyalty that their differences were casual and superficial, never fundamental.

I have seen Mr. Wilson humorously assume the rôle of a brow-beaten and hen-pecked person, unallowed to hold an opinion, when his wife would say in her impetuous way, "Woodrow, you know you don't think that!" and he would smile and say, "Madam, I was venturing to think that I thought that until I was corrected." At one time, when the girls were growing up, he used to laugh and quote Chief Justice Fuller, who remarked that his "jurisdiction extended over all the United States except the Fuller family." I have sometimes wondered how a family composed of varying and very positive elements ever contrived to live in such absolute and undisturbed harmony as did the Wilson family, and I have come to the conclusion that such a result can be attained only in one way, not by any prescription or plan or domestic "scheme" of action, but only by enthroning love supreme — that where love is always master, every day and every hour, there must be harmony. In the Wilson household love is always law.

It has always been love mingled with delightful humor and good nature. Of all the fictions that popular fallacy would weave around a conspicuous man, surely those who knew Mr. Wilson must find it the strangest that he is supposed by some to be a cold and mirthless man.

Those days of the mid-nineties were the abundant growing days in Woodrow Wilson's life. But the seeds of change were in him. He had come to the end of his development as a writer of academic histories and essays upon men and government. He seems to have talked to his Princeton classmate, Charles Talcott, who was mayor of Utica and later Congressman, about some loose organization of men who "knew what they were thinking about," who should raise a united voice in such periodicals as they could enter to make public sentiment for a more intelligent view of political affairs in America. Wilson at that time had the entrée to the best American magazines. It seems to have been his idea to gather about him other writers and speakers and public men who cared more for ideals than patronage. He hoped they might form some sort of a loose political phalanx that would set America thinking about politics rather than men in politics. This idea was not important. It never developed into anything more than correspondence, but it shows how his inner spirit was hearing the call to larger duties. The second phase of his life was foreshadowing itself. Mrs. Wilson must have sensed this feeling of unrest and dissatisfaction with the professorial life, for when he had a nervous breakdown in 1896, some form of a nervous exhaustion which was sapping his energy, she packed him off to Europe alone. The family could not afford to go with him, she could not leave the children, so he took his bicycle and roamed through England for a summer. The trip invigorated him. He came back eager for larger things. The afternoon talks and walks with his father and brother-in-law ceased to interest him, and his brother-in-law remarks that:

> He came back somehow different. He had less and less time for our after-dinner sessions. The old Doctor noticed it and would say: "Something has come over Woodrow; he is restless. He can't sit down happily and talk as he used to."

Probably the ambition of a boy to teach, to write, to be an interesting figure in the embroidery of life was satisfied. His hereditary urge, the grandfather who was a railroad promoter and a bank director, who fought Andrew Jackson and who belonged to the doing, ruling class in Ohio, the Celtic blood which is unhappy taking orders, was stirring in him, moving him to this predestined development, an embryo unfolding into events. Stockton Axson says:

Often in those days I have heard him cry out: "I am so tired of a merely talking profession. I want to do something."

It was that spirit of unsatisfied achievement that set him to work writing the address on behalf of the Princeton faculty which gave him an enlarged place in the academic world — the address upon the occasion of Princeton stepping over the boundary from a college to a university. With this address Wilson moved up a peg.

In the meantime, Woodrow Wilson as a Princeton professor was becoming a college hero. Even when he first came to Princeton to teach, tradition declares that Booth Tarkington, a senior, exclaimed, coming out of Wilson's class: "Say — there's a man!" He put more and more work on his lectures and the charm of a winning personality into his schoolroom manner. He used excellent English and spoke with a trained voice. Youth glowed in his presence and the boys of Princeton came to love him. Four times the seniors voted that he was the most popular man in the faculty. He hungered for the affection of the students as he did in later years for the affection of the American people. He was, in those areas of his soul where he touched life about him, his father's son. It was the Woodrows who were shy, repressed, friendless, punctual, and prim. And the Woodrows — the doers of things — were in leash.

In the late nineties, Dr. Joseph Ruggles Wilson began to grow restless. Often he left Princeton and went South — unconsciously, maybe, looking for his lost halcyon days. Sometimes he went to Augusta or to Rome, Georgia; often he appeared at Columbia, where Janet Woodrow of the curls was buried. But most frequently he appeared at Wilmington, North Carolina, where he had reached the climax of his career. He lived in a boarding-house kept by a parishioner of other days and Dave Bryant came to wait on the old Doctor. They had long talks together, and Dave remembers that many times the old Doctor used to talk about his eldest son. He need have no restraints with Dave. One afternoon, lying weary and half-sick on his bed, the Doctor — pretty badly shattered by his seventy-eight years — poured out his heart to Dave.

"Mr. Tommy is a smart man, Dave!" There was none of the Woodrow nonsense between these two. It was Tommy, when they were alone. Naturally Dave agreed with the father about the ability of the son.

"Dave, he's one of the smartest men in this country." Again Dave agreed.

"Dave, come here," said the old Doctor; "let me

tell you something. One of these days Mr. Tommy will be a candidate for President of the United States! I won't be here, Dave, but you will. Are you still voting, Dave?" The colored man was and is one of the few, less than two hundred, men of his race who qualify as electors in Wilmington. "Dave, promise me this: When I'm gone and Mr. Tommy is running for President, you will go down to the polls and put in my vote — not yours, Dave, but mine — mine!" And being an old man his old Irish eyes filled with emotional tears. And David Bryant says he remembered his promise.

Now this narrative of the two old men doddering over the apple of their eyes has only this significance in history: it seems to foreshadow the coming change in Wilson's life which those near him seemed to sense. Bridges, the friend of Wilson's youth, sensed political ambition always "in the back of his head." Stockton Axson, his faithful kinsman, saw the stirring in his heart that came in the late nineties. Wilson, himself, realized the limitations of his work and chafed under them. "I don't have to stay here," he said to a Princeton trustee in a discussion of University affairs, "I can go into politics!" So his father's Irish intuition told him what urgent voices were clamoring in the son's soul — that the time was drawing near when the happy, peaceful days of Woodrow Wilson's life's apprenticeship were closing.

Doubtless no deep mysticism is needed to account for this sense of portent. America was cutting loose from her mooring of national isolation. The Spanish War was making us a world power. In our home affairs dramatic questions had arisen, fearful doubts in the hearts of millions of Americans who were asking: Is our imperialism divinely sent? Have we solved our home problems well enough to warrant our taking on new duties? Is the plutocracy that governs us wise enough and honest enough to rule the world? If not — if imperialism is wicked, if our domestic politics is rotten, if our plutocratic leadership is mad — what shall we do to be saved? These questions, like great alarms in the night, were clanging through the souls of thinking men, disturbing their peace, calling them to action. Is it strange that Woodrow Wilson, historian and publicist and Celt, a born world ruler, should pace his college walk in vague, restless discontent?

It was but a few weeks after Doctor Wilson and the old servant had formed their covenant to vote for "Mr. Tommy" that the Doctor, losing strength rapidly, was unable to make his wonted rounds of Wilmington. He lay on his bed or sat by a window in his room, and on pleasant days went down to the porch of his boarding-house. His son came to Wilmington to take his father North. The old man knew it would be the last trip and protested his desire to stay in the South: "But don't you want to be with me, father?" asked the son. And Dave said, "Surely, Doctor, you want to be with your boy." So Dave prepared the old man for the trip. But he demanded that Dave should go with him. Tenderness impersonated was in the son as they prepared him for the journey. Going to the station the son explained to Dave that his father needed a trained nurse, and, slipping into the colored man's hand twice as much money as his fare would be, told him just how to miss the train. So the Wilsons left the South together for good and all. Woodrow Wilson returned to the South in 1906. He was the new President of Princeton in a high hat. He brought his father's body back to Columbia to lie beside his wife!

Thus ended the romance begun behind the paling fence in Steubenville when the gloves on the hands of the young theologue, mowing the lawn, made Janet Woodrow smile. If the geese whose quacking saved Rome have gained immortality, why not celebrate forever those gloves which started events that may one day save the world! "Well," sighed the Angel in charge of the Celestial and Earthly

Love Department when he saw *Finis* written after this love-story as the earth covered the mortal remains of two old lovers — Joseph Wilson and Janet — "Well," repeated the angel in pride at the son of their loins just stepping across the new cycle of his destiny, "there's one good job I did for the world anyway!"

PART TWO

The Conflict

CHAPTER VIII

THE LECTURER BECOMES THE ADMINISTRATOR

WOODROW WILSON became President of Princeton University in 1902. Six years before, when Princeton College was dedicated as a university, Professor Wilson's paper proclaiming his belief in the humanities as against the sciences as the motive element in education had marked him as the leader of idealism in education. The German scientific movement was shaping the American college curriculum, and the Princeton University address of Professor Wilson, reprinted in "The Forum," edited at the time by Walter Hines Page, afterwards Ambassador to England, made a stir in the college world. The appointment of the author of that address to the presidency of Princeton, therefore, had significance. It meant that at least one American university of the first rank would consider education, not as a means of livelihood, but as an adornment of the spirit. This Princeton attitude, as set forth by the choice of its new President, was a challenge to the tendency of the times. Too many American colleges were becoming high-toned business colleges. They boldly professed to teach men and women how to get on in the world: how to make "good money" as scientists, as lawyers, as engineers, as physicians, as administrators, as teachers. This utilitarian spirit in education was particularly the pest of our State universities, and the larger the university, the deadlier the pest! The Wilson challenge from Princeton was a revolutionary pronouncement. And the new President at once took leadership of a cause. Never was a leader of the cause of idealism in education better equipped for leadership. He knew, from nearly thirty years' experience in the college world, as student and teacher, what strength his cause had, and, being unquestionably of an open and scholarly mind, he knew the weaknesses of his cause. Moreover, he believed in it profoundly, and because he wrote well and talked well, having entrée to every source of publicity in America — the magazines, the newspapers, the lecture platform, and the higher academic councils of the country — he was a powerful advocate. He surely helped to check the Germanic invasion of our colleges, and certainly he did exalt education, not as a means of getting on in the world, but as a means of understanding and enjoying the world. Woodrow Wilson's stride into the national arena was strong, determined, inspiring. All the pride in him of his Princeton class of '79 was justified; all the love that the Princeton students of a decade had lavished upon him girded him, and he had a confidence in his bearing that shone like an armor upon a young warrior.

So he emerged from the sheltered life, coming for the first time in his career to grips with reality. The aloofness of his childhood, the shyness of his youth before he came into the world of books, and of spiritual things where he would take leadership among his fellows and come by grace of his qualities of heart and mind into full fellowship with the leaders of his world, were in large measure repeated in his professorial years in his contacts with the world outside of the college. But as an administrator dealing with faculty men, as a college president dealing with rich trustees, he found new problems. As a man among men facing unpleasant realities and overcoming them by force when force would suffice, by finesse when finesse was called for, by humble compromise when neither force nor finesse could go further, the new President of Princeton, forty-six years old, a gladiator of righteousness, was singularly, by training and habits of life, like Tommy Wilson; a poor ball-player in spectacles diverting the "Lightfoots" to parliamentary law. And he must have known his weakness. For he had a distaste for personal disputes. He was timid before brawling or rascally opposition, and also he was quick-tempered and ruthless sometimes with opponents whom he judged as enemies. But he was a Woodrow who worked hard, kept his own counsel — which was generally good — never veered, held his ideals inviolate, and so made bitter antagonists out of mere adversaries and sometimes gave them a victory which they ill-deserved.

His administration as President of Princeton opened in a blaze of virtue. It was decided that too many young men were coming to Princeton who considered it little more than a Junior Union League Club. "I'll not be President of a country club," quoth the new President. So academic requirements were raised and stiffened, and a hundred and more of the thirteen hundred students were sent home for failure in their studies. Naturally, many of the hundred would come from homes where the superiority of mere wealth as a means of social salvation was most blatantly emphasized. So trouble camped at the front gates of Princeton and President Wilson went out to meet it. He conquered it without compromise, amid resounding plaudits of the world inside and outside the college gates. The whole episode was entirely to President Wilson's credit. Princeton was better for his victory. Yet the fathers, being publicly shamed through their sons, bided their time.

We are entering what may well be called a secondary phase of the career of Woodrow Wilson; the time of combat. The tempo of his activities changes, and not mysteriously. His lines, up to his forty-sixth year, had been cast in pleasant places, literally in green pastures beside the still waters. The days had moved smoothly, the years had come gently, not because he was a fine and gentle soul, but because the fine and gentle soul was engaged in speculative and sedentary work. When he became an executive, an administrator of important affairs, when the fortunes of thirteen hundred students, when over one hundred members of the teaching force, and when the disposition of a million and a half dollars of endowment came into his hands, his relation to the world changed. Other qualities had to emerge from his character that had lain dormant in his life as a teacher. He had to speed up his soul to meet the procession of new duties hurrying forward to wrestle with him. That is why his life's tempo changed, and why a new man stood forth as President of Princeton. The same man went with slight changes — for experience in eight years could teach him little — out of Princeton into the turmoil of American politics. But this we must bear in mind in considering the regenerated Wilson: he carried with him certain fundamental qualities, purely Wilsonian qualities, as opposed to those from the

Woodrow strain, that stood him in good stead. Always he was a gay spirit. Always he was a brave spirit, though the physical man shrank from strange, unpleasant contact. Always he was a wise, calm spirit, save for the bedevilment of a vicious temper which cost him many a friend and brought him much remorseful sorrow. And above all else, he was a faithful spirit who, with all his handicaps of the flesh, his physical shrinking from rowdies, his waspish temper, and those blistering hates that scorched the victims of his wrath, with all the superficial faults, desired passionately and with devout and consecrated ardor to do the will of his God without a selfish reservation. His contribution to his times was not his mind, which was good, but of no rare timbre; not his talents, which were useful, but never extraordinary; nor his character, though that was of a better texture than his mental equipment. His great contribution to his times was his faith — his unshaken, majestic faith in the goodness of God and the essential nobility of man. If ever he should be degraded from a human being to a hollow statue in a park — disemboweled and dehearted — a symbol instead of the splendid human creature that he was, he should symbolize faith — faith in the moral government of the universe, and in the expanding wisdom and kindliness of men. Only with this prevision of the man in mind may we go forward to examine his life and avoid the pitfalls into which his enemies have so piously fallen.

After winning his fight for higher standards of scholarship in Princeton, the new President began to oppose the forces which seemed to make higher scholastic standards difficult. He felt that the first engagement should be with the aristocratic collegiate societies — the Princeton expression of the common college fraternity that infests American institutions of higher learning. In Princeton, all freshmen eat in the college commons. But in their sophomore year, something less than half of them are taken out of the herd and segregated in eating-clubs. These clubs are beautifully built and handsomely furnished, more or less replicas of the clubs of the boys' fathers in towns and cities. These college clubs are exclusive, and President Wilson believed that they promote snobbery in the one place on earth where intelligent democracy may be maintained. It was his idea to take over these clubs, through lease or purchase by the University, and make them serve the democracy of the University life — not a bad idea, but expensive. About 1905, he introduced another expensive idea into the life of the school when he established what is known as the "preceptor" system. This experiment provided for the American adaptation of the

English tutorial system. The students were grouped under preceptors, who would counsel with them and guide and stimulate their intellectual growth. It cost about seventy-five thousand dollars a year. The sum was provided, but the annual deficit of the College which is, after all, only the sign of collegiate vitality, grew. The Wilsons had no traditional belief in money. They had plenty, but let it go easily as it came easily. President Wilson's opponents declare that he said the way to finance a new thing in a college is to try it and it will finance itself. Probably he said it, and it is a shocking thing for a man to hear who is dollar-minded — a ribald, irreverent, almost obscene remark. And doubtless it set the hair of certain trustees against him. A growing deficit followed the introduction of the preceptorial system and it increased after the reduction of matriculation fees and laboratory fees that followed the restriction of scholastic standards. Therefore, when the new President proposed this other new-fangled idea, to buy or lease the luxurious clubs, that would cost several hundred thousand dollars, the trustees agreed to it in principle — for the new President was a powerful exhorter and his arguments were unanswerable — but deferred the adoption of the proposition to take over the clubhouses until a more favorable time. The Wilson plan looked, eventually, to some provision for additional dormitories, eating-commons, and living-quarters within a Gothic quadrangle — most lovely and highly desirable. It became known as the "quad" system. It was the dream of a democratic school, the realizable vision of an idealist. Wilson's plan brought down upon him the maledictions of those who enjoyed the special privileges of the club system. Obviously they would be the sons of rich fathers — or at least and always the socially favored. A fine row began. In the clubhouses were dormitories retained for the club's alumni who might be wandering back to Princeton. But the chief hegira to the town was to see the football games and other athletic contests. So the sporting alumni, who feared that their privileges would be curtailed, joined the row. They are a noisy but unimportant crew, the spiritual legatees of the slow-brained, leather-necked, brass-lunged campus contingent with little cultural background, and an obstreperous sense of the power of money. But they were out of college and their "kid-brothers" in college began hooting raucously at Wilson: "What — has an American no right to choose his associates? Must a gentleman eat with a mucker?"

They ignored the fact that as freshmen the gentlemen and muckers ate together without contamination, and that they slept together during the entire four years, and also studied and worked together. But the "mucker" battle-cry was raised, and, until the trustees postponed action on the "quad" system, the battle-cry filled the air of Princeton and was first-rate publicity for President Wilson. Thus he became the exponent of democracy in education. And vastly more important than that, he became a convinced democrat in the educational field. His writing, his teaching, his lectures, before he became President of Princeton, revealed no great enthusiasm for the doctrine of democracy. The philosophy of a benevolent aristocracy is revealed in much of his thought in the eighties and nineties. That was the theorist expounding. But the man of action headed pell-mell for democracy. It became the corner-stone of his faith — the political phase of his Calvinism. The equation read thus: The open Bible required the free school, the free school, the open ballot box; the free ballot, the open mind, and the free man demanded a noble material environment for his soul's growth. Social evolution became the first need for spiritual salvation. So reasoned the Calvinist democrat.

But Woodrow Wilson took his democratic ideal for Princeton up and down the world with him — the Princeton world — to alumni meetings, to college dinners, to anniversary celebrations, and, being a powerful orator, he forced it into intellectual conviction in quarters where the heart could not follow the head. For Princeton was one of the strongholds of whatever aristocracy America had in the first decade of the century. An attractive but dangerous phrase delighted Wilson when talking to the alumni in those days: "The side show" — meaning the club snobbery — "seems to be trying to control the performance in the main tent!" It drew forth applause from the sixty per cent outside of the clubs. But the forty per cent inside the clubs, having wealth and social prestige and a desire to maintain wealth and prestige as the pursuit of happiness, were more powerful in the kingdoms of this world than the majority, so the phrase, by its very plausibility and popularity, became a deadly poison which Wilson brewed for his own destruction. His strength as a public man, as a speaker, writer, administrator, idealist in education, was sufficient to throw off the poison. For he was riding a popular wave. Roosevelt, in the White House, was preaching to the country the same philosophy of life that Wilson was giving to Princeton, and the people were devouring the democratic pabulum greedily.

It was in his personal relations that Wilson came to grief in Princeton. The story of that journey to grief is worth telling here in some detail; perhaps not for the importance of the matter at issue. It was trivial; it is interesting only because it was, in small, the replica of a larger journey that affected the history of the world — if there are "ifs" in history.

This grievous part of the journey of Woodrow Wilson as President of Princeton began over a difference between him and Dean Andrew F. West, of the Graduate School of Princeton, over the methods of organizing the faculty of the Graduate School. Ostensibly the difference arose over the location of the proposed buildings for the school upon the College Campus. But one who examines the old quarrel carefully, sighing over its futile bitterness and assessing much blame and little merit — or the reverse if he will — to both parties to the contention, is left uneasy if he accepts the issue as it is stated upon the surface. One cannot see why the quarrel was so bitter over so unimportant a detail as the location of the buildings — which at most were mere dormitories and dining-rooms. Set down in simple and fairly undisputed terms, the apparent issue of the location of the Graduate School is about this: Andrew F. West, who was, as a fellow faculty member, a friend of Wilson, was made dean of the Graduate School in 1901. The Graduate School was established in 1896 when Princeton College was expanded into Princeton University. Later, Dean

West was sent by the trustees to Europe to study graduate schools there, and to report to the President of the University and the trustees a plan for the organization and advancement of the Graduate School at Princeton. Naturally, he came home full of plans and enthusiasm and probably also full of human ambitions. He would have been unworthy of his trust if he had been too anæmic to hope to grow with the Graduate School. His report was read by President Wilson, who seems to have made some slight changes in the manuscript and later in the printer's proof. A beautiful brochure printed by DeVinne, the greatest American printer of his day, was made of the report. In the brochure were photogravure pictures of collegiate architecture in Europe and architects' plans for a similar "Post-Graduate Hall of Residence for Princeton." President Wilson wrote a preface for the brochure. The preface seems upon casual reading to commit President Wilson officially, and, therefore, the University, to Dean West's report. But carefully embedded in the President's preface are phrases which seem to indicate that he did not propose to stand unequivocally for a Graduate School not merged definitely into the organization of the University. President Wilson seems to have felt even then — in 1903 — that Dean West was planning a separate school, a school with a capital S, somewhat outside of the President's control, responsible largely to the trustees, something such an organization as the Theological Seminary was. The brochure was printed beautifully and expensively as a piece of salesmanship. Dean West was approaching his problem not as a dreamer, but as a Scotch-American business man. It was his job to get money for the Graduate School, and he set out to sell his dream to rich givers.

Right here let us stop the narrative and consider Dean West, for he was the first human being whom Woodrow Wilson, until his fiftieth year, had met in combat, not physically, of course, for that would have settled much and helped greatly. (Parenthetically, one who follows the Wilson story feels like clamoring wildly, like a gallery god in a melodrama, for a brawl, for a bitter contest, for some one to come and release the festering rage in our hero's underconsciousness, by a whacking blow, spiritual, or even physical, to give his soul relief and to restore wholesome circulation of his moral blood.) Dean West is a tall, robust man — a two-hundred-forty-pounder — with a sea captain's ruddy skin, large features, hearty voice and manner. He speaks in the indicative, goes to the point, and spits it out. Under emotional pressure he could roar like a bull and also close his eyes and charge as blindly. Given fraternal relations in the faculty, relations based upon equality of power and authority, he and Woodrow Wilson might have been friends for a hundred years, each openly respectful of the other's good qualities and secretly enjoying each other's vices. But in the relation of man and master, their vices would rise inevitably and start a row. Now the word "row" is not a nice word for a difference in a university faculty over a purely academic proposition, but row it was, good and hot and vicious on both sides. Dean West started out frankly to get funds for his Graduate School.

President Wilson apparently decided that the kind of a Graduate School that Dean West was trying to establish would not be a good thing for Princeton. So at many points of his endeavor the Dean felt, but never could exactly define, presidential opposition to his School. The kind of organization that President Wilson desired was that adopted generally by American universities for their graduate schools: a dean, and a faculty taken from the body of the faculty members of the college. The dean in such an organization might be a teaching professor in a department of the college; and the faculty members of the graduate school nearly always taught undergraduates in other departments of the college. The graduate school, typically in the American university, is a paper organization inside the college under the control of the President of the college or university, and little more than a department of the college. Dean West's idea seems to have been — and no turpitude attaches to holding his views — that the graduate school should grow more independently of the college than the American type of graduate school, and should be housed apart and live, actually and spiritually, in its own atmosphere. In the two ideas is no cause for a clash. They are easily compromisable. Surrender under amicable give-and-take should be honorable.

But during three years, the quarrel over these two divergent opinions smouldered in the faculty and among the trustees. In his contention the President had the tremendous advantage of his prestige, his power of life or death over faculty men. Dean West had the strength of an indomitable nature; one to whom combat brings gifts. The President went out appealing to donors to help the College. Dean West went out with his beautifully printed brochure soliciting funds for the Graduate School. In 1905, Moses Taylor Pyne, one of the trustees who admired Dean West and approved his plans, gave anonymously to the Graduate School a large private residence near the campus capable of housing a dozen graduate students and of boarding as many more.

About the same time a bequest of $300,000 came to the Graduate School, with which it was decided by the trustees to erect a new building near the site where the President's house stood. In President Wilson's preface to the West brochure, above referred to, he commits himself to a place that will house "a community of scholars set at the heart of Princeton." He declared, even in his inaugural address three years before, in favor of keeping the Graduate School "at the very heart, at the geographical heart of the University." Always there seemed to be lurking in his consciousness the fear that Dean West, out soliciting funds for the Graduate School, would get money enough to set up a separate school in all but competitive relation to the University — perhaps overshadowing it! With him probably in this dread were his friends in the Board of Trustees, notably Cleveland H. Dodge, Cyrus McCormick, and others, making a safe majority; while, with Dean West, upon the Board were Moses Taylor Pyne and Grover Cleveland, both resident trustees. It was during this submerged academic quarrel that an offer came from the Massachusetts Institute of Technology to Dean West to go to that institution as its President. Dean West went to President Wilson frankly recognizing the status of the quarrel. And the President asked the Dean to remain. His friends among the trustees brought up the Massachusetts offer and the trustees voted to ask him to stay. President Wilson, himself, wrote the resolution of confidence which requested Dean West to remain in Princeton. But it was a stage reconciliation; it signified that the Wilson trustees did not care for an open break with the West trustees, who were in the minority. For in the minority was Grover Cleveland.

Dean West was justified in thinking that in the Board's request that he remain at Princeton was a charter of freedom to proceed with the organization of his Graduate School upon the lines he had mapped out. A graduate council was organized — a group of alumni who had been working as a committee of fifty to raise funds to meet the annual deficit. The Graduate Council, of course, had small use for the quad system. It would cost them a lot of money. It would also destroy the caste system in the University upon which they had been bred. So, inevitably, the Graduate Council, realizing the row in the faculty, the trustees, and the University generally, came to support Dean West. In 1908, President Wilson went to the alumni with his plans for the so-called "quad" system. He found his chief support among the alumni west of the Alleghanies. There they were numerous, but only well-to-do. In the East, where the alumni were rich, where they kept in touch with the University — attending foot-ball games and various intercollegiate sporting events — the alumni were against the "quad" system, and, having no place else to go, lined up with Dean West. The Graduate Council gained an official relation to the Board of Trustees and so Dean West had direct access to the Board. Before that he had had only a right to meet with the Board's commitee on the Graduate School.

It is one of his contentions that at a meeting of his committee, Cleveland H. Dodge, in an enthusiastic moment when it was decided that Dean West should remain at Princeton, offered to find financial support for five professors hired specifically for the Graduate School at five thousand dollars a year — a good academic salary in 1905. Mr. Dodge remembers nothing of this; nor do others of President Wilson's friends. Yet, the thing may have happened. They would easily realize, upon reflection, that five men exclusively in the Graduate School would promote exactly the kind of a graduate school that they opposed. And the thing, which they deemed not a promise but the verbal expression of a wish, would soon pass from their minds. But it would naturally stick, and being denied would rankle, in Dean West's mind, and in the minds of his friend. So quarrels are bred.

It is quite possible, without conceding any villainy upon President Wilson's part, that he did make it obvious to his supporters on the Board that endowment for Graduate School professors was exactly the thing which Princeton University did not need, if his theory of its interests was correct. He had faith in a great democratic university rising upon the site of a rather limited aristocratic school. His faith required for its realization millions for endowment and buildings — to house and care for the youth, to give them preceptorial guides, to give them the advantages of close contact and daily association with all the inspirational elements of the school, the upper-class men, the graduate students, the preceptors, and the faculty — as many as were unmarried. It was to be a hive of culture where every environmental influence should work for democracy and culture — a noble vision. This Graduate School, conceived and promoted by Dean West and supported by West's friends, isolated, remote, deeply divisional, and as Wilson saw it, intellectually snobbish, fell across his hope as a black shadow; because it divided the funds available for Princeton. From this situation, based upon the entirely creditable purposes of two strong men, it is easy to see how enmities rose. It is easy to understand how the Wilson partisans damned West as a marplot appealing to the base passions of base men. But to understand why, when they had a chance to let him go his way, they did not, we must remember that here was a man as President of Princeton whose whole training had been unexecutive — to coin a word, indeed, anti-executive! President Wilson, of Princeton, was out of Professor Wilson, and he was out of the writer, and student, and he was out of frail, aloof, and lonely Tommy Wilson, "a bundle of nerves and mischief," who never had a fight in his life and always strove to win by pleasing or diplomacy, never by bull strength. To understand why Dean West did not go to Massachusetts, we must remember that he was a knock-down-and-drag-out fighter. With him was Grover Cleveland, another of the same kind, only more practiced; and Moses Taylor Pyne, evidently another of the same kind. Mr. Pyne's picture shows him with his hands folded — not across his abdomen, but high across his chest — a pugnacious, masculine creature, clearly obsessed by great visions and happy in fighting for them. It is easy to understand how those three regarded President Wilson as a canting visionary, afraid to fight in the open, hiding under subterfuges, fleeing for defense to words, phrases, and, if too proud to fight, at least not too proud to intrigue.

CHAPTER IX

GOING THROUGH THE FIRST FIRE

It was President Wilson, of Princeton, not Professor Wilson, of Princeton, who became Governor of New Jersey. And it was the Governor of New Jersey, and not the President of Princeton, who became President of the United States. Progressively from his collegiate days to the very end, Woodrow Wilson was learning about life. His first years as President of Princeton were calm enough. His campaign as Governor of New Jersey ran as smoothly and as merrily as a pageant. His first years as President of the United States ran fairly smoothly. Always his destiny seemed to give him a peaceful prelude as life changed the scene and led him along a rougher road. Grief came undisguised to the President of Princeton in the second half of his administration. After he had learned a little of the technique of administration, he had to use his technique complicated with bitterness.

Discord begot hate. Princeton, in those late years of the first decade of the twentieth century, was sizzling with malice. The bitterness of the conflict was telling upon President Wilson's mind and heart.

Once or twice each year he had to get away from the misery of the strife. Heated words flew about in trustees' meetings, men became harsh in their personal relations, and many a night in those years from 1905 to 1909, Woodrow Wilson trudged home to Ellen Axson, his wife, broken, battered, and weary. She, it must be remembered, was a serious person. She, no less than he, took to heart the rancor and resentments that were growing around them. But because she knew that her man was right, she did what any other wife would do, urged him to stand for the right. No man ever had a more faithful ally than Woodrow Wilson had in Ellen, his wife. It was in 1907 that she packed him up again and sent him on a journey; to Bermuda this time, after a particularly hard campaign in which blows fell and he gave blows, but from which he came out worn and weary.

In Bermuda he sat around for a few dull days upon the veranda of the great hotel, reading a little, resting much; an outsider looking in upon the gay life of an insular British society, detached from London, but reflecting the sophistication of London. It was bright, happy, a bit irresponsible, certainly a different type of association of human beings from any that Woodrow Wilson, boy and man in the Presbyterian manse, in the academic shades, in the higher and lonelier walks of the American educational Olympus, had ever seen. To him the female of the species was the faculty woman, passing rich at from three to seven thousand a year, with a small family and a vast pretense of respectability to maintain. A harried woman, earnest, eager, sometimes baffled, but always gentle and wise, was this faculty woman who epitomized the sex to Woodrow Wilson. There, on the veranda of the big hotel, he saw another kind of lady-bug; many brilliant-hued, bright-faced, care-free lady-bugs. For the most part they were married, detached from husbands for various reasons, generally good; sometimes naval, military, or political reasons; reasons of empire if they were British, reasons of business if they were Americans. And one fine night Woodrow Wilson found himself on the other side of the window looking out at the empty veranda.

They took him in, these social Samaritans, him who had been on the Jericho road on the other side of the glass. And they bound up his wounds and made him very comfy, indeed. Of course, he was a somebody — the President of Princeton. The female of the species, detached, sometimes even bored, always yearning for some joy she could not define, found in this impeccable Princeton President something new and strange and wonderful. At the end of a few days he was walking, talking, expanding his soul, and expounding his philosophy — a gay and whimsical Irish philosophy it was at that time — spun in joyous rhetoric out of the moment — and as it were minueting through the high and lovely galleries of the lady's mind. The lady's name was Mrs. Mary Hulbert Peck, the wife of Thomas B. Peck, of Pittsfield, Massachusetts, a wealthy American business man.

Now Mrs. Mary Hulbert Peck appears in this narrative for two reasons: first, because for seven years she afforded Woodrow Wilson one of many outlets for the play of his mind. And, second, she appears because, by some utterly inexplicable cruel chance, her name was linked with Woodrow Wilson's in baseless slanders whispered about during two presidential campaigns; slanders as foul and unfounded as were ever peddled about in any campaign. To ignore such a wicked injustice to a man is no part of a biographer's duty unless the biographer wishes to countenance slanders by ignoring them. During the seven years in which Mrs. Peck and the Wilsons were friends, many letters and other evidences of cordial regard passed between them. It was Mrs. Peck's habit, when a letter came to her in the official envelope of the President of Princeton, or with the seal of the Governor of New Jersey, or with the plain blue line of the White House on the envelope, to open it immediately and read it to whatever friends might be near her when it came. For the letters, which ran into the hundreds, were not particularly intimate. In reading them as a whole one has no sense of any emotional climax or rise or fall in the emotional attitude of the writer. These letters have been seen and read by many people. They reveal a man orienting himself by expressing himself. Probably some of those who have read the letters — and Mrs. Peck naturally felt no compunction in lending them to those who were interested — have copied them, and some day, of course, they will be printed. And this biographer of Woodrow Wilson feels very keenly that the friendship of these two people, Woodrow Wilson and Mary Peck, was of so fine and noble a quality that no future commentator of those letters should be able to twist by innuendo that friendship into anything less lovely than it was. Hence Mary Peck enters these pages.

She had been married, before she met Mr. Peck, to the father of her child, whose name was Allen Hulbert. A gracious and bewitching creature was Mary Hulbert Peck, with a light and lovely sympathy in her voice, with noble eyes that looked not too seriously out of an understanding heart, and lips that smiled easily and never spoke malice nor even harbored ungenerous thoughts. She moved in the insular society a lovely butterfly playing in utter unconsciousness of the realities of a world that did not touch her. It was her habit to walk and talk with men who pleased her, to match their minds with hers, to dance with them through the labyrinth of speculation and noble conjecture upon the nature of the cosmos; the Governor of the Island, the Admiral of the Navy, here a general, there a potentate. And wives knew that Mary Peck was safe. She was one of a dozen or a score of her kind that made the insular society of the Island lovely. Woodrow Wilson's letters home told of the exquisite spiritual prowess and facile charm of Mary Peck. And very soon after President Wilson's return to Princeton, the Wilsons visited her and she visited the Wilsons at their summer home in Connecticut. The Wilson daughters visited her, had gifts from her, wrote notes to her; and Mrs. Wilson, who had always realized how much the Irish play-boy needed a joy and exuberance of contact that she could not give, was glad when younger women could supply it. So once or twice a week, sometimes oftener, Woodrow Wilson sat him down at his typewriter and hammered out the things that were pressing upon his life, the problems, the pleasures, the puns, the plays, the prayers, the puzzles of his soul, to Mary Peck. Once or twice again they met in Bermuda, and there were long walks upon the sands of the South shore, where the red-clad soldiers preened themselves in dress parades, where babies in perambulators and pretty nurses and happy mothers were going by; and then and there, being under the eye of the wide, wide world, they talked, somewhat like the Walrus and the Carpenter, of many things, none of which were of vast importance, but some of which interest this narrative. It was there on those sands, on a bright day of 1909, that Woodrow Wilson first told her of a definite proposal that had come to him to get into politics.

In a letter recalling the time and place, Mrs. Peck writes:

There comes through a frame of rose, of oleander, and gray-green cedar, a picture of shore and sea and reef, never to be forgotten. It was there, looking down upon riders, their horses, children playing in the sand, the world strolling by, that we began to talk, so serious — so solemn, that every word is stamped indelibly on my memory. He began thus:

"My friends tell me that if I will enter the contest and can be nominated and elected as Governor of New Jersey, I stand a very good chance of being the next President of the United States. Shall I, or shall I not, accept the opportunity they offer?"

After a moment, trying to realize the deep significance of this talk, I replied:

"Why not? Statesmanship has always been your natural bent; your real ambition, all your life."

"Of course you know I am not a rich man, and while for myself money means little, I have my dear ones to consider. As President of Princeton, I have a dignified home, their proper background, and enough to give them some of the ease and luxury they deserve. Would it be just to them?"

I said: "If I know anything of your wife and daughters, they would rather scrub to earn their bread than to have you do less than your best work in life; your full duty."

He continued: "And then those fine fellows at Princeton who have stood by me during all this bitter, heart-breaking affair of the College, wouldn't I be deserting them?"

I told him, what seemed to me to be the truth as seen by an outsider, that his work there was really done. After this it would be only a grim fight to hold the line, no real advance.

"If your ideas and ideals are right ones, they will endure. You have made them clear to all."

Then he said: "The life of the next Democratic President will be hell — and it would probably kill me."

"Ah! But you would rather die in harness fighting for all the great things for which you stand than live less than up to the best you know."

The talk drifted away from the concrete subject before them, and Mrs. Peck says that they began talking of life and destiny. There on the sand they stood; she a woman in her glowing maturity and he a handsome man; and about them the beauty of the sea and the odor of the cedars and the glory of the Southern winter day. Then, reverting for a moment to his future in politics, Wilson had another of those inexplicably prophetic moments when he seemed to see far ahead into his own life, as he saw back in his student days when writing of Lord Chatham's tragic end. Turning to Mrs. Peck, he began quoting from memory a poem, an anonymous poem at the end of the "Oxford Book of English Verse." The poem itself, better than pages of description may do, defines the character of their friendship. And it also throws across the years ahead the shadow of coming events in his life. The shadow, of course, was cast by his own spirit working upon circumstance. In his clear, mellow voice, he recited:

"In the hour of death, after this life's whim,
When the heart beats low and the eyes grow dim,
And pain has exhausted every limb —
The lover of the Lord shall trust in Him.

"When the will has forgotten the lifelong aim,
And the mind can only disgrace its fame,
And a man is uncertain of his own name —
The power of the Lord shall fill this frame.

"When the last sigh is heaved, and the last tear is shed,
And the coffin is waiting beside the bed,
And the widow and child forsake the dead —
The angel of the Lord shall lift this head.

"For even the purest delight may pall,
And power must fail and pride must fall,
And the love of the dearest friends grow small —
But the glory of the Lord is all in all."

There these two stood in one of the high moments of life, amid the charm of an alien and exotic civilization, surrounded by scores of their fellows, little realizing that a momentous decision for myriads of men was forming in the heart of that long-jawed, bright-eyed, forthright, middle-aged Irishman, in his shore clothes, as he stood calling out the grim and fateful song, from his heart, to the sea. It is no wonder that Mary Peck could not forget it.

The suggestion that he go into politics came from Colonel George Harvey. He had, of course, talked it out with Ellen Axson, and with Stockton Axson, about the same time he had talked it out in the same way with Robert Bridges. Those who were near and dear to him felt the prescience of some great change in his life; but he was in the midst of a fight at Princeton which engaged all of his strength, took all of his time and attention.

In the meantime, Dean West, very properly, was shaping his plans. In May, 1909, William C. Procter, of Cincinnati, offered to the University half a million dollars for the Graduate School contingent upon another half-million being raised by other friends of the School. The offer came to the Board, through Dean West, and it contained a provision that the Graduate School buildings should be located where Mr. Procter, and presumably Dean West, desired to locate them. The proposed Procter building and endowment, offered to the Graduate School, were in addition to a building provided for by a $300,000 bequest of 1906, which had not been erected largely because of a quarrel about a site. Dean West desired to take the buildings that would rise under the Procter gift to a point rather far removed from the College Campus. The President's vision would vanish if West's dream came true. It was up to the Board of Trustees to decide between the President and the Dean. To go with the Dean meant to leave all the earnest endeavor that the Board and the President had been striving for during seven years; to desert a leader who had been advertising Princeton as the hope of cultural democracy; and to risk dividing the School by creating a unit off the campus which would need great resources for its maintenance. To follow Wilson involved refusing a million dollars for Princeton; and to refuse a million dollars for Princeton would seem, to the sporting alumni who had raised the half-million to meet the Procter gift, like mocking God. But so strong was the loyalty of the trustees to their President, so convincing was he in his plea for democracy, that they did, by a substantial majority vote, practically endorse the Wilson position.

The vote came, as similar votes came during the

long years of controversy, generally upon a dilatory motion making a counter-offer to that of Mr. Procter. But while the offer was pending, and while the misgivings of the trustees were evidenced by their delay in accepting greedily the million-dollar gift, some one distributed to the alumni, returning for the 1909 Commencement, a pamphlet rather viciously attacking the social order at Princeton, and reopening the controversy about the "quad" system which the trustees had closed by deferring it, not from want of agreement with Wilson, but because funds were not available to put it in operation. Probably, however, so far as the trustees were concerned, the "quad" system was indefinitely deferred. The pamphlet enraged the sporting alumni. The hesitation about taking the Procter gift on any terms embittered them, and President Wilson's arguments for hesitation insulted them. For he protested against the interference of mere wealth in the affairs of the University. The answer was, of course, obvious: those who object to mere wealth when it opposes their plans are glad enough to use it to fill the deficit made by their own schemes. The griddles of hate were popping in Princeton that night in June before the 1909 commencement!

After commencement the Board still seemed undecided. And it took considerable parliamentary jockeying to bring the Board to the vote declining the gift. The Board first accepted the gift, but insisted upon the donor withdrawing his strings from it — the condition as to the location of the building. This, of course, he refused to do. The Board plainly was playing fast and loose with a million-dollar gift. And for a college of the first rank to hesitate about a million-dollar gift was newspaper copy. Moreover, the quarrel in Princeton was growing old. In his lifetime Grover Cleveland was leader of the faction in the trustees which had been overridden by President Wilson and his friends. So the old quarrel brought the name of Cleveland over into the new controversy.

The President of the University who was questioning the Procter million-dollar gift was one of the most convincing of American orators, a writer of national reputation, who made his plea defending the trustees upon the ground that money was trying to dictate the educational policy of the colleges of America. He talked and wrote much. The Roosevelt régime was at its climax. The people eagerly accepted the Wilson story. But those who were grilled in the fires of the passions which President Wilson was arousing, basted their blisters in wrath which was more violent because it had no great voice. The friends of Dean West naturally opposed the prestige and distinction of Wilson with the name of

Grover Cleveland, conjuring with it. It was said that, shortly before his death, Mr. Cleveland had written a letter to a friend for posterity, in which he eased his mind about Doctor Wilson. When that letter is printed, if it really exists, it should be discounted. It was written in the fever heat of a malignant controversy. Mr. Cleveland's friend and neighbor, Dean West, had been promised support in a project which Mr. Cleveland considered worthy; and then, for reasons which Mr. Cleveland could not understand, had been refused the promised support. And above all, the personalities of Wilson and Cleveland were profoundly antagonistic. They were the cat and the dog. Neither ever had a friend like the other. They were doomed to mutual suspicion which in any contest was bound to develop malicious mutual contempt!

President Wilson's statement of Christmas, 1909, to Moses Taylor Pyne, who had succeeded Mr. Cleveland as chairman of the trustees' committee on the Graduate School, had become the issue in the contest. He declared that such gifts as the Procter offer were destructive of academic freedom by permitting rich patrons to dictate educational policies. He closed with these words:

I am not willing to be drawn further into the toils. I cannot accede to the acceptance of gifts which take the educational policy of the University out of the hands of the trustees and faculty, and permit it to be determined by those who give money.

How those words rang through the country, which was cheering Roosevelt, and what bitter gall they were to Wilson's enemies! For they felt that he was an opportunist. He had not been a conspicuous democrat in his teaching days. His books certainly are not patently Jeffersonian. And his objection to the Procter offer, because it attempted to locate the buildings of the Graduate School, was not raised when another gift, locating the Graduate School objectionably, was offered in 1905. But the earlier gift, as a matter of fact, had not been used, and the building site proposed had not been in Dean West's control. At bottom it was not the site that aroused Wilson's opposition. It was the organization of the Graduate School under the ideals of Dean West. But of course the President could not make a public cause out of the danger of Dean West's plan for a separate collegiate unit. Though probably he had convinced his friends in the Board of Trustees by his reason, his excuse dramatized itself best for the public upon the issue of the interference of money in academic affairs. This was not conscious demagogy. The heat of combat melts fine distinctions. The menace of wealth to the academic world was an issue, but it was a side issue. To stress it, made it a winning issue. To stress the other issue — the real issue, the West issue — would have appeared to intrude a private quarrel into an academic question. The side issue was a great cause. But, alas, for Woodrow Wilson, he was so unschooled in rough-and-tumble conflict that often he was unable to keep his great causes from degenerating into private quarrels.

The year 1910 opened stormily for Woodrow Wilson. No one can doubt that he had become by 1910 a convinced democrat, and that he was making a real fight for democracy in education. It was out of the mouths of his enemies and by the logic of their deeds that he was convinced. He went into Princeton a student, later as a professor, and still later into the presidency of Princeton, fairly well satisfied with the order that was. Wealth ruled, and had the special privileges of royalty because, upon the whole, wealth deserved to rule and to administer the special privileges of royalty. Once he may have confused the possession of wealth, whether by heredity or by acquisition, with brains, character, and good-will. But he left Princeton with those illusions gone. So in the first months of the year 1910 came the battle days.

And we must not think of him in those months as

the stern and rather austere man whom the country afterwards came to know as its War President. That sternness even then was a veneer. Always in his heart, he was Joseph Wilson's son, the scion of the Irish Kings, loving greatly and ever eager for the love of his kind; with a light word and a merry countenance for the run of the day, and only his dour features for the heavy hours. But the Woodrows, grave, disciplined, industrious, punctual, and serious, were intruding more and more into his conscious moments. They were called by the duties and spiritual hardships that came with executive work. But most of his time, even in the stress and struggle of the eight years before 1910, he had been a gallant Irishman, nimble but strong. Among those he loved, his friends, his family, his casual associates, he was always a bit of a play-boy.

The hall in which he sometimes met the Graduate School Committee staged the controversy. That hall must have sustained his Celtic soul like a fighting draught. It is the chapel of Old Nassau — a big hall, perhaps a hundred feet long, forty feet wide, with marble floors and heavy dark-oak paneling rising twenty-five feet off the forty from floor to ridgepole. That is held up by oak beams, giving the room a baronial character. About Nassau Hall raged the battle of Princeton in the Revolutionary War. Here a cannon ball broke through the wall and tore out a portrait of George II from its gilded frame. Washington took this hall from the Hessians, lost it, and retook it, and the old hall was battle-wrecked. After the Revolution, Washington gave the college a purse which they spent upon a portrait of Washington that fills the frame from which the cannon ball tore out the royal figure. Here in this hall Madison came to chapel, and here Lafayette and Washington met to cement their friendship. The Continental Congress, fleeing from Philadelphia, came to Princeton and met in this hall to ratify the Declaration of Independence. Here Aaron Burr, whose father had been President of Princeton, came to spend the lonely, dishonored years before his death, and in this hall had his touch of the only balm in his gall and wormwood when his college society invited the dishonored old man to rejoin it. Here came John Adams on his way to the Continental Congress. Here generals, supreme court judges, American statesmen of the last century, received religious instruction from the grim and gloomy Calvinists of their times. It was such a hall as Tommy Wilson would have gloried in, and surely Woodrow gave him a peek at the picture of this other Princeton statesman, as he fought the first real hand-to-hand, man-to-man struggle of his life. But most likely, in spite of the romantic setting of the battle-field, when the shindy began, Tommy turned tail and left the field to the Woodrows.[1]

[1] Perhaps a chronology indicating certain official actions both by the Board and Mr. Wilson may be appended for the use of those who are addicted to dates.

May 10, 1909, A. F. West gave to Woodrow Wilson, William Cooper Procter's letter offering the gift of $500,000 to Princeton, contingent upon a similar sum being raised by the alumni. The alumni quickly met the offer.

May 12th, a special committee composed of Mr. Wilson, Mr. Caldwater, Mr. Pyne, and Mr. Sheldon, considered the Procter offer.

June 4th, a sub-committee met, with Mr. Procter present.

June 7th, Mr. Procter by letter indicated that he wanted the site of the Graduate School on the golf links.

June 14th, the Board presented hearty thanks, and the resolution was lost to put the Graduate School near Prospect, a site under consideration for a previous gift for the Graduate School.

October 20th, Mr. Procter offered to withdraw his gift after talking to Mr. Wilson, who explained why he wanted the Graduate School enveloped within the University.

December 21st, a large informal get-together party was held at which Mr. Procter, Dean West, and pretty generally representatives of both sides of the controversy were present. Nothing was offered on either side except tall talk. Mr. Wilson declared he wanted Mr. Procter to stay over so that they might talk further the next day. Mr. Wilson then made an appointment to meet Mr. Procter at the Jersey City station, where Mr. Wilson proposed to have two Graduate Schools, one on the golf links and one at Prospect. There is a question as to whether or not Mr. Procter accepted this offer. His friends say he did. Mr. Wilson's friends have no knowledge of it, nor of the offer.

December 22d, Mr. Wilson wrote to Mr. Pyne that Procter had refused to adjust his offer to the Wilson proposal.

December 25th, Mr. Wilson seems to have written several letters setting forth his views in the matter.

December 28th, he declared that certain counter-proposals of Procter left "West in the saddle."

January 10, 1910, seems to be the date of a meeting when four members of the faculty committee on the Graduate School met and sent a letter to President Wilson which lined up a majority of the members of the Graduate School against the West idea of organization.

On January 12th, the trustees' committee met to consider a "recom-

It was on January 13th that the first real clash came. The trustees had been dallying with their refusal of the Procter gift and its contingent offer; the alumni had been stormy; the liberal givers to the University had been dubious and divided. When the committee for the Graduate School met in Nassau Hall, President Wilson was hag-ridden by fears, and flinching raw from friction with the doubts of weak supporters. He sat on a high bench looking down upon the committee of the trustees who supported Dean West. Dean West was there, being secretary of one of the committees of trustees or of the alumni

mendation to the Board of Trustees concerning the acceptance of Mr. Procter's gift."

On January 13th, Mr. Pyne presented to the committee a letter from Mr. Procter asking the Board to decline his offer, virtually withdrawing his gift. The same day a resolution was adopted by the trustees' committee of five to consider "the whole matter involved in Mr. Procter's offer."

February 6th, Mr. Procter wrote definitely withdrawing his gift.

February 10th, a see-sawing report was presented by the special committee. It was accepted, but not adopted. The committee hoped that Mr. Procter would renew his offer. About that time articles appeared in the *New York Times* and *Post* which were attributed to Mr. Wilson, although they shocked the finer sensibilities of many Princeton graduates. They were anonymous articles, but good evidence seems to exist that he inspired or wrote all or part of these articles. He was fighting and fighting hard in those days.

Shattered in nerves and distraught in mind and soul, he went to Bermuda for a rest. Returning late in February, he began his famous campaign among the alumni, hitting hard from the shoulder at the impudent arrogance of wealth which sought to control the academic world. These speeches at the Princeton Club in Gramercy Park, New York, at Pittsburgh, and at Chicago revealed the Woodrow, full-panoplied, stern, unyielding, cold, and deadly.

concerned with the Graduate School. The President notified the committee of his position on the Procter gift. Then came a letter from Mr. Procter, which the friends of Dean West contend was in effect a surrender of the Procter contention as to the site. It would have made a sensation, surely, and the opponents of the President declare that it did. He rose, white and agitated, and said: "This offer is too — too — too complicated. The time has passed for compromise. At any rate —"

Maybe this story is apocryphal, for none of Wilson's friends were there to recall it, but his opponents aver that he stood with quaking hands and exclaimed:

"I can't accept this."

Then he got hold of himself and said earnestly: "This matter of the site is not essential. Under proper auspices my faculty can make this school a success anywhere in Mercer County. The whole trouble is that Dean West's ideas and ideals are not the ideas and ideals of Princeton!"

Now Wilson's friends deny this declaration. Yet it is, on the whole, the perfect justification for his course. Site was, indeed, unimportant; faculty organization and administrative control of the Graduate School were the essentials. If rich men could enter Princeton and establish a school off the campus, a school which might be at the same time out of administrative control of the President and faculty of the College, virtually naming their own Dean, where, indeed, were "the ideas and ideals of Princeton"!

If Wilson had only spoken thus when Dean West had been invited to Massachusetts, what turmoil he would have avoided! But by holding the Dean from advancement and, in effect, keeping him in Princeton on the Dean's own terms, and then by quietly ignoring those terms and holding him upon terms which the President deemed wise, though galling to the Dean, a great unnecessary embroilment followed. As the meeting, almost impromptu, went on, there in the hall, in the midst of Princeton's oldest traditions, the committee and the President wrangled to their hearts' content. They asked him why he had written the preface to the Dean's brochure used to gather money for the Graduate School. He answered that he had written it without seeing the book, justifying himself probably by the reservation that the manuscript and the proof did not foreshadow the gorgeous elegance of the assembled pages and the alluring photogravures printed and illustrated to sell a school which the President of Princeton could not approve. His later explanation that he wrote the preface good-naturedly and offhand also is not nearly so adequate as the truth, which is that the preface carefully and unmistakably expresses the Wilsonian attitude to the School, which, knowing Wilson for the hard-purposed man revealed by the later controversy, should never have deceived or befuddled Dean West or his friends. If Wilson had only stuck doggedly and openly to the cause he made in that preface, instead of trying to mollify and placate and wear out his adversaries, his cause never would have degenerated into a quarrel.

But he would never have gone through the fire; would never have come out a champion of educational democracy against the assumptions of what Roosevelt loved to call "aggrandized wealth." Woodrow Wilson stumbled into the truth walking a rather devious path. Damascus is no very high goal for a journey's end; yet on the road to Damascus Saul of Tarsus saw a great light. The miracles of God are not done only for "just men made perfect."

A few weeks later, in early February, 1910, the Board of Trustees met and, upon the advice of the President, declined finally to accept the Procter gift, which was then formally withdrawn. But the declination and the withdrawal were met by a turmoil of protest.

Suddenly up bobbed the "quad" system again;

those who objected to the refusal of a million-dollar gift to Princeton made new and lusty clamor against having to "eat with muckers," as if in deadly fear that the President, having committed profanation to Princeton by refusing money for it, was going to lead their gold-plated children by the ears to a trough where they would have to swill themselves with the proletariat! Students, the alumni, the reactionary press, the various union league clubs of the country, croaked with despairing fear for the safety of the Republic when such things as the refusal of the Procter gift by Princeton could be. Somewhat in response to this violent outbreak of feeling in the Princeton world, another meeting of the Board was called a few days later; another vote was taken. It was too close for Wilson's comfort. He was losing ground with the trustees. Wilson at that second meeting had himself well in hand. From time to time he turned his powers of persuasion upon the group. From the minority came wicked thrusts at his veracity, at his integrity of purpose, at his sincerity in turning the issue upon the hinge of educational democracy. Never before in his life had he endured what his adversaries put upon him that day. He saw his friends weaken. He had but sixteen of the thirty trustees, and his narrow majority had heard him reviled by innuendo, and the heart of the man was bruised and hurt. So a few days after the meeting of February 16th, Ellen Axson sent him to Bermuda.

While he was gone, the tempest raged. All over the East the alumni held lodges of sorrow and indignation at the Procter sacrilege! Dr. Henry van Dyke addressed a meeting of alumni at Philadelphia, March 4th. Dr. van Dyke took a middle ground of disagreement with the President. He felt that the Graduate College should not become the first of a series of separate colleges introduced into the student body of Princeton, though he did not wish to have it so far from Nassau Hall as it finally was located. He opposed the "quad" system upon principle. His case is notable, for his opposition was vigorous and frank. Yet his personal relations with Wilson were not affected. As President of the United States, Wilson appointed his former adversary Minister to the Netherlands. This must always be remembered when his enemies say that Wilson could not brook opposition. He could not endure certain kinds: direct, impassioned, reckless — the kind most masculine creatures love to set up when they are convinced that they are right. In addressing a meeting of alumni at Montclair, New Jersey, Doctor Hibben spoke moderately, cautioning the alumni against hasty conclusions. Hibben had been an intimate friend of Wilson's for many years, but Wilson broke with him. It is hard to say just why.

The anti-Wilson faction set up a candidate for trustee, Adrian H. Joline, a railroad director and New York business man of a conservative cast of mind. The immediate battle turned upon the election by the alumni of Mr. Joline. Wilson returned from Bermuda in March, refreshed in body and militant in soul. His faith in his cause was flaming. He set out on a mission, visiting the alumni of the West. There was his strength, and he knew it. He had turned the issue directly upon educational democracy.

Lord Bryce has called attention to the fact that nowhere else in the English-speaking world do leaders of education, college presidents and their kind, have so much weight in public affairs as they have in America. Doctor Wilson, on his mission for educational democracy that spring of 1910, made a stir in America. He was, of course, in unison with the spirit of his times. The insurgents in Congress were defeating Speaker Cannon and preparing for the defeat of President Taft. The plutocratic control of Government was breaking; and Woodrow Wilson, in his fight against the domination of money in education, was part of a national offensive against the rule of materialism in our national life.

His speeches were models of controversial eloquence. This was his thesis:

I cannot accede to the acceptance of gifts upon terms which take the educational policy of the University out of the hands of the trustees and faculty, and permit it to be determined by those who give money.

On this thesis he spoke with fire and yet with rhetorical finish. At Pittsburgh he said:

You can't spend four years at one of our modern universities without getting in your thought the conviction which is most dangerous to America — namely, that you must treat with certain influences which now dominate in the commercial undertakings of the country.

The great voice of America does not come from seats of learning. It comes in a murmur from the hills and woods and the farms and factories and the mills, rolling on and gaining volume until it comes to us from the homes of common men. Do these murmurs echo in the corridors of universities? I have not heard them.

The universities would make men forget their common origins, forget their universal sympathies, and join a class — and no class ever can serve America.

I have dedicated every power that there is within me to bring the colleges that I have anything to do with to an absolutely democratic regeneration in spirit, and I shall not be satisfied — and I hope you will not be — until America shall know that the men in the colleges are saturated with the same thought, the same sympathy, that pulses through the whole great body politic.

I know that the colleges of this country must be reconstructed from top to bottom, and I know that America is going to demand it. While Princeton men pause and think, I hope — and the hope arises out of the great love I share with you all for our inimitable Alma Mater — I hope that they will think on these things, that they will forget tradition in the determination to see to it that the free air of America shall permeate every cranny of their college.

Will America tolerate the seclusion of graduate students? Will America tolerate the idea of having graduate students set apart? America will tolerate nothing except unpatronized endeavor. Seclude a man, separate him from the rough-and-tumble of college life, from all the contacts of every sort and condition of men, and you have done a thing which America will brand with its contemptuous disapproval.

He came back to Princeton from his Western trip a victor assured of Joline's probable defeat.[1] Mr. Joline typified to Woodrow Wilson all that he was combating in Princeton. Mr. Joline was a New York lawyer, with clients in that precinct of the American market-place known as Wall Street. He was a director of the Missouri, Kansas & Texas Railroad, and by training and environment stood in considerable scorn of all the things to which Woodrow Wilson aspired. They had been acquaintances for years, and had exchanged views about matters political. In the latter part of the first decade of the twentieth century, many evidences may be found that Mr. Wilson was thinking of things political. He had written to Mr. Joline a letter about the leadership of Bryan. About the same time he had written to Mrs. Peck along the same lines, regretting

[1] Joline's actual defeat occurred in the election in June.

the fact that the Democratic cause was in the hands of a man whose intellectual processes he so thoroughly discounted. The Joline letter was, however, a link in Wilson's destiny. The defeat of Joline as trustee of Princeton came three years after the letter.

When Joline had been defeated for trustee by the alumni, and it was evident that President Wilson had the majority of the alumni back of him, he walked the campus with his old stride. The years sloughed off. The lines of care, and the pain that had shadowed his face in the winter, vanished. When he stood up in chapel to pray, it was in the old manner — the way of a man who has the ear of the Lord.

> I can still see him [writes a student of those days], a fine, straight, tall figure of a man, vital with pride in his faith. Behind the pulpit in Princeton Chapel, he lifted up his voice in prayer as one sure of his communion. He knew he was of the elect. It radiated joyously in his clear voice with words so carefully chosen, with manner so perfectly poised. The outstanding impression one got from hearing him pray was the impassioned earnestness of the man, his deep belief in the underlying purpose of God. His prayers breathed the firm hope that we young men might be worthy and effective tools in the hands of an Omnipotent Will. His prayer was always extemporized, but no matter what the occasion, he always concluded with a section from the Book of Common Prayer. It ran:
>
> > "Almighty and most merciful Father; we have erred, and strayed from thy ways like lost sheep. We have followed too much the

devices and desires of our own hearts. We have offended against thy holy laws. We have left undone those things which we ought to have done, and we have done those things which we ought not to have done. And there is no health in us. But thou, O Lord, have mercy upon us, miserable offenders. Spare thou those, O God, who confess their faults. Restore thou those who are penitent; according to thy promises declared unto mankind in Christ Jesus our Lord. And grant, O most merciful Father, for his sake, that we may hereafter live a godly, righteous, and sober life, to the glory of thy holy Name. Amen."

The bruise of the blow which fell in February, when his hold on the trustees seemed to be slipping, had gone. He was healed and happy. He had won his fight by the courage of his faith. The alumni had sustained him, confused his enemies, and strengthened the purpose of the trustees. Then to this Job came another messenger who brought bad tidings. It was at commencement. An old man, Isaac C. Wyman, whose father had fought in the battle of Princeton, and was rich enough to give Washington forty thousand pounds, died May 18th. Ten days later his will was read. He left the bulk of his fortune to Princeton, but —

It was late twilight when David Lawrence, a student correspondent of the *New York Times*, tapped at Wilson's study door in Prospect. He handed Doctor Wilson a telegram from the *Times*. It read:

> Isaac C. Wyman, of Salem, Massachusetts, died leaving an estate valued at over ten million dollars to the Graduate School at Princeton, naming his attorney, John H. Raymond, and Dean Andrew F. West, executors. Ask President Wilson for statement to use in connection with the announcement in to-morrow's paper.

Doctor Wilson held the telegram under the electric bulb and re-read the words. He put his hand on the table with the telegram between his fingers and grew rigid, then paled.

"Lawrence," he said, "this means defeat. We never can overcome ten millions." He picked up the paper, handed it back, tried to smile, and said: "Nothing to-night, Lawrence — you'll understand."

The fight was over — lost.

To all intents and purposes that was the last day of his service at Princeton. He remained on three months longer drawing the salary as President, but his heart was not in the work. That period of his life was closed. In estimating what Woodrow Wilson did in his first executive position, it may be well to quote from Vernon Lansing Collins's volume on Princeton in the "American College and University Series," on page 282. He writes:

To sum up the progress made during the seven years from 1902 to 1909, the internal discipline and rules of administration had been stiffened, a carefully devised course of study based on the Princeton theory of practically required under-class years, followed by two years of a coherent and assisted elective system, had been installed, an effective method of instruction had been introduced, the teaching force had been greatly strengthened, the library equipment had been increased, honor courses had been instituted in mathematics, physics, and the classical humanities, McCosh Hall, containing recitation and lecture rooms, had been erected, as well as the great gymnasium and the well-appointed laboratories in natural and physical sciences, Guyot Hall, and Palmer Laboratory, the Faculty Room had been remodeled and given a dignity worthy of the historic associations of the apartment, while Holder, Patton, Blair extension, the Seventy-Nine and Seventy-Seven dormitories had been erected, Lake Carnegie had been constructed, and acquisitions to the campus had extended it from two hundred and twenty acres to six hundred. During this period of feverish activity, over four and a quarter millions had been received by the University, of which sum, roughly speaking, only $2,400,000 had gone into endowment, including dormitories; buildings not producing income had cost $1,700,000, additional campus $100,000, and laboratory equipment $80,000. Through the Graduate Council the alumni were contributing annually approximately $100,000 for current expenses, or nearly what the preceptorial method was costing. The non-productive buildings required $40,000 a year for maintenance, and the upkeep of the campus was an increasing expense. The faculty had grown from one hundred and eight in 1902 to one hundred and sixty-nine in 1909, most of the growth occurring in one year, while the student body during the same period had fallen off from one thousand three hundred and eighty-three in 1902 to one thousand three hundred and fourteen in 1909.

There was a record of substantial achievement, a record of which any man might be proud. And yet, because he saw his ideals wrecked by the Wyman gift, he felt that his work was done.

The next day after the telegram came announcing the Wyman gift, the world knew it. When the trustees met, they had before them the renewal of the Procter offer. President Wilson formally asked the Board to accept it. The ten millions afterward shrank to something less than two, but the promise of so large a sum as the bequest at first appeared to be, made another situation. Even at the risk of establishing a separate college unit at Princeton, the President could not ask the Board to decline the Wyman gift. He called Dean West to Prospect and said: "Now, listen — don't speak till I finish. I wish to say that I desire to coöperate with you generally and in every possible way in working toward the success of the Graduate School under this bequest. The size of the gift entirely changes the perspective." He paused; evidently he had said his say.

Dean West replied: "I shall carry on my work," and turned away.

A few nights later, President Wilson attended a

dinner at Dean West's house given to celebrate the reception of the Wyman bequest. He presented a silver cup to Moses Taylor Pyne, the trustee who had supported Dean West, to commemorate his twenty-five years' service on the Board. He played the game.

An ancient custom draws the Princeton Seniors to the steps of Old Nassau a few nights before commencement to sing. That year, when they sang, the usual crowd gathered under the trees in the dusk to listen. From immemorial time they had put local faculty hits into their songs. Princeton wondered how they would handle the situation made by the day's events. They sang of Professor John G. Hibben, "We call him Jack — the whitest man in all the fac." Then, "To Stockton Axson, who works us hard, but lets us through." Then a clear voice rang out with the lines:

> "Here's to Andy eight million West,
> Sixty-three inches around the vest,
> To get him Boston tried her best,
> He winked his eye — you know the rest."

Then up sang another imp by the cauldron:

> "Here's to Woodrow, King divine,
> Who rules this place along with Fine.
> We have no fear he'll leave this town
> To try for anybody's crown!"

They had sung it even the year before — in 1909. How could they know about the crown that was so near? Glamis was not even Cawdor then! What urged them to deny that he should seek a crown hereafter?

CHAPTER X

IN WHICH WE SHIFT THE SCENE

THE only comedy that colored the somber drama of Woodrow Wilson's middle life was set in 1910 — a romping, knock-about interlude with the New Jersey Irish; coming as a gala relief after the tragedy of his Princeton defeat, and before the powerful morality play, reminiscent somewhat of Prometheus, that hurried Wilson, as a test of his faith and as a punishment for stealing its fire from the gods, into the lonely, clouded days that marked his exit. To understand the comedy, we must go back in our story nearly a dozen years. The year 1910 saw his entry into politics. But the events of that year had various roots in his life and the drift of the times. His yearning for a career in politics which his friends in college noted, the feeling of his father, his letters to Mrs. Peck and his talk with her, his significant remark to the Princeton trustee, his suggestion to Charles Talcott, the mayor of Utica, all indicate that, back in his subconscious mind, a politician was developing as the man in the upper consciousness read and wrote and lectured about the science of government.

Contemporaneous with these evidences of his

political ambitions, but quite apart from them, came the upheaval in our national life: the Populists questioning the divine right of property to rule, the Spanish War, giving us the burden of imperial administration of the affairs of backward island peoples. The election of 1900 saddled imperialism upon us. The Populist questioning submerged to reappear as the Roosevelt policies. And the first decade of the new century brought with it a pandemonium of voices clamoring for economic adjustment in our national business, for political reform which would give the average citizen more power in the control of government. The dammed waters of national progress, that for three decades following the Civil War had been held by bigoted partisanship sustaining greedy individualism, were bursting their bounds, and the old economic and political structure of America was crumbling in the flood. A new nationalism, later to be known as a new freedom, was rising in the hearts of the people. The old order entrenched in both parties was making a death struggle, bitter and fierce. Generally it controlled both party organizations in the cities and in many of the States, particularly in in the Eastern cities and States. The conservative forces everywhere were eager to find a local Moses, some one with an attractive personality and no particular sense of the controversy, who would lure the aroused electorate from their local insurgent heroes. Good men outside of the party organizations, illustrious persons who could be depended upon to wear plug hats well and speak fittingly upon public occasions, were sought by party managers whose party tills were stuffed with money from insurance companies, railroads, telephone and telegraph companies, food packers and grain manipulators.

Woodrow Wilson, from the day he became a national figure by reason of his fight for educational democracy, seemed to be the perfect flower for these gardeners of reaction to transplant into politics. He was eminently respectable, had no embarrassing business connections, was not aware of the import of the struggle of the revolutionaries, but had been engaged in what to the politicians appeared an amusing sham battle at Princeton, the account of which would sound well if advertised in a campaign. As early as 1903 he had been mentioned as a presidential possibility by reporters casting about idly for a Democratic candidate against the inevitable Roosevelt of 1904. In 1906 George Harvey, a newspaper man who had done some good messenger service for the Wall Street crowd, furnishing more brains than Wall Street ordinarily needed — George Harvey had met Woodrow Wilson, his plug hat, raglan coat, single eyeglass, in New York, where Wilson was the guest of honor at a Lotus Club dinner. On that occasion Colonel Harvey had introduced Wilson as a potential president. The Lotus Club was, and is, one of the soft seats of the tired plutocracy of our metropolis, perfumed by a literary air which sometimes fools guests into trying to take seriously questions at issue between the March Hare and the Mad Hatter. But nothing ever happens. President Wilson, having had the benediction of a Lotus Club dinner, the "Brooklyn Eagle" nominated him for President a few months later, and in 1907 George Harvey introduced Wilson's name as a candidate for the Democratic senatorial nomination in New Jersey—an empty honor which carried the endorsement of a hopeless minority. But even this honor was denied him. He did not like the "honorable mention," and wrote letters to friends expressing the fear that messing in politics was weakening his position in the University. In 1909 George Harvey, who was then editor of "Harper's Weekly," again mentioned Wilson as a presidential possibility. In the meantime he had become an important figure in the academic world — partly through the advertising that came to him as the result of the Princeton quarrel; but chiefly because, as a writer, a lecturer, the head of a great school, and a man of exceptional talents and charm and a clear vision of the educational need of the times, he had shown force of character and intelligence which entitled him to his academic leadership. He was of full man's size in the world in which he moved.

Now for his immediate political environment; namely, the Democratic Party in New Jersey and more particularly in Mercer County. It was outwardly in the control of the Irish. They were the governing classes. They held the power as bosses, State and local. They held all the offices, in which they took orders from the industrial corporations and the financial concerns that controlled the industrial corporations. So the Irish represented the plutocracy of the time and place, but the control was veiled, and from year to year many a fine row raged among the Irish for leadership, with no thought of turning the State over to the voters for an experiment in self-government. The Irish controlled the cities, and gave the public service corporations the kind of franchises which they desired. The Irish controlled the forces that controlled the legislature. These Irish gave the financial leaders in banking and industry laws which would create the special privileges and immunities they required. Sometimes the Irish used the Republican Party and sometimes the Democratic Party. But the governing classes were generally

Irish and of the Holy Faith, and the ruling classes were always of the older American stock and of no faith in particular.

In 1906–08 the American Revolution of the decade touched New Jersey. It came first in the Republican Party and was called the New Idea. It was a faction led by George L. Record, Everett Colby, Gilbert Roe, and half a dozen strong men who determined to take the fight for free government, which was waging in the West, into New Jersey. Naturally the fight attracted the Irish, and they, being for the most part Democratic, made the fight in their party. But they were in a sad minority. The State Democratic machine was in the hands of what was known as the "Jim-Jim" crowd and "Little Bob" Davis; meaning the Honorable James Smith, former United States Senator, his kinsman, the Honorable James Nugent, and the Honorable Robert Davis, city collector of Jersey City; all honorable men and vicegerents of Mammon in New Jersey. A fine lot they were, these Irish bosses, sub-bosses, and satellites; emotional, impulsive, acquisitive, but as honest as their rulers would let them be. The division in the Republican ranks, due to the New Idea, made it seem likely that the Democrats would win the governorship in 1910 and possibly the United States senatorship. A strong current in the Republican Party had set in, a rising tide from the West which promised to overwhelm Mr. Taft's leadership in Congress, and in June, 1910, Roosevelt, returning from Africa, was giving comfort to the enemies of the Republican organization everywhere — and notably in New Jersey. So the Irish in the Democratic Party saw their chance.

The talk of Wilson for Governor began early in the year. George Harvey was its mouthpiece. He had Wall Street contacts that were in communication with the Jim-Jim organization. There is a suspicion in Princeton that the wealthy opponents of Wilson, as, for instance, Moses Taylor Pyne, leader of the West faction in the trustees, fostered the Wilson gubernatorial boom. But the evidence for this is purely circumstantial. They certainly were glad to be quit of him in Princeton — these trustees of the opposition. It was in June that the Honorable James Smith began talking to the other Irish about Wilson as a gubernatorial candidate. Smith, lacking any point of praise for his candidate which his followers would understand, kept referring to him as "the man of the hour"! Now, as the phrase was used by the Honorable Jim No. 1, "the man of the hour" meant to his Irish cohorts nothing except that "the chief wants him," which was enough. So the word went thrilling down the line that the "big fellow" desired the nomination of Woodrow Wilson, President of Princeton.

All this happened in July, 1910. But before it happened, negotiations were opened between Doctor Wilson and the Irish, something of this nature: Colonel George Harvey frankly asked Mr. Wilson if he would accept the nomination. He indicated that he would be glad to consider it. He went upon his summer vacation to Lyme, Connecticut. He wrote to his friend, Dean Fine, of Princeton College, that he was seriously considering the Democratic gubernatorial nomination. The New Jersey newspapers began mentioning Wilson as a candidate in obviously inspired editorials. A reporter for the "Newark News" went to New England to see Doctor Wilson. Wilson said he was undecided. Then he came down to New York City, and in a prominent club he met Colonel Harvey in a conference with five others. Harvey was sincerely Wilson's friend and became a sort of liaison officer between Wilson, Wall Street, and the New Jersey machine. He could speak the three languages needed in the conference; academic, commercial, and political. The others in the conference represented the Democratic machine of New Jersey; Little Bob Davis and the two Jims; James Nugent was easily the most forceful man there. But the others at the conference were Millard

F. Ross, a county leader under Smith; R. V. Lindabury, also representing Smith, and Eugene F. Kinkead and Robert S. Hudspeth, probably representing Little Bob Davis, of Jersey City. These conferees were authorized to tell Doctor Wilson that there was a real demand for him as a candidate, meaning, of course, that Colonel Harvey's friends were anxious to put Wilson in the race and had persuaded the Jim-Jim machine, one way or another, to accept him. And that meant money to finance the campaign; probably not much — a few thousands. Of course Wilson knew little of the masonry of the work they were putting on. He probably accepted the whole performance at its face value. The conferees talked up in the air for a time — about buncombe issues and unrealities. Then up spoke one of the men and said:

> Doctor Wilson, there have been some political reformers who, after they have been elected to office as candidates of one party or the other, have shut the doors in the face of the organization leaders, refusing even to listen to them. Is it your idea that a governor should regard himself free of all obligation to his party organization?

At least that is what this friend told Josephus Daniels, and Daniels quoted Wilson's reply as this:

> Gentlemen: I have always been a believer in party organizations. If I were elected Governor of New

Jersey, I should be very glad to consult with the leaders of the Democratic organization. I should refuse to listen to no man, but I should be especially glad to hear and duly consider the suggestions of the leaders of my party. If, on my own independent investigation, I found that the recommendations for appointments made to me by the organization leaders named the best possible men, I should naturally prefer, other things being equal, to appoint them, as the men pointed out by the combined counsels of the party.

Very likely the dialogue was not set in that kind of third-reader rhetoric. But at any rate Doctor Wilson was clever enough to side-step the trap and the Irish were fools enough to let him get away with his tall talk, instead of pinning him down to cases. This was in mid-July. The "Newark News" reporter, just back from New England, was explaining to the managing editor that Wilson was undecided, and probably was not a candidate, despite the fact that the Irish had given the newspaper office a tip that Wilson had decided — when the telephone rang. It was Doctor Wilson calling the reporter to give him the announcement; and then the fun began. The announcement was made July 15th, that if it was "the wish of a majority of the thoughtful Democrats of the State" — that phrase "thoughtful Democrats" particularly galled the Irish and cost the Jim-Jim machine a pretty penny in good beer and free lunch — he would accept the nomination. He went back to his New England bungalow and did not turn a hand for the nomination.

But the organization had a hard summer. The difficulty in the Wilson pre-convention campaign lay somewhat in the fact that he could not control his home county. He had never identified himself with the organization, and the leading candidate of the anti-machine crowd was from Mercer County, where Mr. Wilson lived! Wilson had never been in the court-house of his county nor the state-house of his State before he was nominated, and his political influence was just one vote. He had never sat in a county convention nor stood up in a ward caucus. He could have done nothing better for his candidacy than go to New England with it and let the Jim-Jim machine get the convention delegates to nominate him.

The reformers in the Democratic Party in New Jersey in the summer of 1910 were against Woodrow Wilson. They had the same opinion of him that the bosses had; that he was an honest, thick-headed, well-meaning innocent who would take orders! The reformers were a shivering little band of Irish who had tried to do for Democracy what Record and Colby had done for the Republican Party in the State: free it from the domination of an organization controlled by Wall Street. The reformers were led by Martin P. Devlin, of Trenton; John J. Tracy, Mark A. Sullivan, W. W. St. John, Joseph P. Tumulty — and a number of other young Irishmen picked by Little Bob Davis as respectables to dress the windows of his machine shop; he nominated them for the legislature. Also with them was James Kerney, of the "Trenton Times," and the editors of four leading daily newspapers of the State. These star-eyed godlets of reform lined up behind the candidacy of Mayor Frank S. Katzenbach, later justice of the State Supreme Court, and picked him to beat Wilson and the machine.

September 14th came. Colonel Harvey brought Wilson down from the cool fastnesses of New England. The State convention was to meet the next day. The political hotel where the statesmen gathered was filled with stale smoke, beer-fumes, sour lunch, and the clamor of marching clubs romping through the halls. The Katzenbach band serenaded the Wilson headquarters in Room 100, where Colonel George Harvey held forth, but never a Wilson delegate from his home county was there to vote for him — not even one from Princeton. Big Jim Smith, standing by the washstand in Room 100, assembled the reporters at ten o'clock at night and declared: "It will be Wilson on the first ballot," and gave out the platform which had been written by the organization for the convention to adopt the next day; a fine gesture of power. "It will never be Wilson on any ballot," declared Frank Katzenbach, conducting his own campaign, and irritated that an intruder from his own county should come in who never had voted in a caucus. "Wilson will have 800 of the 1413 delegates," replied Smith when the reporters came back from Katzenbach's room, and Smith announced the names of the counties from which the delegates would come.

In the meantime, Woodrow Wilson in Prospect, the presidential home of Princeton, was working through the hot night on his speech of acceptance. He knew, what every one knew, that if Smith, Nugent, and Davis could not nominate him on the first ballot, they had lost the fight. The morning papers printed the conflicting claims, votes by counties of the rival camps, and Senator Smith's defi ran thus:

> Doctor Wilson will have 800 delegates on the first ballot and in November will sweep the State. With Maine gone for the Democrats, it looks like a Democratic year in New Jersey. I had no desire to get into this contest at all; but it was like an old fire horse hitched to a milk wagon hearing the alarm bells! So here I am. We can win with Wilson, a man of high attainments, not an office-seeker — a man who rose from the people!

It was a perfect clarion note of its kind. The streets of Trenton, leading to the Taylor Opera

House where the convention assembled, began to liven up by ten o'clock on the morning of the 15th. The contest for the preliminary organization of the convention was won by Smith, Nugent, and Davis. Their platform had been written and printed the night before, but a platform committee was solemnly named. The platform, among other things, provided for a programme which would catch the Liberal Independent vote. This vote was becoming stronger and stronger in New Jersey: direct primaries, civil service extension, giving the rate-making power for public utilities to the State commission, an employers' liability law, and a corrupt practices law were the things which the Republican reformers were demanding in their platform. These things were incorporated by Smith and Nugent in the Democratic platform. At one o'clock the decks were cleared for the big fight. The convention took recess until half-past two. It was fairly certain that Wilson would win, but the contest was still open.

At two-thirty, hot, red-faced, full of heavy food and too much rebellious liquor, came the delegates stamping into the close, stuffy opera house. Tension made their hearts beat quicker. Their nerves were raw. A thousand fans fluttered. Men let down their wet suspenders and unbuttoned their sweaty shirt fronts. The nominating speeches began. The speech for Wilson was greeted with enthusiasm; that was a part of the machine programme. Enthusiasm is one of the things in a convention that a machine always can produce. Clarence L. Cole, of Atlantic City, made the Wilson nominating speech. He was a recent convert to the Wilson programme, but the managers of the convention had to have some one from Atlantic City to make the Wilson speech; first, because no one from his own county would do it, and consequently: second, this fact had to be minimized by having Wilson's name presented at the very beginning of the roll-call. Cole's speech, therefore, was a surprise, and in politics surprise always brings anger to some one. At the end of Cole's speech, in the midst of the mechanical demonstration for Wilson, John J. Crandall, an old and picturesque lawyer in the Atlantic City delegation, arose to protest the nomination of Wilson. The Atlantic City delegation was divided. Cole was regarded as an apostate from George A. Silzer, later Governor of the State, the "favorite son." A man slumping in a chair near by woke up, hearing the row in the Atlantic City delegation, rose, and tried to pull down Crandall. The waking delegate failed. He tried again. Crandall, white with rage, broke his cane across the head of the Wilson man, and as the crowd howled its joy at the fight, the claquers went on with the demonstration. It was a great day for Mr. Wilson's "thoughtful Democrats"!

Mayor Frank Katzenbach's name, when presented, also rocked the building. The convention was in Mercer County. The galleries were for Katzenbach. The other candidates were named. Silzer with the others received the conventional claque. Then a third delegate from Atlantic City, J. Thompson Baker, unknown to those controlling the convention, rose and began to make "a man who" speech, setting forth glowingly the virtues of his candidate, but withholding his name. The tired, sweaty, nervous delegates rebelled. "Name him!" they cried, and, "Put 'im out!" and other disrespectful yowlings. The little, old, bald-headed man, hurt and scared, answered, "His name is Woodrow Wilson." The tension snapped. The convention roared, then howled, then organized a demonstration of its own, and the opposition knew by the spontaneity of the clamor that Wilson had the votes. They came in the first ballot; Smith's 800 prediction was only a little short. Wilson got 747 and a half, the opposition got 665 and a half. Wilson had forty more than a majority, a narrow squeak!

After the balloting, the platform came from the platform committee as it had been written, and was adopted. A delegate from Atlantic City tried to inject the liquor issue; but failed amid a great caterwauling of "thoughtful Democrats," but the contest furnished exactly the time needed to bring Mr. Wilson into the convention.

He had been playing golf — a sort of Scotch Cincinnatus — on the Princeton links, waiting for the call of the masses. The call came. He went home, discarded his golf trousers and cap, put on a soft hat, gray trousers, a dark sack coat, and kept on his gray knitted golf sweater. He motored quickly over the twelve well-paved miles between Princeton and Trenton, but in that trip he crossed a chasm abysmal. He waited for a time in the room of the hotel around the corner from the hall. Then when the convention was ready he came to it. At the door of the Taylor Opera House he met the committee appointed to escort him to the hall. Eagerly he asked: "Well, how was it? By what majority?" The Irish committeeman, realizing that a majority of forty in a vote of 1400 was not a bragging matter, shook a patronizing head and said: "Enough!" Then, taking the neophyte by the arm, led him to the altar.

As the crowd saw the committee come into the hall with their hero, the "thoughtful Democrats" began to whoop and clamor. They did not know their candidate, but they did know George Harvey and Big Jim Smith and Little Bob Davis. When they came crowding down the aisle with a stranger, the Democrats knew it was time to yell. The stranger mounted the stage steps and stood before them. It was the first political convention he had ever seen. He was not flustered. He stood there, self-contained, almost complacent, the soft gray hat in his hand, meticulous as to linen and tie, and creased trousers, and above it all the cool, engaging countenance of the Irish Kings, the affectionate and benignant smile of the Irish gentry, electric with the democracy of an unquestioned aristocrat. There smiled Joseph Ruggles Wilson, moderator of his church, orator, preacher, and punning professor; and James Wilson, bank director, railroad promoter, editor, and leading citizen. There amid that bawling mob the decent, repressed Woodrows of the cloister and counting-room, the Woodrows who for eight years had stood sternly by while he did his hard administrative work amid his unseemly quarrels, left him for the hour as he entered that hall. Out of his cordial visage glowed the heart of the western cross-channel Celts. He put out his hand gayly to quiet the crowd, and in his slowly articulated, carefully chosen words began to talk to the red-faced, disheveled roomful of bogtrotters, the great unwashed Democracy before him. He reached them. The supporters of the organization who had accepted him without conviction at the dictates of the bosses came first. Then he got the visionaries — the progressives, the anti-machine Irish, and bound them to his wheel. Indeed, he turned the steam roller into a triumphal chariot. Yet, reading the speech after fourteen years, one does not find it an important speech. He said the usual things that candidates say about being free of pledges, and he exalted his freedom. But many a partisan bound-boy before had hidden his chains. The thing that captured that convention was the soul of Woodrow Wilson — wholesome, aspiring, brave, with a radiance that shone upon his face and gave a glowing air of youth to his middle-aged fifties. The man whom the Princeton boys heard in their classes, and saw in a bright aura as he prayed in chapel, the man who went forth to the college alumni with his cause and convinced them of its righteousness, stood there in that torrid room that stank with fetid air, in that room where men had brawled and raged like beasts. When he spoke a few minutes, they surrendered, gathered about him, regenerated by his faith in life and hope for its dignity. They knew their master right gladly. And he knew that he had them. The oratorical instinct told him that; but alas, it could not tell him what he had. And all his life he never knew. As a master, he was royal; as a fellow, he failed.

And in that hour, when he stood upon the stage of the opera house in Trenton, it was as if he had walked upon a magic carpet. He came up the opera-house steps a middle-aged college president, he came down those steps into a new order. He looked about him — the college had vanished; the faculty had disappeared; the students were gone. He was in another world. It was all changed — gravitation, values, relations of men, habits, standards — everything was different. The neophyte was puzzled at first. He could talk; all that held over from the elder world was his gift of speech! As the hours became days and weeks, he talked and talked. He tried to hear what men said in reply. But often they used a dull idiom that confused him and finally bored him to impatience. So men said he was cold or petulant, or worse.

That we may know better this man who walked out of one world in his mid-fifties into another, let us for a moment consider the two worlds. Woodrow Wilson was reared, and until he was fifty-four lived, among scholars — exact men as the word goes. They knew things were true, because they had examined the facts. He had the scholar's respect for facts, and upon assembled facts founded whatever truth he held. That was the academic way of acquiring knowledge; even wisdom. The laboratory, the library, the research table, all sources of facts were the scholar's altar. Wilson knew no other. He came at things quickly sometimes; but only because he covered backgrounds quickly, not because he ignored them. The world out of which he stepped on September 15, 1910, was a solid, logical, material world, more or less fluid but ponderable; more or less changing but according to law.

Politics is another world. Here men base their actions upon intuition. Here men go for their reasons, not to facts, but to the judgments of other men. Here loyalties are changed from ponderable things to friendships, to prejudices, to hatreds, to traditions, to opinions. In politics life shifts back ages and herd instincts govern. A kind of voodoo craft senses things political, or pretends to, and truth is left in the fountain where Pontius Pilate, himself a politician of parts, washed his hands and left it.

This cool, nattily dressed professor, in a business suit over a gray knit sweater, left the golf links casually one afternoon, mounted some dirty wooden steps and faced a pair of double doors. He crossed the threshold, when bang! slammed the door on his whole life, his training of fifty years, his ambition, his friends, his daily habits — wiping out everything.

There he stood, apparently composed, facing a shrieking den of devotees of a strange cult. Is it a wonder that he was dazed sometimes as the years wore on in his new world, a bit timid at heart; seemed aloof, cold and repellent often, and at the end distracted at the antics of mad men in the mad world wherein he wandered?

Was it for this that he was made Thane of Cawdor? Was it over Bedlam that he was to be king hereafter?

CHAPTER XI

A THREAD OF DESTINY IS WOVEN

ONE bright afternoon in early autumn, 1910, after Woodrow Wilson had been nominated for Governor of New Jersey, former United States Senator James Smith, of New Jersey, bedecked as became a statesman and the boss of New Jersey, called at Prospect, the home of the President of Princeton University. With Senator Smith was a delegation from Mercer County which had been the home county of Woodrow Wilson for twenty years. The delegation was composed of the local party workers, followers and cohorts of Frank S. Katzenbach, whom Wilson had defeated in the convention at Trenton. Excepting when he stood on the platform in his two-piece suit and knit gray vest, to deliver his speech of acceptance, these party workers in Mercer County had never seen President Wilson of Princeton. They were ushered into his workroom, a large book-lined place, and then and there he and they went over that queer, vague essence of nothing in particular that politicians call "the situation." For an hour or two Woodrow Wilson and the Mercer County gang talked it over. In the meantime the Honorable James

Smith, ranking boss of New Jersey, strolled out upon the terrace overlooking the garden. The garden is walled with evergreens — save where a vista opens. In the garden the autumn flowers, dahlias, zinnias, cosmos, goldenglow, cannas, and the whole gorgeous flare of autumn blossoms stretched below him on the hillside. And through tall evergreens on either side, a vista of the New Jersey hills gently rolling, crowned here and there with clumps of woods, led away into a far horizon. A beautiful place it was, that terrace overlooking the garden of Prospect! Ellen Axson, an artist, made that garden, composed it, tended it, loved it. James Kerney, editor of the "Trenton Times," standing by the big boss, took in the placid scene with the garden in the foreground.

"Jim," said the big man pathetically, "what in hell a man wants to leave this for to get into politics is more than I can see."

It was that he might anchor in that kind of a harbor that the Honorable James Smith had been wrangling in politics for thirty years. It is for something of the sort — peace, glory, self-respect — the thing for which all politicians think they are in politics; just as gamblers think they gamble for the gains. But it is really the game and not the stakes that holds them. The other lads of Mercer County had no such delusions as bothered Senator Smith.

If they saw the vista, they paid no heed to it, and looked upon the garden with blinded eyes. They had fallen in love with Woodrow Wilson. Going down the front steps, through the tall trees and graveled walks that led from the front of Prospect, through the shade of the Princeton campus, these husky young governors of the sovereign people gave their verdict: "That's a go-through guy!" — their choicest blessing.

Thus he was initiated and became one of the elect. During the campaign, Mrs. Wilson and her husband, at home, often talked about the years that brought the conflict that was closing. She seemed to realize how completely life had changed for him when he stepped from the academic world into politics.

Stockton Axson declares that Ellen Axson Wilson asked her husband to promise her that as he went into politics he would try to avoid actual personal conflicts with men, conflicts of the kind that had come with Dean West and that were threatening with Doctor Hibben. They had seen, during the decade, friends grow cold, then bitter. They had seen associations of a lifetime wither and break. And it all disturbed Ellen Axson because she knew that it pained her husband. He was at heart sensitive, easily wounded, and his scars never calloused. Mr. Axson feels, and probably there is justification for his feeling, that this promise which Woodrow Wilson gave Ellen Axson there in Princeton in 1910 accounts for the fact that many times during the dozen years that stretched before him, Woodrow Wilson broke friendly relations, sometimes without explanation, where he felt that he could not hold them without a quarrel. Possibly he distrusted his temper.

There can be no doubt that he went into the gubernatorial campaign in 1910 with a light heart. He stood before his audiences with a certain grace of youth in his figure; spoke easily; more like a teacher than a politician. For teaching was his second nature. He was at his very best in that campaign. He sent for Dave Bryant down in Wilmington, North Carolina, and let him work among the colored people of the New Jersey cities. He was always felicitous in expression and usually really happy. He had a bad day when the trustees of Princeton snapped up his resignation as president without waiting until after the election. But bad days were few. Fate, in choosing Wilson's enemies, made him a liberal. In passing, let us note this significant thing about Wilson. He has been helped more often by the maledictions of his enemies than by the benedictions of his friends. So being at the moment, in the campaign, of a liberal mind and proud of it, even exuberant about it, he spoke his liberal mind splendidly. He was stealing the thunder of the New Jersey Republican liberals, men inspired by Roosevelt; translating the Roosevelt policies into New Jersey terms; the New Idea crowd, of which Everett Colby and George L. Record were the responsible leaders of the day. They listened to the blithe talk of the intruding professor and decided to test him. Publicly they demanded to know — and Record was the man who sent the questions — whether, when Wilson was talking of bosses, he meant exactly the Democratic bosses, namely, Jim Smith, Jim Nugent, and Bob Davis, et al.[1] The

[1] During the campaign in 1910 for Governor, Wilson's academic speeches led ex-Governor Griggs in a public speech to speak of him as being a mere recluse and bookworm. This nettled Wilson, and he in his next speech referred to Griggs's criticism, and issued a blanket challenge to any politician in the State to meet him on the stump and discuss any public question. Mr. Record was running for the Republican nomination for Congress that year and, believing that Wilson had been put up by Smith and George Harvey as a camouflage for Wall Street, Record jumped in with a public acceptance of Wilson's challenge and agreed to meet him at any time or place. After a rather embarrassing delay, Wilson stated that his engagements would prevent this, but he would debate any public question by letter. Whereupon Record wrote Wilson a letter asking a series of questions, such as the following:

1. Where do you stand upon the direct primary?
2. What is your position upon the subject of the establishment of a Public Utility Commission with the power to fix rates?
3. What is your position upon the subject of railroad taxation?
4. If as you say the Republican leaders are the representatives of the railroads and the utilities and other interests, which I admit, is it not a fact that the Democratic leaders, such as Jim Smith, also represent the same interests? And if so, what do you propose to do about it?

In this way Record put up to Wilson the programme for which the

Democratic bosses were cut from the same piece of cloth that furnished the Republican bosses. Both crowds believed in the wisdom of the great corporate interests which were using the State of New Jersey as a sort of fence, where, under the corporation tax laws, many corporations were avoiding shamelessly their moral obligations to society. It did not occur to Smith and Nugent that their candidate would pay serious attention to Mr. Record's questions, and one day a car full of amiable bosses dropped in at some local "opera house" to hear their candidate talk. For he was always a delightful talker; always worth hearing. They sat in a box above the stage. Their candidate appeared, walked easily down stage, smiled gayly at the box, began his speech, and produced the questions sent to the public prints by Mr. Record. Without oratorical flourish, without vehemence or anger, Mr. Wilson declared to the crowd that, when he spoke of Democratic bosses and de-

Progressive Republicans in the State had been fighting for years against the Republican leaders.

To the astonishment of everybody, including Record himself, Wilson pledged himself unequivocally to every measure which the Progressive Republicans had been advocating. It was a dramatic thing and unquestionably contributed to his great majority. It is a characteristic thing, however, that never again in the campaign did Wilson refer to these issues.

After election, when it became plain that he would have to fight Smith, he called several meetings in the principal cities of the State and went directly to the public with his side of the controversy. This was a brave, dramatic, and extremely effective thing to do.

nounced them, he did mean exactly Jim Smith, and his allies. The crowd lifted the roof with applause. The bosses in the box smiled, and, as they rode away in the car, chuckled and congratulated themselves upon the sporting blood of their candidate, never remotely suspecting that he meant what he said. So Wilson was elected.

Apparently Senator Smith did not think it worth while to surround his Governor-elect with a background that would color him. And the Progressive Irish, encouraged by the candidate's words during the campaign and taking these words at their face value, gathered about him as their hero.

James E. Martine had been declared the primary nominee of the Democratic Party for United States Senator. The legislature was morally bound to vote for the primary nominee. In those days American United States Senators were elected by legislatures, not by a direct vote of the people. Former Senator Smith began to prepare his own candidacy for the United States Senate, insolently ignoring the action of the primary which had named Martine. He felt that he controlled the Democratic legislature which had been elected with Woodrow Wilson. He knew no legal reason why he should pay the slightest attention to the primary majority for Mr. Martine. And probably at first, Governor-elect Wilson did not see the moral obliquity of the candidacy of Smith as he came to see it later. But the progressive Irish surrounding Wilson, James Kerney, of Trenton, Martin P. Devlin, W. W. St. John, Joseph Tumulty, and that faction of Progressive Democracy were fired with the zeal of the new cause. They were shocked at Smith's assumption that the will of the New Jersey Democrats in their primaries should be ignored. Sounding Wilson, they found that he was entirely unaware of a revolt abroad among the Democrats of New Jersey. He read no New Jersey papers. He saw few New Jersey politicians during the time between his election and his inauguration as Governor. And the Progressive Democrats found that he was getting his political information chiefly from the "New York Evening Post." So they delegated one of their number, W. W. St. John, to write rousing and indignant letters to the "Post" about the candidacy of Smith. The Governor-elect swallowed the bait, hook, sinker, and pole. Then they set about to see that he had a proper private secretary. It was a lively Irish intrigue running through a visit to Kentucky and back which landed Joseph P. Tumulty as the Governor's private secretary.[1]

[1] Nothing better illustrates the gay crusading spirit of these Irish Progressives than this story: The bishop is calling on Kerney, of the

Joseph P. Tumulty, a stocky, blond, blue-eyed Irishman with thin, soft curly hair, in his mid-thirties, was Woodrow Wilson's man Friday for ten years. His affection and loyalty were never questioned, and considering the tremendous responsibility he had, considering his training and early environment in Jersey City politics, his record of errors was exceedingly small. There can be no doubt that Wilson loved, understood, and greatly trusted him. Neither can any one gainsay the fact that Tumulty was of immense service to his chief. They were two handsome Irishmen — master and man — who hunted in pairs through ten years, and in those years — certainly in the first of those years — no other man had as much influence with Woodrow Wilson as Joe Tumulty. Other men were closer to Wilson at times; other men he trusted infinitely more because their judgment warranted it and their intellectual background inspired deep confidence. But day in and day out for ten years this stocky, earnest, honest, decent Irishman was a big figure in a big world, and before this narrative closes we shall hear more of him and understand him that we may realize better his chief.

Trenton Times, a faithful son of the Church, on behalf of a senatorial candidacy. Says Kerney: "Now see here, Bishop. I believe your candidate is a crook. And I'm not above supporting a crook, but he must be a Protestant crook. I don't propose to have my church loaded up with him!"

When Wilson was thoroughly convinced that the mandate of the New Jersey Democrats in their primary nomination of Martine for the United States Senate was politically irrevocable without dishonor, he straightway went to the home of James Smith and quietly told him that the Governor of New Jersey would support Martine for the Senate.

After visiting Smith, Wilson gave out a statement to the press that he believed Martine should be the Democratic nominee for Senator rather than Smith. Smith countered the next morning with a lovely statement to the press to the effect that the campaign had been too much for Wilson, and that he needed a rest. Just that, and nothing more!

It was rather a large order, this demand that Smith give up his ambition. A first-class fight ensued. At first the State Democratic bosses, Davis, Nugent, and Smith, and their followers merely sniffed at the obstreperous academician who was taking them to school in practical politics. But Wilson could talk; that was his major talent. And he took his talent over New Jersey again in behalf of Martine. His talent multiplied because of his prestige as Governor. Democratic governors have been rare in New Jersey. His defiance of the bosses in the campaign, followed by a definite defi of a particular boss in his crowning ambition after the election made Wilson a dramatic figure. When he talked, he was cast as a hero in spite of himself. He had no quarrel with Smith, no bickering. He called no names. The scenes at Princeton were not repeated in this campaign against Smith, and he won it easily, and winning it became a national figure.

He went to work putting his party platform through the legislature. Just before he was inaugurated, he and the Irish held what Woodrow Wilson regarded as a confidential meeting at the Martinique Hotel in New York City to discuss the platform and to get such planks as seemed important drafted into bills. George Record was there, a seasoned campaigner of many New Jersey battles, the veteran of insurgency and reform, a man of fine courage, splendid legal talent, and exceptional civic consciousness, with a rare sense of the currents of public opinion. James Kerney, of the "Trenton Times," was one of the moving spirits in that day. The planks of the Democratic platform which should make the Wilson programme were agreed upon at that meeting, and Record was asked to draft the planks into bills to be submitted to the legislature. Wilson in those days had no idea how a bill was drafted and leaned upon Record heavily. James Kerney, being a plutocratic publisher in Trenton and a sort of host and general manager of the Martinique meeting, paid for the lunch rather by process of elimination than by spontaneous generosity on Jim's part. Wilson beamed through it all, a happy student in the kindergarten of politics. Going down the elevator from the confidential meeting, Mr. Wilson suggested to a few of the henchmen that probably it would be better if nothing were said of the meeting. Whereupon James Kerney, having just been separated from the major part of a fifty-dollar bill, and wanting something substantial out of it, said:

"Why, Professor, Tom Dill, he has probably been sending half-hourly bulletins of the meeting all day to Jim Nugent. Man, he would as soon kill you as look at you if Jim said so."

Wilson batted no eye, but gulped, and Kerney got his thrill. It was thus that the Irish disciples of the Holy Faith liked to disturb the heretic follower of John Calvin. It was worth the fifty-dollar bill to know that the moral gladiator had his physical qualms!

When Record had his bills prepared, he came to the Governor's office with them. Wilson was busy; Wilson kept busy. And finally Record left the bills without seeing the Governor. The story of the meeting in the Martinique had got out. Wilson did not enjoy it. He shrank characteristically from sharing credit with others. He did not want the public tc know that Record had prepared the bills; hence this ducking of his head in the sand. We must remember that, after accepting Record's challenge upon the bosses and the issues, Wilson dropped them. He disliked to play another man's game. All his life he was feeding his "Lightfoots" parliamentary law because he knew it better than baseball. He did not break with Record, of course, and during the rest of his life held him in high esteem.

The job of putting his legislative programme through was not difficult. He was the unquestioned leader of his party. By defeating Smith, he had demolished the Smith machine. Jim Nugent, enraged at Smith's overthrow, came to the Governor's office to brand Wilson as an ingrate; also to call him "no gentleman."

"You're no judge," quoth the bland and punctilious Governor, showing Jim Nugent the door. It was a great day for the Irish!

In the legislature his whole programme was put before the Democratic caucus, where it was likely to be beaten. Wilson, who always considered that a governor or president was more of a premier than an executive, walked into the caucus uninvited, which is contrary to all precedent, and there took up the cudgels for his measures. His audacity, coupled with the prestige he had acquired by winning the Smith fight, turned enough Democrats to him to enable him to control the caucus.

In those days and nights of wrestling with the legislature, he used all of his charm. He sat up with the politicians at night, and inhaled their smoke by day. On the last night of the first session, George Record, who had been working with him through the session, says that the Governor came out into the outer offices in the early hours of the morning and joined those who were looking over the bills. Every one was telling stories, waiting for the legislature to act, and Wilson turned in and told a great string of stories, most delightfully, all, however, taken from books, not from the experiences of his own life. But according to Record, his very graciousness gave one a curious impression, not of insincerity, but of aloofness. By trying to get close to his fellows, he made it evident that he was far from them. Men knew, even then in 1911, when he was making his fight for the regeneration of New Jersey, that he was an odd fish, but powerful. All over the United States his name became a symbol of the Progressive cause in the Democratic Party.

The basic thing which General James B. Weaver, the Greenbacker, started in Iowa, which the Populists stimulated in the nineties, which Bryan proclaimed in '96, and which Roosevelt preached as the New Nationalism in 1912, had its Democratic apotheosis in Woodrow Wilson's New Jersey campaign. That basic thing when separated from the chaff of local issues — some of which were untenable — was a demand for a redistribution of the benefits of an industrial civilization among those whose work produced the civilization. Voicing this demand, Woodrow Wilson became the leader of the Democratic aspiration of the day. Still, his friends who disagreed with him, friends who held to the doctrine of Cleveland and Alton B. Parker, were loyal to him, chained to him by his charm and grace and eloquence. He went over the country after his New Jersey legislative programme had been achieved, expounding it. From one end of the land to the other his name — the Wilson spirit — began to stand for the new cult in the old Democracy.

At this period of Wilson's career we begin to pick up threads of a dramatic story; threads that led back three or four years into his life and that spun forward, with widening power and consequence, into the large web of his career. In October, 1911, Wilson went to Texas to address the State Fair at Dallas. A certain Colonel Edward M. House had become interested in Wilson, but had not met him. House wanted to give the New Jersey Governor a try-out. House had been a liberal leader in Texas and a supporter of Bryan, believing more in the implications of the Bryan creed than in its surface manifestations. The Wilson speech at Dallas pleased Colonel House. It was thus that Wilson first knew of the power of House in Texas politics. Wilson sent two friends, Mr. McCombs, who was one of his chief heralds, and William G. McAdoo, a trusted agent, to arrange a meeting with Colonel House and Wilson. Several days later at the Hotel Gotham in New York, where House was staying, Wilson called. The ostensible object of the call was, on Wilson's part, to ask Colonel House to be one of his campaign committee; a sort of a stucco pillar of a house of dreams which Wilson at that time was creating under the theory that it was a political organization. It was mostly names in a paper structure. Their meeting developed a case of love at first sight. They talked the hour of the appointment away, and forgot all about the subject of the meeting, except that the Colonel said incidentally that such campaign committees as Wilson was assembling only attracted the enemies of the supporters and did not bring their friends. And that matter was dismissed. But they talked about responsible government, about the needs of the times for leadership in the Democratic Party, and leadership in Washington when the Democratic Party should control there. Wilson's talent for talk, the fine, large, graceful embroidery and embellishment of ideas, stood him in stead that afternoon. The two men became cronies in an hour. The next day and the next week they exchanged notes many times and visits also. It was one of those sudden, deep friendships with which Wilson, who had always been a lonely man, often restored his soul. They were to him what a flirtation would have been to a lonely woman. Unquestionably Wilson's life was deeply affected by his attachment for Colonel House.

Let us observe Colonel House in that day; a man of slight figure, perhaps five feet six in height, of a thin, oval cast of countenance, adorned by a short, gray, stubby mustache over a firm and yet sensitive mouth which in turn is carved above a strong chin. The whole countenance bursts into illumination with beaming, kindly eyes below a rather higher brow than one expects from the remainder of the face; and the voice, when it comes from this gentle, interesting, and intelligent face, is soft and low and modest. A certain almost Oriental modesty, a Chinese self-effacement, abides with the personality of Colonel House. He seems to be in constant and delightful agreement with his auditor. And this delightful agreement, as one knows him, expresses itself in a thousand ways in an obvious and unmistakable desire to serve. He is never servile, but always serving;

gentle without being soft, exceedingly courteous with the most unbending dignity. He is forever punctuating one's sentences with "that's true, that's true"; and stimulating candor among men, which is the essence of friendship. But probably the quality in House which attracted Wilson was the imagination — the brilliant imagination of the Texan, a quality akin to genius. That he should have called out the finest qualities of Woodrow Wilson's heart was inevitable. Their friendship for eight years was one of the beautiful things of modern American politics. Their affection was genuine, whole-hearted, and forever expressing itself in devotion and care. Neither side gave more than the other. Wilson's letters to Colonel House in that period contain his noblest expressions. They are affectionate to a degree, and when they are printed some day will reveal the inner aspirations of a noble soul. In the meantime Colonel House became greatly interested in the Wilson presidential candidacy.

So much for thread number one. Now let us take up thread number two. Colonel George Harvey was probably more than any other one person responsible for the fact that Wilson was Governor of New Jersey. He was the editor of "Harper's Weekly" and head of the Harper & Brothers' publications, a firm which at the time was supposed to have certain obligations to the Morgan banking house. With an admirable and unselfish devotion, Harvey was proclaiming the candidacy of Wilson and at the same time making a frankly reactionary paper out of "Harper's Weekly." To one who realizes Colonel Harvey's keen perspicacity, it seems odd that he should have felt any interest in the Wilson presidential candidacy, holding the views which Colonel Harvey expressed in the editorial pages of "Harper's Weekly." By that time he must have realized that Wilson was thoroughly committed to the Progressive cause. He must also have sensed the determination on the part of Wilson to go his own way which had been characteristic of all of his public actions for nearly a decade. It was obvious that Wilson was not biddable to the counsel of his friends nor the cudgeling of his enemies. And yet Colonel Harvey stuck to him. Their personal relations were close and pleasant. Perhaps the Wilson charm of manner and grace of spirit held George Harvey loyal against his judgment. But Wilson, as a politician of something more than a year's practical novitiate, realized that "Harper's Weekly" was doing him no good in the West and South. Being at odd times a candid man, he said so. Colonel Harvey heard that Wilson had declared that "Harper's Weekly" was hurting him. Harvey had his proper pride, and meeting Wilson in New York at the Manhattan Club, along with Colonel Henry Watterson, of Louisville, Colonel Harvey asked Wilson, bluntly, if it was true that he felt that "Harper's Weekly" was harming him.

An account of what actually happened at that encounter, Colonel Harvey has written in a memorandum. After he and Colonel Watterson had brought the conversation to a proper place, Harvey asked:

"Is there anything left of that cheap talk during the gubernatorial campaign about my advocating you on behalf of the interests?"

Governor Wilson replied with great positiveness: "Yes, there is. I lunched to-day with two of the young men in my literary bureau, and they both declared it was having a serious effect in the West. I didn't ask them for the information, they volunteered it."

Colonel Harvey asked: "Have you thought of any way to counteract this harmful effect?"

Governor Wilson replied: "I have not. In fact, I am greatly perplexed to know how to do it. I have been able to satisfy those I can reach, but there are thousands, of course, whom we cannot reach — I have not yet been able to devise a way to meet the situation."

Harvey asked: "Is there anything I can do except, of course, to stop advocating your nomination?"

Governor Wilson answered: "I think not. At least I can't think of anything."

Colonel Harvey said: "Then I will simply sing low."

Wilson made no reply. An embarrassed pause followed, which Colonel Watterson broke with: "Yes, that is the only thing to do. The power of silence is very great — for myself, too, I shall not say a word for the present."

A long pause; it must have been icy. Governor Wilson said: "Good-bye, gentlemen."

The two insulted Colonels, Harvey and Watterson, nodded responses.

W. W. exit.

Wilson evidently felt that nothing important had been said, and went from the club to the home of Colonel House, where, after discussing other things, casually he mentioned what he had said to Colonel Harvey. Casually he told Stockton Axson and Mrs. Wilson the next day of the conversation, apparently attaching no importance to it. But Colonel Harvey was wounded to the heart. Perhaps no small part of the pain of the wound came from the fact that a few weeks afterward, either with Wilson's knowledge or at least without his effective attempt to stop it, the episode was used by the press agents of the Wilson presidential campaign, and Wilson was represented, in a highly virtuous attitude, spurning the help of a reactionary friend. There again it is difficult to assess blame, if there is blame, intelligently.

Later he wrote a letter to Colonel Harvey, which was published two years afterward in the "New York Evening Post" with Mr. Wilson's consent, in which he spoke of his one-track mind and observed that it could run only one train of thought at a time. He added:

A long time after that interview, when you asked me that question about the 'Weekly' and I answered it simply as a matter of fact and business, I remembered that I said never a word of my sincere gratitude to you for all your generous support or of my hope that it may be continued — forgive me and forget my manners.

Colonel Harvey waited two weeks, and answered that he had been pouring devotion upon Wilson out of a kind heart and a "belief that I was rendering a distinct public service." It is evident that Harvey was cut deeply, for he closed his letter thus:

The real point at the time of your interview was, as you aptly put it, 'one simply of fact and business.' And when you stated the fact to be that my support was hurting your candidacy, the only possible thing for me to do in simple fairness to you, no less than in consideration of my own self-respect, was to relieve you of your embarrassment by ceasing to advocate your nomination. . . . Whatever little hurt I may have felt, as a consequence of the unexpected peremptoriness of your attitude toward me, is, of course, wholly eliminated by your gracious words.

The poignant sarcasm of that last sentence, thrust in and twisted by the words "of course," is one of the classics in the history of broken friendships. A week later Wilson wrote to Colonel Harvey a letter also widely published with Wilson's consent, which indicates that the sarcasm did not reach him. Ending his letter he writes:

> All that I can say is that you have proved yourself very big, and that I wish I might have an early opportunity to tell you face to face how I really feel about it.

What the public got of the Wilson-Harvey episode was the slop-over from the quarrel. There can be no doubt that the political use of the episode marked a distinct advance in the Wilson candidacy for the presidency.

Now we come to thread number three, and the threads begin to weave together. Colonel House, upon meeting Wilson, was convinced that here was the leader of the evolutionary liberal movement in the Democratic Party. Without consulting Wilson, House went straight to William J. Bryan, who for sixteen years had been voicing the new creed in the Democratic Party and so had become the national leader of the liberal faction in that party. House had supported Bryan; Bryan trusted House. He spent several hours with Mr. and Mrs. Bryan, telling them about the career, the personality, and the aspirations of Woodrow Wilson. House made a deep impression. Naturally House did not tell Bryan that Wilson was House's choice as a new leader in their common cause, but he planted in Bryan's heart a trust in Wilson. Then the Harvey episode became public. It was an affront; a deep, grievous affront to the conservative forces in the Democratic Party. These forces had been led by Grover Cleveland, and in 1904 they gathered under Alton B. Parker's banner. This conservative group hoped again to control the party in 1912. Its members at first were not definitely opposed to Wilson. Men like Harvey had felt that they could take him as a just compromise. But when he broke with Harvey, and when his campaign publicity bureau made capital out of that break, his action enraged the conservatives. Bryan, seeing the break with Harvey, rejoiced. Wilson, supported by Harvey, and through Harvey by the Morgans, and through the Morgans by the thing which Bryan called Wall Street, was sticking hard in Bryan's craw. When Wilson broke with Harvey, that impediment was gone. Then into the woof of the cloth woven by the fates came Adrian H. Joline, whom Wilson had defeated for trustee of Princeton in the spring of 1910. Mr. Joline appeared with a letter from Wilson, written in 1907, denouncing Bryan. It was a letter that became famous in the campaign as the "cocked-hat letter," in which Wilson expressed the pious hope that something dignified and effective might be done "to knock Bryan once and for all into a cocked-hat." The letter was given out evidently to hurt Governor Wilson with the Bryan faction in the

Democratic Party. But the very fact that it was given out from that estate known as Wall Street, to hurt a liberal, strengthened Bryan's feeling that Wilson was genuine. House, being bedfast at the time, sent Josephus Daniels to see Bryan and explain the Joline episode. Bryan, being a liberal first and a human being somewhat later, rose magnanimously. January 8, 1912, before the guests assembled at a Jackson Day banquet in Washington, Bryan met Wilson for the first time, shook hands with him, and put an arm around Wilson and gave him the Bryan benediction! The support of Bryan put more vigor into the Wilson presidential candidacy than had all the outriders, cohorts, and heralds in half a year, blowing their paper horns through their paper organizations. Harvey, House, Bryan, Joline, each woven with the other, united to make an anchor rope that weathered many storms in coming days and years.

Wilson was then an avowed liberal — a Progressive Democrat. He was bidding for the strength of the Progressive faction in his party, even as Roosevelt was leading a similar faction in the Republican Party. The legislative measures which Wilson forced through the New Jersey legislature, almost by sheer power of his will and the prestige of his national leadership, were counted radical in their day. A few of them did not stand up under the test of time, but they were in the main just measures and such measures as were common in the more progressive States of the Union.

It was in those days that he became the conscious militant liberal. No man could hold in his heart for a dozen years the ambition to be President as Woodrow Wilson held it, and not respond definitely to that ambition when realization kept coming nearer and surer as it came to him in 1911 and the early part of 1912. He would be more than human if his ambition did not urge him, guide him, embolden him in all that he did.

It was in those hours that Ellen Axson's fear struggled with her pride. She knew how frail his body was. She understood how deeply he aspired to high service. She shared his ambitions and desired him to be a power for good in the world. No one could question but that these two walked humbly, even trembling, before the things that were ahead. His eagerness to grasp the prize sometimes was checked by a profound reserve — the reserve of one awed in the presence of his responsibility; yet at other times half unconsciously he reached for the prize greedily. His was a complicated and contradictory personality. For in his own soul he had a dual nature, and added to the puzzle was Ellen Axson, a strong, serious

GOVERNOR WILSON IN HIS STUDY AT PRINCETON, WITH MRS. WILSON

woman, his counselor, his friend, and his spiritual partner. If the Woodrows were coming out of five generations of the Calvinistic ministry and intruding into this life, dethroning the Celtic dreamer, also close in his life and heart was all that Ellen Axson had planted there, her inheritance from a long line of Calvinists and Puritans. No wonder the man baffled his intimates and often was cast as a hypocrite to his enemies. Motives are mixed in all of us. In every man's decisive moments come conflicting forces in his life. But in those days, when Woodrow Wilson went forward to meet the call of his blood and inheritance, he did walk as straight a course as it is given to stumbling mortals to follow. The things he sought were high things. Even then the faith that made him a world leader was the impulse that led him on.

CHAPTER XII

THE LIBERAL LEADER ARRIVES

PROBABLY no other American ever learned so much politics in twenty-two months as Woodrow Wilson learned from the Irish of New Jersey between September, 1910, and the spring of 1912. He had seemed not to be playing a practical game. As Governor, by way of functioning premier, he was inclined to turn most of his patronage over to Joe Tumulty and James Kerney, his private secretary and the editor of the newspaper which was advocating his cause, who were appalled, but flattered and delighted with the responsibility. He appeared to care little about the things that interested organized party men. Yet he did not know what interested them. He did know what motives controlled them. All that he had read as student, as teacher, as writer, came back to him and stood him in great stead. He was, of course, academic, but the vicarious experience one gets from the library was vitalized in him by two years of vigorous struggle in as active and as dirty politics as America at the time could afford; a struggle in which he was, of course, human and sometimes foolish, but upright, clean, and without reproach. If he had traveled the road that other politicians used in coming to the White House, he might have learned the game of politics differently, but he could not have learned it better. Roosevelt came to the White House after wrestling in the ward caucus; after fighting through his county and State conventions; after leading a struggle in his party's national convention; nearly thirty years before the climactical struggle in which he met the foes of liberalism. Roosevelt had championed civil service as a commissioner; had bickered with crooked policemen as their chief; had been in Washington; was familiar with the White House; had been Governor, and was acquainted with all the byways and avenues of politics that led to his goal. Wilson had never been in a county convention when he was nominated for Governor; had never been in his State capitol until he stepped across the threshold as Governor; had never been in the White House until he was its master. Yet in those days of the spring and early summer of 1912, when he was a candidate for the presidency, his genius directed the fight. He needed no Jim-Jim machine to nominate him, and he had no Colonel Harvey as a liaison officer between politics and business. Wilson had his managers, but they were for the most part stage supers.

By the spring of 1912, the presidential year, the

Wilson candidacy no longer required stage supers for its support. The Wilson spirit was abroad in the land — one of those moving currents that sweep through democracies moving men to loyalties that are translated into events. Always, in considering these years of the ascendancy of the Wilson spirit, the years between 1910 and 1912 during which Wilson became a figure in national politics as he had been a figure in national education, we must remember something of the emotional stir of the times: the Theodore Roosevelt theme, one motive, one tune; a preachment for a larger participation for the common man in the common benefits of our common life. As a corollary of that demand, of course, there would have to be some surrender of larger benefits to those who had been enjoying smaller. Hence anger came into the situation from those who were asked to give, and the political atmosphere was charged heavily with enthusiasm and hates, aspirations and denunciations, altruism and greed. For Roosevelt was a powerful man, a convincing exhorter, one of the world's voices in the wilderness. Bryan, before Roosevelt came, had voiced something of the doctrine which Roosevelt expounded, but Bryan's intellectual equipment stalled him as a national leader, and he became a leader of a faction inside the Democratic Party. The faction was overthrown by the conservatives in the Democratic Party in 1904. Bryan, still strong with his crowd, was not a leader of a united party. He was a factional leader and a strong and indomitable leader, for a cause which held him emotionally rather than intellectually. Inside the Democratic Party he kept watch over his flock.

Chiefly his followers came from the South and West, but in every State they were challenged by the strong conservative Cleveland and Parker forces. So the stage was set in 1912 when the spirit of Woodrow Wilson came into the Democratic Party as a considerable factor for the presidential nomination. It was not exactly Woodrow Wilson the man. For all his personal charms, for all his notable achievements in Princeton, which were localized by the college and by the narrow educational realm, for all his good work as Governor of New Jersey, chiefly as the leader of the legislature rather than an administrator, Wilson as a man had no great following. But that swift current of liberalism that was running across the civilized world here in America was revealed as the Progressive movement, and in the Democratic Party was localized as the spirit of Wilson, the spirit of a constructive evolutionary statesman who believed intelligently and with some passionate interest in the new doctrine which Bryan had preached and Roosevelt had explained and championed. The Wilson spirit was more than an echo of the struggle which Roosevelt was maintaining in the Republican Party. It had its own organism, its own definition, its own spiritual status. But surely the clatter, jammer, and row in the Republican Party in that spring of 1912, when Roosevelt was wresting one great Republican State after another from the conservative forces in the primaries, could not but affect and strengthen the work of the Wilson spirit which was moving in the Democratic Party.

The Wilson spirit, like any other strong current in our politics, manifested itself in most practical ways. Colonel House through adroit manipulation secured the Texas delegation for Wilson. Then the New Jersey delegation, the Minnesota delegation, the Delaware delegation, a large block from Pennsylvania, the Wisconsin delegation, one after another were secured in the campaign of practical politics for the Wilson candidacy. Parts of delegations in a score of States came to Wilson. It was evident that he was to be the hero in the dramatic clash between conservatism and liberalism at the Baltimore National Democratic Convention in late June. The conservative forces were divided, but not seriously. The candidacies of Congressman Oscar Underwood, of Alabama, and of Governor Judson Harmon, of Ohio, seemed to unite the strongest forces of conservatism. Tammany in New York City was, of course, conservative to a reactionary point. Probably it was the Tammany leadership that conceived the idea of stalking Speaker Champ Clark, of Missouri, against Wilson. Champ Clark was personified politics. He had come to the convention over the beaten dirt paths from the county court-house. He was a rural statesman who observed punctiliously all the rules of the political game. He talked in vernacular, dressed conventionally, thought in one syllable, and was not ashamed to advertise his love for corn whiskey and the plain people. He was the idol of the temple Pharisees of both parties, who marveled at his easy, instinctive regularity. He had been county officer, and a Congressman, and was Speaker of the House of Representatives in Washington; in politics a just man made perfect personally, loving and lovable, loyal and dependable. He brought to the convention the Missouri song, "You Gotta Quit Kicking My Dog Around" — the hound-dog tune, a perfect musical expression of the Clark candidacy! Clark had no great faith in the doctrines of either faction of the party. He was a partisan Democrat. He worked under the leadership of Grover Cleveland. He supported Alton B. Parker. Later he was to work under the leadership of Woodrow Wilson. A Democrat was a Democrat to him, and nothing more. But he had been friendly with Bryan; had supported Bryan. Bryan liked him, for Bryan generally was a grateful man. So the candidacy of Champ Clark appeared in the pre-convention struggle and loomed large there. Clark had the support of New York and Tammany. It was odd that Tammany did not know how that support would alienate Bryan. Very likely Tammany had no great use for Clark, preferring either Underwood or Harmon. It would have taken either if the fortune of the convention had led to a conservative victory that way. Wilson's candidacy had no entangling conservative support. It was the outward and visible sign of the inner and Wilson spirit in the heart of the Democratic Party.

Just before the Democratic National Convention assembled in late June at Baltimore, Bryan sent to all the candidates a letter protesting against the nomination of Judge Alton B. Parker, an avowed conservative, as temporary chairman of the convention — a nomination that had been made by the Democratic National Committee which had held over from the Parker campaign of 1904. Bryan's letter was one of those delightful Bryanesque things; quixotic, irrelevant more or less, and highly improbable if not absolutely impossible. But it had a righteous spirit behind it; Wilson was the only candidate of first magnitude who endorsed the Bryan position. That strengthened the anchor rope which had been woven at the Jackson Day banquet in January from strands which House made, strands which Harvey made, strands which Joline made, all unwittingly, in other days and other years.

The Baltimore Convention assembled. Bryan, in alpaca coat, white vest, clerical tie, with thinning hair above his dome-like head, still youthful, still carrying the air of the Boy Orator of the Platte who came out of the West in 1896, was leading rather grotesquely the forces of insurgent liberalism in the convention. At first, and perhaps because of his fumbling leadership, he seemed to have only a minority. Wilson kept his hands off, though there must have been anxious hours down at Seagirt, New Jersey, where the Wilsons were spending their summer, as they watched the awkward work of the great-hearted bungler at Baltimore who had the cause of the Progressives in his keeping. Of course, Wilson had his managers on the ground. Colonel House was not of them. Being a practical man, he knew how futile convention managers are, so he had sailed away for Europe just before the convention, realizing that Wilson had the only compact minority gathered around an idea in the convention. House believed that this minority would gather to itself enough strength to become a majority and dominate the convention. But House's talents were not those which could gather those delegates and make that majority. He had done his work. Placidly, and with a certain Chinese dignity and faith in fate, Colonel House sailed away across the sea.

The Wilsons at Seagirt heard hourly the story of the convention. Of course, they were admonished in impassioned tones to cut loose from Bryan. All sorts of good and bad advice was sent over the wire to Seagirt. The first roll-call resulted in the defeat of Bryan's resolution against Parker, the conservative leader. But in that roll-call it was obvious that Bryan had the Far West behind him, with the Middle West well in Bryan's favor. The South was Parker's. New England and the Atlantic Coast were much more unanimously for Parker. Clearly the country was cleaving in the Democratic Convention as it had split in the Republican Convention — the conservative South and the East against the liberal Middle West and the mountain States and the Pacific Coast. Clearly the Wilson spirit was the Western spirit. It appeared during the first day that Wilson, who had taken pot-luck with Bryan, would rise or fall with Bryan. In the machinery of the convention, certainly a material contrivance full of the steel cogs and copper cans of hate and envy and ambition, the Wilson spirit had to dominate and express itself. The bosses of the convention, Murphy, of New York, Taggart, of Indiana, and Sullivan, of Illinois, men who represented the governing powers of the great cities and through them the commercial rulers in the background, scorned the Wilson candidacy. In a Democratic convention, it is always necessary to get a candidate who can do two important things; first, get campaign money; second, carry New York, Ohio, and Connecticut. These States with the Solid South can pick up from local Republican defection enough votes for a Democratic victory. Because Champ Clark stood for party regularity, Clark was the hope of those powers which cared least for the Wilson spirit — the party high priests who stood by the collection boxes and the party Irish bosses who controlled the great cities. What a whirlpool of diverse antagonistic interests and issues and aims is a great party convention! There they rallied that first day at Baltimore, in a huge hall that seated ten thousand and more, eleven hundred delegates on the floor, ten thousand spectators in the gallery — hooting, howling, hissing, roaring, cheering, laughing, performing some mystic psychological Caucasian war dance that we call politics; probably as rude and barbaric and footless as the savage medicine jamborees of our remote ancestors in the black forests of

Germany two thousand years ago. Into that maelstrom, the Wilson spirit had to go; and from it, grinding through the complicated human machinery of a great parliamentary mass, that spirit had to come victorious or beaten.

The galleries were filled with the insurgent liberals. When Judge Parker began his speech accepting the temporary chairmanship, although the afternoon of the first day still was young, the galleries rose and walked out, a brutal, noisy crowd, and left a rather dazed old gentleman reading a long manuscript, nervously looking over his glasses occasionally at the vanishing crowd. Finally, in sorrow and despair he cut his speech in two, but the crowd waited at the evening session until it thought he had finished his speech before it came back. On the second day the liberals regained control of the convention by a vote of 555 to 484, a harrowingly narrow vote which came upon a proposition to modify the old Democratic unit rule to conform with new primary laws. Shortly before the roll-call, a portentous Wilson demonstration rose during a debate upon the rule. And that second day of the convention it was evident that Bryan's star was rising. It was also clear that the convention was frightened by its reactionary vote of the first day. The Wilson spirit had laid hold upon the machinery of the convention. Obviously Clark was the greatest loser in the rise of Bryan, and Wilson the gainer. Bryan, of course, had not put the curse upon Clark that day, but it was in his heart, and men knew it. Tammany's support of Clark had set Bryan against the Missouri leader.

Down at Seagirt, New Jersey, Woodrow Wilson watched the proceedings. In the main he did little that changed the course of things. Most of the advice he had was bad, and for once in his life his habit of working out his own salvation in his own way stood him in good stead. When Bryan offered an insolent resolution directed at Thomas F. Ryan and August Belmont, delegates in the convention, a resolution which questioned their patriotism because of their wealth, it would have been easy for Woodrow Wilson to cut loose from the Bryan leadership because it was foolish. The resolution was unanimously adopted after a considerable section of the galleries, and perhaps a majority of the delegates, had hissed and jeered at Bryan. But the unanimous adoption turned into a joke what he had regarded as a serious matter, and placed Bryan in a rather weak and ridiculous position. Wilson at Seagirt could have lost the presidency by following foolish advice to desert Bryan then. The quarreling and bickering in the convention, the roar of laughter that went up when Bryan's resolution against Belmont and Ryan was passed, the long days, tedious, meaningless, see-sawing with the credentials report, meant nothing, although breathless advisers to Wilson gasped over the telephone awful tales and direful threats of what would happen if he did or did not do this or that thing. He sat at Seagirt with Mrs. Wilson reading aloud, walking along the shore, riding in the cars of his friends, talking to the reporters camped on the lawn, a perfect picture of the poise which the country afterward came to know so well as Wilsonian detachment. Three times in the convention before his name was formally presented, explosions of genuine enthusiasm burst out during the routine work of the delegates. It was evident that the Wilson spirit, quite apart from Wilson the man, was moving somewhere deeply in the heart of the convention. When the first ballot came during the third day of the convention, it was evident that Clark, who had almost a majority of the convention from the start, and Underwood and Harmon, who together had something over three hundred votes, at least a third of the convention, could dominate the convention if Clark's men were as conservative as Harmon's and Underwood's, leaving Wilson's strength a little more than a third. Thus Wilson could have prevented a nomination that was not Progressive because, under the two-thirds rule under which all Democratic National

Conventions are held, he could have vetoed a conservative. Ballot after ballot went by, Wilson gaining little, Clark gaining considerably. Clark at last polled more than a majority of the votes of the convention, but not the necessary two-thirds majority. He was in the lead strongly. Bryan was in a fighting mood all the fourth day of the convention. And Friday it became evident that he would not support Champ Clark. Clark began to break after the fifteenth ballot. At the end of the twentieth ballot, Wilson was slowly gaining. Harmon had all but passed out; Underwood was failing. Obviously it was a contest between Clark and Wilson. Clark dropped below five hundred on the twenty-fourth ballot, and Wilson's vote rose above four hundred. There the deadlock stood over Sunday.

That Sunday the Governor and Mrs. Wilson went to church as usual. Coming home, they fell in with former Governor Fort and Mrs. Fort, of New Jersey, and said Governor Wilson, by way of making talk:

"Bryan tells me I should withdraw, and McCombs also advises that. What do you think?"

The families of the Governor and the ex-Governor had been friends of long standing. Their wives were walking on ahead. Fort considered for a moment. Wilson said:

"Mrs. Wilson thinks I should stay in. She says I've nothing to lose."

Fort agreed, and Wilson laughed and said:

"Well, I believe I shall."

So in a casual noonday stroll down the pleasant streets of Seagirt, far from the madding crowd at Baltimore, as an incident of small talk of old friends, Wilson made one of his momentous decisions. Upon what trivial hinges do great events swing their doors! Did Bryan try to scare Wilson out so that Bryan might win? Bryan often did things that his enemies were inclined to misconstrue. They would have said that Bryan, seeking to eliminate Wilson, was playing a sly hand for Bryan, which is probably not the truth. That Sunday at Seagirt, when the convention was adjourned and the hotels at Baltimore were rife with rumors and seething with intrigue, Woodrow Wilson read his modicum of poetry, had his spiritual frolic with his friends and family, and went about the orderly routine of his daily life. He was as gay as an ordained ruling elder of the Second Presbyterian Church at Princeton might be on the Holy Sabbath; told such stories to the reporters as comported with the dignity of a potential President; chatted with his callers, and, with such ardor as a man might exhibit of a Sunday, damned the telephone when it rang. If the Wilson spirit was to win in Baltimore, it had no aid or comfort from Wilson the man. The Wilson spirit was in a current that had passed far out of his control.

So the days dragged on, and the balloting continued through the twenties, through the thirties, into the forties. Gradually Clark sank after a Tammany demonstration for him in the early part of the convention. Gradually the Wilson spirit became more and more manifest. It was odd to see that spirit feeling its way into control of the convention as Clark disintegrated, Underwood remained stationary, Harmon grew negligible. Wilson did not pass five hundred until the thirty-ninth ballot. Among the Clark delegates, who in the forty-first ballot numbered 424, were men who sympathized with Wilson, but were held to Clark somewhat by the unit rule, somewhat by State loyalty.

It was late at night when the forty-second ballot was taken and an adjournment was forced by the friends of Wilson. Overnight Wilson developed a majority of the Convention, but not the necessary two thirds for nomination. Clark was down to 329, Wilson was up to 602 on the first ballot Tuesday morning, July 3d, and the Wilson spirit was in control of the convention. Hours were spent in wrangling over preliminary details. The fighting heart of the conservatives still was pumping hard. No more gallant band in a lost cause ever assembled in a convention. On the forty-fourth ballot, Wilson received 625 votes. No stampede was that, but a slow searching of the soul of the convention. The call of the times, the voice of Roosevelt, the liberal spirit of the age, the fine, upstanding personality of Wilson, the dream of a nation for life, liberty, and the pursuit of happiness, all those deep, unvoiced yearnings for social justice that were in the air of the era, grappled with men's consciences in the hall that hot summer day and slowly, surely drew them to a political expression of the vision of the hour.

Colonel Harvey is authority for this sidelight on the Convention. Before the last session of the Baltimore Convention, in the morning, Harvey went by appointment to Bryan's room. The two men stood in the bathroom each with a foot on the tub, and Bryan proposed to Colonel Harvey that he pass the word to the friends of Clark to propose the adjournment of the convention for thirty days, when the deadlock might be broken, which otherwise might be broken by the nomination of Wilson on the forty-fourth ballot. Bryan, according to the Harvey interpretation of the story, felt that with Clark exposed as the Tammany candidate and Wilson cut down at the height of his strength, Bryan would be the nominee of the convention. Louis Siebold, reporter for the "World," said that a short time after this bathroom discussion, Bryan met Siebold and told Siebold the convention would adjourn for thirty days. Bryan was expected, as a Wilson leader, to support the Clark adjournment motion. During the preliminaries of the day, Bryan kept his eye on Harvey in the press box. Harvey did not pass the tip.

Between the roll-calls the excitement was so powerful that it was expressed in silence. The forty-fifth ballot registered: Clark, 306; Wilson 633. Clark's friends could not cheer; Wilson's were afraid. The forty-sixth ballot began. Then the convention realized that it was about to see the rise of a new dynasty. Cleveland had passed with Parker. Bryan's star was setting. Senator Bankhead, of Alabama, rose before the roll-call started and withdrew the name of Underwood. Senator Stone, of Missouri, the floor leader for Champ Clark, released the delegates that had been pledged to Clark. The announcement was followed by terrific applause — hysterical. The convention knew that the death struggle was done. Fitzgerald, of New York, an old campaigner who had been the floor leader of Tammany, rose to move that the roll-call be omitted and that Wilson be nominated by acclamation. Another outburst of frenzied applause arose. Senator Reed, of Missouri, objected because Missouri wanted to vote for Clark on the last ballot. The call of the roll began. Senator Harmon's name was withdrawn. State after State fell into line for Wilson. At the end of the ballot, Clark had 84 votes: 24 from California, 5 from Florida, 2 from Louisiana, 36 from Missouri where Clark's men went down unconquered, 6 from Nevada, 4 from New Jersey — the Jim-Jims who had left Wilson early in the balloting — 1 from Ohio, and 6 from the District of Columbia. Wilson polled 990 votes — more than the necessary two thirds.

Far back into the heart of events — five years back — the finger of circumstance was writing this name upon the page — back to Joline, back to George Harvey, back to Colonel House, back to Bryan. With even one slip of the hand, some other name than Wilson's might have been written that day upon the scroll in Baltimore. The spirit of Wilson, the spirit of the times, had come into that convention. Then, after seven days of wrestling and seven nights of vain conspiracy and bickering, by some miracle beyond explanation under any psychological science we know now, without the aid of great strategies on the floor, without the aid of wise managers in the convention lobbies, the Wilson spirit had dragged this thing out of the hearts of a reluctant party. So Wilson passed upward to the next stage of his journey.

The campaign which followed Governor Wilson's nomination as the Democratic candidate for the presidency in 1912 was a bitter yet profitable campaign. The Republican Party was frankly conservative. Its nominee, President Taft, set his face hard against the New Nationalism of Colonel Roosevelt and the New Freedom of Governor Wilson. Theodore Roosevelt was running as the nominee of the Progressive Party, a party created by his own hand for his own purpose; and yet no party ever exhibited more enthusiasm, more intelligence, more industry in caring for the details which are necessary to go through an election with dignity than did this Progressive Party. The creed of the New Nationalism of Colonel Roosevelt had been set forth in a speech at Osawatomie, Kansas, in August, 1910. In effect the New Nationalism declared for the strongly centralized government to which the Hamiltonian Republicans had been committed for sixty years; but this strongly centralized government was to be used to guard the average citizen against the exploiting instinct of what Roosevelt pleased to call "aggrandized wealth." A number of measures were suggested which would check the oppression of the great aggregates of capital. In the main these suggested measures were the eight-hour day; abolition of child labor; a mothers' pension; a minimum wage for women; a trade commission which should stand guard over commerce and demand that it cease and desist from illegal, unfair, and monopolistic practices; a tariff commission which should revise the tariff after considering the cost of production in other countries; a remodeled currency that would insure against panics; the initiative, the referendum, and the recall, and the direct primary which would place government more directly in the hands of the voter; the direct election of United States Senators; and the income tax. The New Freedom as defined by Woodrow Wilson largely took this programme. But the New Freedom held that the programme should be consummated, not by a strongly centralized government, but through Jeffersonian methods in the several States and communities as might be worked out by the genius of the people.

Between the New Nationalism and the New Freedom was that fantastic imaginary gulf that always has existed between tweedle-dum and tweedle-dee. The astonishingly large vote for Roosevelt indicated a liberal sentiment inside the Republican Party which was unquestionably a majority of the party voters. That Wilson also received a large vote for President, and enough presidential electors to elect him, might or might not mean that the Democratic Party was committed to the idea of liberalism.

Party loyalty brings many votes to any presidential candidate. Probably Clark would have polled almost as many votes as Wilson; though, of course, the Progressive Democrats who might have voted for Clark would have been unhappy and possibly would have voted for Roosevelt. But no one knows whether their defection would have been sufficiently important to defeat Clark. If Divine purpose takes cognizance of American politics, it must have singled Wilson out as the Democratic leader, provided, of course, that the Lord was voting the liberal ticket that year. Certainly the rise of Wilson and his control of his party gave to the Democratic Party, which had been only eight years before in conservative hands, a liberal trend which, taken with the Bryan leadership from 1896 to 1904, put a distinctly liberal brand upon the Democrats and almost effaced Cleveland's influence.

In the three-cornered fight which ensued after the nomination of Theodore Roosevelt by the Progressives in August, 1912, naturally Colonel Roosevelt, the liberal rampant, attacked each of his adversaries. He slashed both wide and deep; his assaults upon the New Freedom, the Jeffersonian liberalism of Wilson, surely forced Wilson, even as George Record's New Jersey challenge did in 1910, to a firmer and perhaps a more advanced liberalism than he otherwise might have taken. President Taft maintained a dignified malevolence toward both the liberals, and harmed neither. Wilson seemed to devote himself with more gusto to the Roosevelt position than to Taft's. And a fine Dutch-Irish mêlée it was. Its one effect was to separate irrevocably the two outstanding American liberals. Neither was a good forgiver. Wilson's academic discussion of crying evils seemed weak and puling to Roosevelt. Roosevelt's swashbuckling, slam-bang, noisy, saber-rattling campaign struck Wilson as rather cheap and ineffective. Yet probably each had a wholesome respect for the talents in the other which he could not himself command. To Roosevelt, Wilson was a rather impotent, generally inept, academic wrist-slapper. Yet the instinctive chivalry of Roosevelt and his bubbling sense of humor put a grand quietus upon one phase of the campaign which might have annoyed, even if it did not injure, Wilson. Whispering slanderers were connecting Wilson's name with the fact that Mrs. Mary H. Peck had secured a divorce. Campaign lying appeals to the moron mind which loves to create myths. The two campaigns of 1912 and 1916 developed what may be called the "Peck myth." It had no more foundation, this Peck myth, than the story which suddenly rises among the peasants of a Latin people to the effect that a baby has been born with hair and teeth who began talking at birth, announcing that it was the Devil's child. Yet thousands of the benighted believe the story and sometimes take long journeys to see the child. The same type of mind created the myth that there were certain Peck letters, letters from Woodrow Wilson to Mrs. Mary Peck, of an incriminating nature; that the letters were offered for sale; that various friends of the President had bought the letters, paying sums varying from fifty to eighty thousand dollars; that Louis Brandeis, as an attorney, had negotiated the sale, and in return was put on the Supreme Bench; that Mrs. Peck held a job in the Treasury Department at Washington, and that Colonel House had taken her to Europe twice to get her out of the country. The basis in fact for this myth was the Woodrow Wilson correspondence with Mrs. Peck beginning in 1907 and ending in 1915. She received some two hundred letters. Scores of people have seen them; publishers and friends of Mrs. Peck. They are such letters as the "Dear Maria" letters which Colonel Roosevelt wrote to Mrs. Bellamy Storer. Indeed, Colonel Roosevelt wrote many letters to wives, widows, sisters, and daughters of friends in much the same tone and tempo that the Peck letters were written. They could have been printed in the "Sunday School Times." Some of the Peck letters are of historical interest. Others apparently are diary notes. All of them are innocuous. It would have been impossible to inject into that series of letters any epistle of an amatory nature, so static are they, so utterly on one key and in one mode and method.

But from this conclusion one must not assume that Woodrow Wilson found no charm in Mary Peck. She brought a rare and lovely grace into his life as she did wherever she came. A beautiful woman she was with a nimble mind; nimble but dainty, full of rare fantasies. When he wrote of a woman of another day and land, in his youth: "She had besides beauty a most lively and stimulating wit; such a mind as we most desire to see in a woman — a mind that stirs without irritating you, that rouses yet does not belabor, amuses yet subtly instructs," he was describing Mary Peck whom he would not meet for nearly thirty years. But a youth who held in his heart a presentiment of such a soul could not fail to enjoy her when he found her. His letters are set upon a monotone, without being exactly monotonous, static without being dull, but always through the letters one finds urges upon urges for her to write. Her letters to him must have been major intellectual calisthenics done to the rhythm of some cadence in her heart. She was exotic, European, although naturally of mid-Western birth and blood, but something quite outside the Calvin cycle. And how fearfully the Scotchman must have backed off scandalized and scared; but how eagerly the Irishman must have run to meet the blessed apparition. But the Peck letters furnished salacious gossip for two campaigns and did a cruel injustice to a good woman and a blameless man. Dean Andrew F. West, of Princeton, who was Wilson's most scornful enemy, testifies to his certainty that there is no dust of the primrose path upon Wilson's feet. Instinctively Roosevelt touched the Wilson defense in his characterization of Wilson as the apothecary's clerk in an affair of the heart. That story is worth reciting. The campaign slanders were brought to Roosevelt's attention by a political manager, and Roosevelt indignantly demanded that so far as his friends and partisans were concerned the whispering stop. Roosevelt proclaimed his fundamental belief in the integrity of his adversary, and then, bursting into premonitory wrinkles until his face looked like a ruddy baked apple, the Colonel squeaked:

"What's more, it wouldn't work. You can't cast a man as Romeo who looks and acts so much like the apothecary's clerk."

Wilson on his part to his friends defended Roosevelt's contention that the presidency carried with it congressional leadership.

"Whatever else we may think or say of Theodore Roosevelt," remarked Mr. Wilson, "we must admit that he is an aggressive leader. He led Congress — he was not driven by Congress. We may not approve his methods, but we must concede that he made Congress follow him."

The two stalwart liberals of that campaign of 1912 might well have been hunting together, beating a different side of the bush, each going in the same direction, each after the same big game: even though each glared at the other and made public "snoots" at each other which did not altogether improve the grace or pulchritude of either countenance. At the end of the campaign, Wilson's electoral college majority was overwhelming. His popular vote was not so significant, but the campaign definitely set America, for four years at least and probably for many more, upon the highroad away from plutocracy into which it had been drifting during the first three decades after the Civil War.

And now that Woodrow Wilson is President-elect, let us look back at the long path he has traveled in fifty-six years. He was the son and the grandson of well-to-do parents, whose work in the world cast their lots with the richest and most important members of the communities in which they lived.

THE PRESIDENT-ELECT WITH HIS FAMILY AT SEAGIRT, N.J.

For all American purposes he was a born aristocrat. He had the best education that America could give a man in the latter quarter of the last century. He went into the teaching profession, one of the gentle professions in this country, and rose rapidly in it. He learned to write, and could sell his writing in a profitable market. He learned to talk, and made a name and money talking. Teaching, writing, and talking gave him distinction, fame, and influence. He went to the top of the teaching profession when he was chosen president of one of half a dozen of the most important American universities. By championing democracy in education, he acquired enough prestige to take him into politics without the long years of political apprenticeship that most statesmen give. And in two moves on the political board he is in the king row — President-elect of the United States of America. What a career!

But this we must always bear in mind. Even as he mounted to his destiny, he traveled, not through bitterness and sorrow, but in a joyous course, straight and steadily rising. From his birth his star had beckoned him; no calamity had broken him. Is it a wonder that his faith in God was strong and his belief in man was hardy? Surely the Satanic cynics may well have gibed, "Doth Job fear God for naught?"

CHAPTER XIII

AN EVIL MESSENGER COMES

THE changes that came into America and indeed the world, between March, 1913, and March, 1917, were epochal. Here, in these four years, the old world of the nineteenth century dropped away and disclosed the new world stark and strange. But before we go into those changes and the events that gave them birth, we must consider in this story the changes that came into the life of Woodrow Wilson. His academic career had fallen from him in 1910. But shifting the scenes from the college world to politics was a change in externals. His home remained, and his way of life. As Governor of New Jersey no important executive task weighed upon him. He sublet administration largely to Joseph Tumulty, his private secretary, and his administrative deputies. He was a leader of the legislature and the people — an exalted schoolmaster!

But when the President-elect left Princeton for Washington, he went down into another level of the abyss that separated his old life from the new existence that was coming. This chapter will be devoted to those personal changes that cut Woodrow Wilson adrift at fifty-six from all the dear and intimate associations of his life. The world story must pause while we take up the events in the life of the man who played so large a part in the larger story. At the end of the four years he found himself across the chasm that opened before him there at the door of the Taylor Opera House in Trenton in September, 1910, in a new world, among new people doing new things. And he was in all externals a new man!

For twenty-two years he lived in Princeton, not counting his four years there as student. He commuted from Princeton to Trenton when he was Governor, yet one must bear in mind the fact that he never really touched the town. He seemed as transient there as he was in Wilmington, or in Columbia, or in Bryn Mawr, or in Middletown. No town tradition binds him with the Princeton town life. When he went away, Mrs. Wilson, who felt this, was hurt by it. So at the suggestion of Colonel David Flynn, of the First National Bank, the townsmen gathered one day before the President-elect left for Washington to give him a loving-cup. In his response he made it plain to them how aloof he had been, declaring that when all the world knew him he went into a store in Princeton, a little town of less than five thousand, and asked to have something charged, and was met by the clerk's query, "What name, please?" The incident illustrating his attitude is a revealing comment upon his isolation in his relations with men. Something of the perennial hoarfrost of the Woodrows always got between Wilson, the son of the old doctor, and his public, whatever it happened to be. Always he was a little blurred, out of focus, never quite clear-cut within the picture. Yet he loved humanity infinitely, and longed to be loved in return. What made the frosty veil between him and life no one knows.

March 3, 1913, he stood a little above the medium height, a little below the medium weight, with a face worn down by the rigors of the campaign, and a frail body shaken but not shattered. Large, glowing eyes, which were not quite steady enough to make them as handsome as they might have been, illuminated his face and gave it an indefinably shifty look which at first repelled the deepest trust from candid natures. Colonel House sensed this. He told a friend after House's first meeting with Wilson that the time would come when Wilson would put him on the scrap-heap. No one ever stood upon the solid rock of confidence with Wilson, and scores of men got this first impression of the isolation of Wilson's soul. Only his smile and the grace of his Irish heart removed that unpleasant impression. His hair, once blond, then brown, was turning slightly gray in those days when he was President-elect; his step was firm; his movement swift but never jerky. His third of a century in the academic world as student, teacher, and administrator had given him poise and self-confidence, and a clarity of casual expression coming from a nice and alert use of words that made conversation with him easy and agreeable. But in the academic world he had gathered little human experience and little cultural experience outside of his texts and research books. For music he had a keen enjoyment. He sang beautifully with a clear tenor. He had no technical knowledge of the art; no wide information about the literature of the art. A Beethoven symphony, so far as he knew or recognized it, might as well have been a Tschaikowsky symphony. "The concord of sweet sounds" soothed him, diverted him, furnished him with a pleasant screen behind which his brain might work felicitously. He knew of the plastic arts only what Ellen Axson had taught him. She had much technical knowledge both as a painter and as a devotee of painting, and she knew the whole vocabulary of the painter's art. She taught him to know a good picture, and he came to respect her technique, her style, her bag of tricks, and to love it. His stomach had been weak from childhood, so he ate food without relish and without much knowledge of its composition. Food was merely sustenance for his body. He took no great joy in good cooking, and bad cooking meant to him only a dread of pain. He loved to walk, to talk, to speculate, to hypothecate upon large subjects and elaborate unique ideas — in short, to gas! This, of course, only in the inner circle of his dearest friends. He called it matching minds, and it was his favorite indoor and outdoor sport. His body was the soft body of the cloistered man.

After the campaign the Wilsons went to Bermuda where Mrs. Peck lent them her house. Following her divorce she took the name of her first husband and became Mrs. Mary Hulbert. At Bermuda Mr. and Mrs. Wilson walked and rode and talked and loafed and invited their souls, letting the scent of the clean air and the joy of the beauteous landscape heal the breaches that the hard months of the campaign had made. Returning, they visited Mrs. Hulbert in New York, where there was good talk for an hour or so and a merry matching of minds.

He brought with him to the White House a stomach pump which he used almost daily and a quart can of some sort of coal-tar product — headache tablets. These were giving him the symptoms of incipient Bright's disease until the White House doctors took hold of him and stopped the tablets. The tinkering with his intestines proved the frailty of the man. Tommy Wilson, the "mischievous bundle of nerves";

Tommy Wilson with the glasses teaching his "Lightfoots" parliamentary law because he could not excel in the rough games; Tommy Wilson, who two or three times during his college career was sent home by failing health, and Woodrow Wilson, who had to quit his academic work time and again because his body was too weak an engine for his mind, went to the White House as President Wilson considerably under the average man in physical energy.

But nevertheless it was a triumphal day for Woodrow Wilson, that 4th of March, 1913, and he enjoyed it. A human creature he was; and he gathered about him with his family a troop of his kinsmen from the South — Miss Ellen McMasters, of Columbia; his cousins, the Bones girls; Stockton Axson; and, because his mind went back to his old father and because he probably had heard of the story of Dave Bryant's promise to cast his vote for Tommy, the President did not forget to have Dave Bryant at the White House on Inauguration Day; in the kitchen, but prouder than Punch of his old friend in the front of the house.

Upon his inauguration he stood before the throng, in the plaza of the Capitol, composed, even placid. A generation as a schoolmaster had obliterated stage fright in him. He took the oath and delivered his inaugural with no self-conscious attitude, as a gentleman performing a conventional function. Mrs. Wilson was tremendously proud of him; that was obvious. And the Wilson girls, standing near by, were big-eyed with joy and wonder. There was the fairy story. In Princeton, where they had grown from girlhood through their teens into young womanhood, they had lived in the college circle. Plain living and high thinking had surrounded their childhood and youth. A family horse with a family surrey coming down country lanes had been their equipage during most of their lives. It was a family habit to pick up wayfarers along the road; the carpenter going to his work, the washerwoman with her bundle, the messenger on his errand, the neighbor on his way. The college boy was no high treat to these girls, but he was their fairy prince; not much of a prince. Then suddenly we have three Cinderellas in Washington in the White House, riding about in three White House cars, golden coaches, and with fairy princes — young army officers, young navy officers, young diplomats, young statesmen, all varieties of desirable young gods — lined up to do their beck and call. And they knew that they could wear their crystal slipper for at least four years. No dancing was allowed in the White House — the ruling elder of the Second Presbyterian Church in Princeton saw to that; but outside they could go to the prince's ball any night they chose. It was a fairy story come true. And no small part of the sustaining delight of the presidential office to the Wilson elders was found watching this story of the three Cinderellas dancing through their happy days. Lovely girls they were, Margaret, Jessie, and Eleanor, who, during all of the eight years of the Wilsons' occupancy of the White House, bore their part with their father's good taste, good sense, and good humor; American young women of the best tradition, the highest type.

Three words out of his inaugural address remain embedded in our thinking, "Forward-looking men." The rest was not important; a liberal message, but not a keynote. He failed to make the welkin ring; he never rang it: perhaps never could ring it; never could produce startling dramatic effects. He undramatized many things, nearly everything he touched. Just as Roosevelt, in apposition, could dramatize himself as a hero buying a newspaper or eating a casual peanut by the way, so Wilson, falling from a balloon, would manage somehow to distract common interest from his fall, and then light undramatically. He felt intensely enough always; but muffled his impressions in their expression. It was Ellen Axson, however, upon whom the impact of duties and obligations at the White House fell heavily. Her serious soul was racked by a thousand cares, a thousand dreads, a thousand duties, that came processioning through her life. The White House is no place for a New England conscience. The months wore upon her. She went out into the city of Washington (the first city, by the way, in which the Wilsons ever had lived, for they were country-town people), and there she saw the poor and neglected, the under-privileged. With all the might of her sensitive heart she set out to relieve them. She stretched eager hands to every duty that beckoned to her. As the months came, the social obligations of the place, necessary enough, crushed her, sapping her strength. She was a sweet and beautiful White House hostess; the academic woman, wise and gentle and unsophisticated amid a hard and formal whirl that had ruthlessly destroyed scores of women before her and took no heed of its toll. While her husband was fighting his battles, and they were many and hard and soul-trying, Ellen Axson tried to stand by, tried to help, tried to strengthen; did her lovely best.

But the time came when he saw that, if he bore all his burdens unto her, the load would break her. So White House people say that often at night he sat at his typewriter alone, hammering out letters to friends. Colonel House had many of these outpourings of his heart, trying to orient himself by expressing himself; to know what he thought by saying it. Mrs. Mary

Hulbert has many of these letters, and his daughters, who were away on visits, had them, and James Kerney, of Trenton, has a sheaf of them. Wherever he could find a sympathetic and understanding heart, he was liable to pour himself out. Issues, bills, policies, took the best of his attention. Patronage irked him. He all but farmed the appointment of his Cabinet to Colonel House, Joseph Tumulty, James Kerney, and a few other friends. Always patronage was to Woodrow Wilson a left-handed job at most; when he did it badly, he did not seem to care, and often he did it badly. The appeal to the heart sometimes caught him. Senator James Reed, of Missouri, once all but shed tears to get a man appointed in St. Louis whose selection shocked the more sensitive of the President's friends. And, for that and other reasons, the President broiled Reed on the slow, inextinguishable fires of his malediction for ten years! The appointment of Bryan in his Cabinet came, they say, against the instinctive judgment of Mrs. Wilson. Her intellect rejected the Bryan type. She feared his blunders of intelligence while she trusted his essential goodness. But the President felt that Bryan, with all his faults, in the Cabinet, where the President could minimize those faults, would be of less danger to the administration than Bryan, with all his strength, outside the Cabinet, where Wilson could not command him.

Always he shrank from strangers. Yet he cried out in his loneliness to Robert Bender, a reporter for the United Press: "It is no compliment to me to have it said that I am a 'great intellectual machine.' Good Heavens, is there no more in me than that? I want people to love me — but I suppose they never will." He liked men in the mass, but was finical about his associates among men in particular. Above everything he disliked to talk shop out of shop. In the White House he had no politicians about him. He feared two things about politicians: first, that they would bore him: second, that they would quote him and so betray him. He refused an invitation to join the Chevy Chase Golf Club, the haunt of the rich and the powerful; and men said he was a consistent democrat when he played upon a public course. Members of his family say he was merely trying to avoid people who would bother him with shop talk. He went regularly to the Keith Vaudeville house for something the same reason that he went to the public golf course. He did not want to meet smart or important people. When he closed his office door, he shut in his official life. Yet he wrote letters full of shop. His letters to Mrs. Hulbert discussed Bryan candidly, even festively, but intelligently. His letters to Colonel House are full of wise saws about government affairs. His letters to Stockton Axson are full of shop. But with strangers he had no confidence; it was his way.

The threat of the Mexican war bore terribly down upon Ellen Axson, his wife. Her soul had no Irish resilience, and the image of her husband bringing on war which should send thousands of her countrymen to death beat upon her like a great spiritual flail and winnowed all the joy out of her heart.

Under the strain of it all, Ellen Axson died, just before the world realized the horror of the Great War.

Then and there came the dread messenger unto this Man of Uz, with his evil tidings. For nearly thirty years he and Ellen Axson had lived together, grown together in mind and spirit. She probably was the stronger soul; his, the quicker mind. Inevitably their aspirations were held in common; the visions of their heart were one. Both, in observing a thousand mutual inhibitions which two people put upon one another for their soul's good and their heart's sake, held themselves in a common way of life — a pleasant path of conduct. Each had made the other. She had done her part to steady his gay spirit and temper the iron of the Woodrow soul to useful steel. Every true marriage of the spirit affects men and women thus at the end of many years. They are profoundly and indissolubly united.

Yet, when the breach comes, a thousand releases

occur. It is as though the brakes were off at a score of places in his life. No longer do the old inhibitions rise at certain points of his contact with life. A freedom akin to madness, poignant, of course, but unsettling to his life, comes to every human being when death breaks from him a companion of long and intimate association. Ellen Axson had done what she could; all that she made stood after she left. And that was her monument, her contribution to her race as much as his. They grew into the public Woodrow Wilson together, and her life lived through him. Those who knew her best agree that she was a radiant woman. Wilson himself said of her:

> She was the most radiant creature I have ever known. Something like an aura of light always surrounded her.

> Light and love [says one who understood her well] were at the very core of her. From them sprang her strength, her sweetness, her clarity of vision, her self-effacement. We must always remember, too, that she was an artist of ability and had the strong emotional nature which goes with the artistic temperament. But she held her emotional nature firmly in control; expressing it in her painting, in her gardening, and in the decoration of her house The garden at Princeton, with its beauty that got under the mellow, Irish heart of Senator Smith, was of her planning and designing, a most enchanting garden.

Three of her pictures were entered anonymously in the New York Academy of Art, the most exclusive of all yearly art exhibits in America, and admitted to a place there. Mrs. Wilson was too modest to send her pictures, but the President and the three Wilson girls forced her to send them. She was amazed and exultant when they were accepted; and the whole family was happy for weeks. It was that kind of a family. That picture of an exulting family, proud of its mother, bright, full of gibes and quips and gayety, we must hold in our minds as we see the Wilson of those first White House years going forward under the deepening shadow of his responsibility to the dark days that came afterward.

Surely if Ellen Axson had been spared, she would have strengthened him in the great hours that were coming; would have persisted even stronger in life than she lived in habit and memory. And the world might have been a better world if she could have stayed in it. Her passing inevitably had to cripple Woodrow Wilson sadly.[1]

"I want you to be the first to know from me," he declared to Mrs. Hulbert a few hours after Ellen Axson's death, "of Ellen's passing."

He wrote a beautiful letter to this old friend out of a heart deeply wounded. She was a family friend who had visited in the White House during Mrs. Wilson's lifetime.

[1] Ellen Axson died August 6, 1914. Mr. Wilson married Edith Bolling Galt December 18, 1915.

Of course he did not try to replace her in his second marriage. No man ever can restore a life's companionship which goes. Wilson was a tremendously uxorious man. He needed a woman around. The love of his kind which he lavished upon men, he could not withhold from some woman when his life was broken.

In Mrs. Edith Bolling Galt, Woodrow Wilson found devotion, high spirits, an infinite capacity for sprightliness, play, joy, and lightness of contact. She gave him these, together with an untiring, beautiful, self-merging common-sense that sustained him for nine years. The wife of a man like Woodrow Wilson is necessarily as much a part of him as any attribute of his mind or heart. Marriage with a domestic man is more than a sacrament, more than a partnership, closer than a fellowship; it is a deep, infrangible union. So that when Edith Bolling Galt came into his life, she also became a part of him; became one with him; became an essence of the Wilson story. Again Woodrow Wilson said to his old friend, Mary Hulbert, "I want you to be the first to know," but this time it was "of my great happiness!" After Ellen Axson's death, several letters passed, urging Mary Hulbert to write. Then they stopped. She never knew why.

In the spring of 1915, after Congress had had a

Copyright by Arnold Genthe, New York

EDITH BOLLING WILSON

year of Wilson, Congressman Victor Murdock, Republican, talking casually one day with Claude Kitchin, Democratic Congressman from North Carolina; Fitzgerald, Tammany Democratic Congressman from New York, and Oscar Underwood, Democratic Congressman from Alabama, asked:

"What do you fellows make of Wilson? How do you get on with him?"

Kitchin replied: "Not a bit. We never get near him."

Underwood cut in: "No more than you do."

Fitzgerald added: "He holds us at arm's length."

Kitchin continued: "He seems to think we are a lot of dirty politicians; contaminating and dangerous."

"Wilson," said a Congressman one day coming out of the White House with a pet scheme squashed, "is a pincher —" And to the question in the reporter's eyes, who met him in the White House lobby, the angered Congressman said: "A pincher's a horse that butts against his keeper who tries to make him stand over." And he stalked out of the room down the steps into the White House grounds, where he took the air.

Now these were congressional leaders of the first order in his party; absolutely necessary men to whom he would have to go in time of need.

This attitude of the politicians to the President never was entirely changed during his eight years. His academic habit of thought, his desire for factual reasons, rather than intuitive, for an opinion, his impatience with convictions that were based upon another man's thought, his loathing of guesses, hunches, and willow-withe-witching of the waters of truth which in politics men follow, put them "at arm's length," as Fitzgerald said. Sometimes his dealings with his Cabinet were almost as aloof as his relations with Congressmen and the smaller fry in politics. At the Cabinet meeting in which Wilson read the message in 1917, wherein he asked Congress to put other commodities as well as coal under the Lever Act, which controlled coal, after he had finished, the Cabinet sat in awed silence without comment. Victor Murdock, who had been invited in with other members of the Federal Trade Commission to the meeting, blurted out an objection to the way labor had been treated. Clearly the Cabinet was disturbed by the Murdock impertinence. But Tumulty, who stood in no great awe of his chief, agreed with Murdock, and the change was made. Wilson recognized Murdock as the expert. The Wilsonian austerity was only for those who had shown emotion in their disagreement with him, or those who wore out his patience; men who told him the same thing over and over at one interview or came back to repeat it at another interview.

"Oh, yes, I remember you," he said to Congressman Lewis, of Maryland, who was calling. "You are the man who paid me the high compliment of assuming that I could absorb an idea in five minutes."

Lewis had organized his presentation, spoken his piece, and turned around and left the White House without palaver. The President made him a Tariff Commissioner as a token of appreciation. But speaking broadly, one may say that in those days of the President's first term, when he was getting used to Congressmen and their ways, his life was hard and full of trouble. He gave the impression by his brusqueness that he was conceited, arrogant, impatient; that he knew it all, and desired no information, or advice. Yet in truth he was not insulating himself against information or advice. He was taxing every ounce of his strength to get information, to receive advice. But most of the people who came to him, came to tell him what he already knew, and to advise him to do what he had already done or would do if he could. So he had a curt, self-protective phrase, "I know that," which he stabbed into many a conversation and ended it. The wound hurt. But sometimes he was too busy to be courteous. We must not forget that he was frail, and had to defend his strength savagely. This protective armor of inconsideration, that passed as arrogance, was only for those whom he cared to call strangers. At home, or among his friends, he unbuckled his breastplate, and threw it aside. Miss Ida Tarbell, who saw him in February, 1916, at the Daniels Cabinet dinner, writes:

While we were at the dinner table I noticed that he was gay. I learned later that he told stories and quoted limericks all through the dinner. It was later, when I had my turn of talking with him, that I knew he was anxious. I suppose I must have said something about its being an anxious time. I remember he said: "No one can tell how anxious it is. I never go to bed without realizing that I may be called up by news that will mean that we are at war. Before to-morrow morning we may be at war. It is harder because the reports that come to us must be kept secret. Hasty action, indiscretion, might plunge us into a dangerous situation when a little care would entirely change the face of things."

I remember he said: "You cannot always know that the reports of the morning are true reports."

He added that he felt his great duty was not to see red, as he expressed it. I know I carried away from that dinner a feeling of the tremendous difficulty, of the tremendous threat under which he constantly lived, and of a man that had steeled himself to see it through. It strengthened my confidence in him.

In the four years that passed after March 3, 1913, the house of Wilson had been completely changed.

The wife of his youth was gone, and the children of the home he had been building for nearly thirty years were married or out in the world upon their own resources. Mrs. Edith Bolling Wilson had come into his life. She made a bright home for him, and comfortable — the only home in which he could have found strength to endure the stress of the days that were bringing their crushing burden upon him. He had, in addition to his work as legislative leader, his national premiership, if one may so say, the work of administration that here he could not ignore. It required him to open new areas of his mind, to develop latent talents, to let a new man rise in him who had a giant's task. The exalted schoolmaster at Trenton was becoming an international figure — the teacher turned preacher, his rostrum set high above the world; his pupils and congregation, civilized humanity. Amid all this change, why should not the man sometimes seem unnatural, impatient, preoccupied, remote from the commonality of men? Maybe he was puzzled at himself. Perhaps in his heart's heart he saw little Tommy and the amiable professor of jurisprudence at Princeton standing apart asking each other who is this strange man in this strange house, in this strange life that has crowded in upon us?

CHAPTER XIV

A LIBERAL LEADER'S TRIAL BALANCE

PRESIDENT WILSON expected to make a record as a liberal President. His first four years in the White House left no doubt as to his liberal intention. Those years left considerable doubt about the efficacy of his liberalism. His inexperience in the business of national politics, his unfamiliarity with the names and characters of men, his vast indifference to patronage and the assumption that he often made of his own mental superiority over others — that is to say, his major delusion that he had a first-class mind — led him into many blunders, many inconsistent positions for a liberal to take. So the liberal record was not clear. It was not so clear as he would have made it had he spent four years in Congress or a term in the Senate, where he might have known national figures, national issues, and the national mind. But the things he did for which he should have credit as a liberal President are his achievements in legislation, carrying out the specific demands of the Roosevelt Progressive platform. Wilson became, after his own fashion and belief, more of a premier than a president — leading the Congress rather than enforcing its acts. He appeared before Congress and read his presidential messages, thus reviving a custom established by Washington which emphasized his legislative rather than his administrative leadership.

If the background of the life of Woodrow Wilson had been changed by the years that began with 1910 and ended with 1916, his country also had been going through a change. Fundamentally it was a changed attitude of the popular mind. The people had lost faith in the divine right of capital to rule the land, somewhat because the country had become convinced that capital is not divinely immune from the selfishness which inheres in human nature. So all sorts of checks and restrictions were being thrown about the rule of capital. America was establishing a new government, a sort of limited constitutional plutocracy. Senators were no longer elected by legislatures, which were easily controlled by politicians serving large aggregates of capital. Instead, the people elected their Senators directly. Nominations for all public offices were made, not by party conventions, but by direct primaries. In nearly half the States the initiative and referendum in one form or another had been established. The right of the people to assess national income taxes was guaranteed by the Federal Constitution. State-wide prohibition and woman suffrage were adopted in a majority of the States foreshadowing the amendments to the National Constitution which established these measures nationally. The railroads were passing under federal control, and federal postal savings banks were set up in the post-offices. Inheritance taxes were common and popular. Everywhere where large aggregates of capital were affected with public interest, they were legally restricted toward the public welfare. The good old days of the good old pirates who built the West and ruled it were passing. Agitators in every American State were educating the people to suspect and subjugate the men and change their methods, whom another generation had exalted. It was a new America — an America in peaceful revolution — that Woodrow Wilson faced when he became President. He joined the revolution. He hoped to make it epochal.

The most notable legislative achievement of his first term as President was the Federal Reserve Act. Wilson knew nothing of currency problems and finances. He barely knew the broad fundamental principles of finance. But he did take good advice, had an open mind for many months, and followed with splendid courage and genuine fellowship the men who did know. The result of his coöperation with the wise men in Congress and out who were studying the problem gave the Nation a measure devised primarily as an insurance against panics. The Federal Reserve Act has stood up under the stress of war and under the greater stress of deflation that followed the War.

Scarcely less important than the Reserve Act was a law establishing the Federal Trade Commission; a commission instituted to prevent unfair methods of competition in business. From the commission have gone to the Department of Justice orders, resulting in suits started and successfully finished, defining along certain lines the path that business may go. Equally important with these suits have been the orders of the commission which have been tested in the courts. Thus a path of business probity is being surveyed and constructed along which business in America may go in justice and honor, with celerity and directness to any good end.

The law providing for the United States Tariff Commission was intended to provide a flexible tariff under executive order. This was another Wilsonian achievement. His stand in favor of remitting the Panama Canal tolls for British as well as American ships was a brave stand. In it he reversed himself and reversed his party platform, squarely, consciously, and in the interests of international justice. Indeed, in most of these important legislative matters just noted, President Wilson reversed Professor Wilson rather brutally. Professor Wilson in 1908 could not have conceived that he would have pushed through Congress the Federal Trade Commission, for he had written that year an article for "The American Lawyer" denouncing regulation by commission, declaring that "it is not regulation by law, but control according to the discretion of government officials." There are other pages in this "American Lawyer" article denouncing the things that Wilson later was proud to do as President. But his mind was rigid, when his Democratic friends tried to change the presidential mind on the subject of a sugar tariff and a dozen other tariff schedules. More that that, he denounced the "insidious lobby" which was trying to make the tariff what Hancock called "a local issue." The tariff bill enacted in his first term was perfected according to the plans and specifications previously made in Wilson's mind. No one could induce him to abandon his plan for a government-owned merchant marine, yet upon the whole subject of the regulation of commerce by commission and the Clayton modification of the Sherman Law, his mind was, as he himself said, "to let." Louis Brandeis moved in. In the summer of 1916, under the threat of a nation-wide railway strike, President Wilson stood for the eight-hour day in the railroad industry which afterward all but legalized the eight-hour day in every other American industry. The eight-hour day came out of the Progressive platform. The law providing for the first rural credits was a piece of genuinely liberal legislation. It is a part and parcel of the Administration's attitude toward finances and money, a genuinely liberal attitude, one which would have shocked John Sherman in his day of financial leadership and would have made General Weaver and the Populists warm with joy.

Wilson's chief blunders as a liberal came from the vice of exalting his faults as virtues. He was proud of his single-track mind, and apparently did not try to consider many things at once. If he were busy upon a note to Carranza, he might let some monstrously reactionary appointment pass unnoticed. Being engaged upon a foreign policy, he allowed one of his boards to be so influenced by the liquor interests of the Capital City as to make it incumbent upon any President, knowing of the affairs for which he is responsible, to remove several of its members instantly. The board continued because there were no sidetracks at the District of Columbia crossings at which the Wilson express might stop. Being preoccupied with a problem of preparedness, he allowed the picketing suffragists taken from the White House gate to be treated with brutal indignities at the Washington City jail, after his friends had tried to get through his idea-proof consciousness that he himself, being at the head of the police of the District, was personally responsible for the outrages committed upon these women.

He appointed Louis D. Brandeis Associate Justice of the Supreme Court. Justice Brandeis was and is one of the foremost constructive liberal American statesmen. And then, as he was thinking of something else, he offset the appointment of Justice Brandeis with the appointment of Justice McReynolds. There could be no question but that Colonel House and Attorney-General Gregory tried to make over the federal bench under President Wilson into a liberal body. They succeeded only when they could get their chief's attention. But his mind, running by on a single track, often let Senators put into the federal judiciary, in its district and appellate branches, men of unconscionably reactionary tendencies. Yet, upon the whole, he left a liberal judiciary. Also, upon the whole, he surrounded himself with liberal advisers. Yet in the campaign of 1916 he had to answer for an astonishingly large number of men whose bitter conservatism was wormwood to his liberal supporters. He allowed a lobby from his steamboat inspection service and the United States

Bureau of Navigation to put obstacles in front of the passage of the Seamen's Act, probably the wisest piece of maritime legislation that any nation had passed up to that time. And while the President was unquestionably sympathetic to labor, while he stood stanchly for the eight-hour day and saw it through Congress and through the Supreme Court, probably he did not take time or energy to realize that his own Attorney-General, afterwards elevated to the Supreme Court, made eight interpretations of federal labor laws and that all of these interpretations were against the side of labor. He spoke beautifully about the white light of publicity, and allowed Congressmen Underwood and Fitzgerald to formulate legislation overnight and pass it before the setting sun; then went out and made inspiring speeches denouncing "a few gentlemen who sat in a private room and played special Providence." He opposed woman suffrage vigorously, demanding that the question be settled by the States and defending his position because woman suffrage was not included in the Democratic platform. Then he overturned the Democratic platform and his own campaign promises and speeches in the Panama Canal tolls matter. He balanced his Cabinet and the assistant secretaries between the two party factions, like boys choosing up hand-over-hand on a ball bat. He gave a strong impression to many discouraged liberals in the year 1916 that he was more of a forward-talking than a forward-looking man.

But amid all these inconsistencies, and they are many and obvious, there is never inconsistency of intention. His mind, which he outwardly trusted, had to change, had even to trek backwards on the single track, but his direction and purpose and righteous intention never wavered. When he changed his mind, it was not for his own glory. He changed it often in humility. That first-class mind, in which he had so much vain pride, had a sorry time in those days of his first administration as he made mistakes and rectified them. He changed always from the worse to the better. Underneath, in the depths of him, his unwavering faith held the prow of his ship to a true course. It was lack of experience, chiefly, that hampered him. Experience was forever teaching him new things, rather obvious things, which many politicians old in the game knew by instinct. In this connection, perhaps it may be well to recall that William McKinley had been in politics for over twenty years before he became President. He had nothing like the mental or academic equipment of Woodrow Wilson, yet his mistakes of patronage were small compared with those of Wilson. Experience guided McKinley; less than two years of political experience were back of Wilson's intelligence when he came into the White House. Roosevelt, who was a poor judge of men naturally and inclined to compromise on non-essentials, in his major appointments probably made fewer mistakes of judgment than Wilson. And then, it is only fair to remember that Wilson came into power as the head of the Democratic Party, which was not a liberal party. There were many conservative Democrats whose title to office was clear, as there were liberal Democrats, and he could not factionalize the patronage of his party. All these things must be weighed when one would exult over the blunders of the first-class mind; over the mistakes of a liberal-hearted President.

For certainly when his four years' work is considered as a whole, when it is viewed in perspective, it may be seen as the fastest-moving four years in our economic and social history. And no one, more than the President, deserves credit for our progress. Some sense of that credit must have been in the hearts of the people during that campaign. For no such long forward trek could be taken by a people unconsciously; nor could they fail to know in their hearts the intention of their leader. The motive power on the single-track mind moved straight and fast and forward.

The Mexican situation, which was left over from the Taft Administration, soon began to bother the new liberal President. The Mexican situation was a part of the world drift away from feudalism into democracy, such an expression of that drift as might come to Latin-American civilization. Diaz, the feudal President, was gone. Madero, his successor, who was introducing economic reforms into the country, had been assassinated. His reforms were scarcely revolutionary from a Northern European viewpoint, but in Mexico they seemed revolutionary. The beneficiary of his assassination, who possibly had inspired the assassination, was General Victoriano Huerta, who had seized the Mexican Government upon such legal pretenses as he could find. President Taft had not recognized Huerta. President Wilson continued to withhold American recognition. A state bordering upon anarchy prevailed in Mexico. Huerta refused to recognize the American flag. President Wilson landed troops at Vera Cruz to demand recognition. The troops were withdrawn without securing the recognition. Carranza succeeded Huerta. The Mexican Government was unable to establish order. Rival bandits and roaming brigands gathered rebel troops about them. One of the choicest of these, Pancho Villa, infested Northern Mexico, conducting a bushwhacking campaign against the Government to justify his looting and murder. He raided Columbus, New Mexico, with some loss of American lives. Troops were sent to the border by President Wilson to guard it and to capture Villa, if possible. General Pershing, in charge of the troops, penetrated into Mexico and returned empty-handed. These were the untoward incidents of the Mexican situation as the new Democratic President found it, and as it developed under his policy.

Now the President's Mexican policy may have been consciously developed in his mind; probably it was not. A Democratic President had not been in office for sixteen years, and Wilson felt that the dollar diplomacy of his Republican predecessors was not to be the diplomatic policy of America toward Mexico. He did not mention foreign affairs in his first inaugural address, although the Mexican situation was fairly acute in March, 1913. But early in March he issued a statement declaring that one of our chief objects would be the cultivation of friendship with the republics of Central and South America. He pleaded for coöperation, which was possible "only when supported at every turn by the orderly processes of just government based upon law, not upon arbitrary or irregular forces."

By August, 1913, he seems to have thought his way

far enough into the Mexican situation to propose as terms of a Mexican settlement: first, cessation of fighting in Mexico under an armistice; second, a free election, in which, third, General Huerta should not be a candidate; and, fourth, all parties should agree to abide by the election. This proposition was rejected by Mexico as interference. Yet it was plain that the President had no desire to wield the big stick, playing the big-brother-with-a-gun for Latin America. Gradually he worked out a policy of neighborly interest. "Clearly, everything that we do must be rooted in patience and with calm, disinterested deliberation. We can afford to exercise the self-restraint of a really great nation which realizes its own strength and scorns to misuse it," he said.

Gradually we see him creeping along the road, feeling his way out, perhaps, as much as thinking his way out. He said definitely "that the United States will never again seek one additional foot of territory by conquest." This was in October, 1913. In an address to the Southern Commercial Congress at Mobile, he used these significant words, key-words of his entire diplomatic policy for this continent: "Human rights, national integrity, and opportunity as against material interests — that is the issue." Upon that line for three years, the years of "watchful waiting," President Wilson formed his foreign policy, hesitating here a bit, backing and filling there as diplomatic need demanded, but always trying to move forward along that line. This policy must have been in his heart as he began considering our European policy and formulating its tenets. Indeed, the whole Mexican policy of the Government is a part of the general foreign policy of the Wilson Administration during its eight years, a policy which puts an unselfish interest in orderly government in the nations of mankind ahead of any material interest of the United States. It is a pacifist policy in that it postpones, indeed, entirely ignores, and produces only at the end of futile discussion, the use of force. It is in direct opposition to the policy of the big stick which would put our ability to use force always in the foreground of our consciousness and in that of our neighbors in discussing international affairs. Naturally this Wilsonian restatement of the American foreign policy was distasteful to those who were anxious to make American commerce an arterial network through which our ideas, our philosophy, our business methods, and our national prosperity itself should flow strongly; directly uniting us by material bonds to the rest of the world in a commercial union. This commercial union of the dollar diplomats would be based somewhat upon business, but largely upon our capacity to enforce our business ethics upon our neighbors if and when they accepted our capital for business development. It was easy for those opposing the President to find inconsistencies between his principles and his practices. It was not difficult to see that he was going slowly, groping his way. So those who disagreed fundamentally with his philosophy, seeing his actual performances zigzagging more or less, seeking points of least resistance in difficult situations, set him down for a fool.

This peremptory disposal of the Wilson foreign policy by its enemies was made easier by the President's obvious delight in his earlier rhetorical achievements. He seemed to like to match minds with his people, with our Latin-American neighbors, with the wide world in the first half of his first term. Also his evident respect for his intellectual processes begot a certain impatience with duller wits; and he scorned the dull as he did the greedy. This intellectual attitude contributed many impediments to his progress in his own country; and possibly obscured the clarity of his intentions abroad. But no one can review those years of "watchful waiting" in the light of the pacifist policy which finally became our policy before the Great War and during the Great War and after the Great War, without discerning a clear, unbending intent in the whole circuitous, and sometimes devious, course which he followed. For these détours, these side excursions, hesitations, and blind stumblings, of course there is this practical mitigation. The President was speaking through Mr. Bryan, for one thing; for another, he moved on the chessboard with his elbow always close to the fingers of a Foreign Relations Committee which was palely hostile; and finally he had to use the language of diplomacy — a language that was new — amid procedure with which he was profoundly unfamiliar. More than all that, often he chose to use men who sometimes failed him, and rarely comprehended entirely the philosophy of his purpose.

The occupation of Vera Cruz by our forces naturally awakened great enthusiasm in those Americans — by no means an insignificant minority — who believed that the United States should extend from the Hudson Bay to Panama. One of these continental Americans was former Congressman John D. Bellamy, of Wilmington, North Carolina, with whom Tommy Wilson roamed through Scott in the Wilmington days of his youth. John D. sat him down and wrote a "Dear old Tommy" letter to the President, telling him never to haul down the flag; an ardent letter from an old friend, thrilling with patriotic national pride at the thought of Funston's army in Vera Cruz. His boyhood friend wrote to John D. a "Dear Sir" letter, so cold, so curt, so sternly rebuking him for his enthusiasm, that Mr. Bellamy held it in his hand for a moment and then tore it up and dropped it in the basket, and no one else ever saw it. The piny woods where the two had stretched out to read and dream and dream and read, the water-front at Wilmington with the tall ships sailing out, and John D. forever hauling his boy friend back to Scott and the chivalry of the past, meant nothing to the man who saw his cause misinterpreted. And so another friendship fell under the wheels on the single-track mind. When any one failed to comprehend Wilson's purpose, he was liable to encounter the train on his single-track mind.

PART THREE

The Victory

CHAPTER XV

OUR FIRST NATIONAL LIBERAL VICTORY

PRESIDENT WILSON was renominated by his party without opposition in 1916 and won the election in November of that year. Three things contributed to his success: first, he was the one statesman in America that year with a constructive programme; second, he had shown, during his three years in the White House, strong qualities of leadership; third, although his programme was not unanimously accepted, indeed, was met with rebellion and contumely, yet it did offer, at home and abroad, the one scrap of moral leadership to which the country, that year, could turn. His party, in Congress and for the most part the people supporting the party, followed his leadership. In domestic affairs he had accomplished definite results; not what the more enthusiastic liberals expected, but something real. In his Mexican policy he had developed, slowly and with rather bad dramatics, a course distinctly Wilsonian, but still a course. In his European policy he was formulating a course based upon the principle which produced his Mexican policy. But in each of these foreign relations he was leading. No one else was gathering a following who suggested any action which could rival the Wilson programme.

The campaign of 1916, in which President Wilson defeated former Justice Hughes, was the first election in which the people of the United States directly endorsed the work of a liberal President. When Colonel Roosevelt was elected in 1904, he had been, for three years, carrying out the McKinley policies; carrying them out with a liberal hand, it is true, but still doing the work of another man. William H. Taft, elected in 1908, made it clear during his campaign that he was not a liberal of the Roosevelt type, however much President Roosevelt might acclaim him as his legatee. But when President Wilson came before the people in 1916, it was after four years of achievement as a liberal President. He was opposed by Charles Evans Hughes, who had left the Supreme Court to run for President on the Republican ticket. Hughes in his campaign undertook to criticize the Wilson record; the undertaking failed. The electoral votes of the West and the South defeated the Republican presidential candidate. The votes of the South have no significance; they would have been given to a Democratic conservative, however reactionary he might have been, or a liberal, however radical. But three States, more or less Southern, voted for President Wilson; States which sometimes have gone to the Republicans — Missouri, Kentucky, and Maryland. The votes of these Southern States may be considered as fairly significant, as the motives that governed these three States may be assumed to be something like the motives that took Kansas, Colorado, and Idaho from the Republican moorings. The votes of these half-dozen States were distinctly against Mr. Hughes. For in 1916 President Wilson still was a remote, rather cold and calculating figure in our politics, hardly a popular hero. Mr. Hughes had the support of Colonel Roosevelt, who in 1912 certainly had been a popular figure. The Western States, where Roosevelt for years was an idol, voted, not for his candidate, Mr. Hughes, but for Woodrow Wilson. But these States returned Republicans to Congress and elected Republican governors and Republican legislators to make their laws. The Republicans in these States carefully picked out the Republican candidates for a majority of the offices of political importance, then squarely turned their backs upon the Republican candidate for the presidency. He failed to interest them because he had nothing of interest to say.

Now, these States of the West which deserted Hughes and came to Wilson, came to him because he was a liberal. The Western people took their politics seriously. For years they had been exercising certain political ideas which their Eastern friends called delusions. Excepting New Mexico, every Western State that voted for President Wilson in 1916 had one of three things in its constitution which Eastern Republicans regarded at the time as lunacy — prohibition, woman suffrage, or the initiative and referendum. Many of these States had two, and several all three of these political institutions. For instance, Ohio had the initiative and referendum, and more than half the State was dry. Missouri had the initiative and referendum, and eighty per cent of the State was dry territory. Kansas had State-wide prohibition and woman suffrage. Nebraska had the initiative and referendum and prohibition. Colorado and Idaho had all three, as had Arizona, Montana, and Washington. California only missed prohibition by a small margin or it would have had the trio. Utah had voted for prohibition. Now, of course, these Western people did not expect presidential candidates in a national campaign to discuss what were then purely local and quite obviously State issues. These new measures came only after long and serious, more or less crafty, contests in practical politics; contests lasting over half a decade which gave the West a broad and rather unpartisan idea of politics. They had to vote across party lines many times to secure their ends.

When Mr. Hughes left the Supreme Court to accept the Republican nomination, the West sincerely believed that a new national leader was coming. The Western idea of a national leader was influenced by Western tradition and creed. The West expected courage and candor. Above all, the Westerners expected their leader to sound the call for a new vital issue. They were listening for a big man to speak important things. Therefore, they were shocked beyond measure when, in his speech of acceptance in July, Mr. Hughes began talking about patronage, about the civil service, and about partisan things. He was expected to produce an issue large enough to unite the Republican and Progressive parties which, as parties, were not united even if many of their leaders were united. Instead of feeding the fire which should amalgamate the parties, Mr. Hughes began playing the hose of his criticism upon the Progressive ardor which President Wilson had been able to kindle in a Democratic Congress. But in spite of his speech of acceptance, the party Progressives in all the States were eager to follow Mr. Hughes. Two million Progressive votes had been cast in 1914 for governors and senators. The Progressives had no predilection for the Democratic Party. The Progressive Party was recruited from the Republicans, particularly in the West, but they were incorrigible independents. Men who had gone out to make long, tedious, and often lonely fights to secure some social or political reform like prohibition or woman suffrage, or the initiative and referendum, found nothing in the Hughes speeches in which to set their teeth. He talked tariff like Mark Hanna; he talked of industrial affairs in the McKinley tongue. He gave the party Progressives of the West the impression that he was one of those good men in politics, a kind of business man's candidate who would devote himself to the work of cleaning up the public service, naming good men for offices, but always clinging to the *status quo* like a sick kitten to a hot brick. The Progressive Convention of 1916 represented the idealism of America. To get the loyalty of the Progressives, Mr. Hughes had to convince them. He took them for granted and failed. When Mr. Hughes, in his July speeches, spoke earnestly of "a great united liberal party," the flippant Progressives hooted, and demanded to know "united with what?"

Naturally they turned to Wilson. He, at least, had Progressive achievement; not what they had hoped for, but something upon which to build. So the Progressives, looking at his liberal record, gave the election to Mr. Wilson. It was not because he kept them out of war. The flaming posters that blossomed over the land in October had their effect. But without the liberalism of Wilson and the confusion of Hughes, the posters would have availed nothing. These Western States, given to what the Republicans of that day were pleased to call radicalism — hitherto mentioned — to the various laws which had interested Wilson in New Jersey, were more liberal than pacifist. Mr. Hughes could not have taken them with the promise to keep them out of war. When the call came for volunteers, a few months after the election, the States which gave Wilson his majority were the first States to fill their quota in the Army and in the Navy; weeks and sometimes months ahead of the fire-eating, war-hungry States which damned Wilson in the election as a pacifist. It was not supine, timid pacifism that elected Wilson, but liberalism. They voted for him, not because he was trying to keep them out of war, but because he was trying to keep them out of plutocracy. He spoke to them a language which they knew, the language which they had been using for ten or a dozen years. Former Justice Hughes spoke to them haltingly in an old vernacular that reminded them sadly of President Taft. Only a more radical liberal than Wilson could have defeated Wilson in 1916.

If our inspection of the election returns of the campaign of 1916 indicate, as they seem to, a feeling among the people that the President had won his election as a liberal President rather than as an interpreter and mediator in foreign affairs, we must not make the mistake of assuming that his foreign policy had no weight in the election. The collapse of the Progressive Party, and the obvious attempt of some of its leaders to take the party Progressives into the Republican Party, left millions of Rooseveltian Progressives dazed and angry. During the two latter years of President Wilson's first term, from August, 1914, until the election in 1916, these Progressives had no common mind upon a foreign policy. Loyal as they were to Colonel Roosevelt in domestic matters, the new issues arising out of the European war left many of them in sad disagreement with their former leader. It is likely that a majority of the voters who followed Roosevelt from the Republican Party in 1912 were not in accord with him in his criticisms that finally became denunciations of President Wilson in the campaign of 1916. By the very nature of the Progressive philosophy, it was a philosophy of reason rather than force. They believed, these millions of Rooseveltian Progressives, in spiritual progress manifesting itself in human institutions, and were opposed profoundly in doctrine to the materialistic creed of the regular Republicans. It was natural, therefore, that these party Progressives should find their place following the policy of President Wilson, for it became evident early in the Great War that his policy would be based upon reason, and not upon force nor the threat of force.

When the Great War burst into a peaceful world in August, 1914, the proclamation of neutrality which President Wilson issued and his statement to the belligerent governments offering to mediate in the interests of peace were, of course, traditional American gestures. His note early in August sent to all the belligerents, calling attention to obvious differences of opinion about the rights of neutrals on the sea, and his proposal, that for the duration of the war the laws of naval warfare laid down in the Declaration of London be accepted by the belligerents, firmly embedded America in a position of neutrality. While the Declaration of London of 1909 had not been ratified by the ten maritime powers represented at the conference, the general approval of its proposals warranted the President in assuming that it might be the object of a *modus vivendi* during the War. The gist of this proposal was not a reliance upon the force achieved by any victor of the War. The President's reversion to the Declaration of London emphasized our American belief that the rights of neutrals upon the sea should be determined by a power greater than the will of any belligerent, victorious or defeated. It was the pacifist doctrine, the doctrine of reason against the acceptance of force. However President Wilson may have wandered in following one expedient or another to avoid conflict, there can be no question that his foreign policy in connection with the European war, as with Mexico, was based upon an instinctive conviction of the might of right as against the right of might. That conviction awakened a responsive echo in the heart of the Progressives of 1912, who had been driven from their party by the right of might. The Wilson philosophy was their philosophy. And while it is, of course, manifest, from reading the election returns State by State in the election of 1916, that States, wherein the voters had been working out a liberal programme for ten years, followed Wilson, it is also well to remember that the philosophy of their liberal programme was the philosophy upon which Wilson based his foreign policy. "He kept us out of war," flaring upon the bill-boards of the land, excited no wrath in the hearts of the millions of party Progressives who felt that, until every possible means was exhausted to maintain an honorable peace, we should indeed keep out of war — out of any war.

Of course, there were minority groups — the Germans and the Irish particularly on one side and millions of descendants from our English ancestors on the other side, together with the small minority of Frenchmen in the United States — who differed from the President. Each group felt that President Wilson should get into the war on behalf of its fellow countrymen in Europe. The proclamation of neutrality came as an offense to these American sympathizers with the belligerents. His refusal to protest upon the invasion of Belgium made a sharp division of public opinion in the country. Two courses lay before him, and each course had its adherents in the clamor of the press and the obvious convictions of the people; though this clamor and these obvious convictions became much more conspicuous a year after the fact. At the time the President's course was not seriously criticized in responsible quarters. But at that crossroads in September, 1914, when he stood before a commission from Belgium asking for the protest, the President showed the way in which he walked until the end of his career; indeed, the way in which he was ordained from the beginning to walk.

He was, in his foreign policy, showing forth in works the Calvinism which impregnated his soul. Perhaps it may best serve to define the two courses that parted there in September, 1914, before that Belgian Commission, by impersonating the alternatives. One was the Roosevelt way, the other Wilson's.

Doubtless the Rooseveltian way would have been to issue the protest, to show force, to make it appear definitely that American public opinion was outraged and that the only satisfaction which that outrage could feel would be in the whack of the big stick. There are no "ifs" in history, but one has a right to guess that this swish of the big stick in the autumn air that year in the beginning of the War would have brought Germany to a realization of her isolation in the world, and its danger. It might have been wise to walk down that branch of the crossroads. But Wilson could not walk there. His faith in the ultimate triumph of reason as the will of God, rather than of force in displaying that will, was the lever which moved the greatest events in the world in those early days of the War. Within two weeks of the outbreak of the War, the United States Senate had ratified treaties with eighteen countries providing for commissions of inquiry to precede war. By the 15th of September, Great Britain, France, Spain, and China had signed such treaties and Secretary Bryan was urging Russia, Germany, and Austria to join with us in similar treaties. It was then that President Wilson first proposed to Germany that he start negotiations looking to peace under the auspices of our Government. The brusque answer of Germany closed that avenue. In October, it was evident that the United States' proposal for the general acceptance of the Declaration of London would be tentatively accepted by Germany and Austria-Hungary, but could not be adopted because Great Britain had too strongly qualified the conditions. After that, America fell back upon the accepted rules of international law and the treaties with the belligerent powers, reserving the right to protest, a right which was used until it broke.

It is well to remember that our first clash in the War was with Great Britain. We entered a general protest to Great Britain against the British naval policy toward neutral shipping. In President Wilson's message to Congress in December of that year, we find no hint of a conviction, even if he had one, that America was moving even slowly in the whirlpool that was drawing the world to war. He asked for the same shipping bill that he had endorsed earlier in his administration, again suggested a larger measure of self-government for the Philippines, and had no harsh words for Mexico. He was the serene pacifist viewing the premonitory tremblings of a martial earthquake. But as a matter of fact, in our hearts, despite our hysteria, which was external, Americans were with Wilson in those days. The campaign of 1912, the Roosevelt campaign itself, had converted us to a philosophy which made us follow Wilson in the foreign policy so far as it had been developed in 1916.

When 1915 opened, it was evident that the European war was no mere passing episode in Europe and that it threatened to become epoch-making in its significance. The partisans of war on both sides of the controversy in America became more and more vocal in their demand for our active participation, but also it was obvious that these partisans were minority groups. The word "propaganda" became the answer to the contentions of many would-be American belligerents. Difficulties with Germany, which arose early in 1915, made it apparent that Senator Stone, chairman of the Committee on Foreign Affairs, was as widely removed in sympathy from the President's attitude as was Colonel Roosevelt; though Stone seemed to be favoring the position of the Central Powers and Roosevelt clearly was sympathetic with the contention of the Allies. In taking that first position of a neutral demanding the freedom of the seas, we had forced ourselves several degrees farther into the whirlpool than we could have realized in the beginning of the War. Yet that position was inevitable to a man of President Wilson's temperament, training, and belief.

In February, 1915, the German Government

seems to have decided upon a departure from the rules of international law in retaliating against the British restriction upon neutral commerce. For the German admiralty proclaimed a war zone about the British Isles and warned neutrals of their danger therein; making it plain by mid-February that the German submarines intended to destroy every merchant vessel found in the war zone without making provision for the safety of crews or passengers. British vessels carried neutral flags. The submarines, in the nature of things, could not visit and search a neutral ship to make sure of its identity, but must sink without warning any vessel found there. Here was a new question. Force was meeting reason with contempt. The Wilson philosophy was thus put to its first practical test; its test as a practicable creed in time of war; its test in the hearts of the American people. Those were hard days for Woodrow Wilson.

Even in tranquil times there is an impact of responsibility, a weight of conflicting opinion upon the White House, which is sure to put askew the vision of the clearest-sighted man in the world. No one escapes it. American Presidents cannot see with the American people. They can only guess, cipher, and hope when they deal with public opinion as a guide for presidential conduct. Of course, no President can ignore public opinion; that also is one of the major curses of the White House. Public opinion comes through newspapers, through Congressmen, through petitions, through letters, through friends, seeping in from every external crevice. In those winter days of 1915, when the Germans had snapped their fingers at our American philosophy of sweetness and light, public opinion boiled and swirled and roared like a maelstrom. And we must not forget that from the bottom of his Irish heart always the motive which most surely moved Woodrow Wilson was the love of his kind. The austere Woodrows who made him punctual at the White House meals, who made him implacable before those who personally disagreed with him, as he felt unfairly, the austere Woodrows who directed his brain and controlled his mind, had no entrance to his heart. That was from the Irish Celts, always yearning for affection, always eager for agreement. In the great storm that beat upon the White House, a cyclone that twisted both ways, from the Allies and from the Germans, out of a land saturated with propaganda, President Wilson held his course. Never once in those days did he stray from the fold of Calvin, an idealist couchant. Roosevelt was a militarist rampant; while Senator Stone, chairman of the Senate Foreign Relations Committee, an opportunist with a German constituency, crawled rather craftily around the picture on the shield. The President declared in a note to the German Government that it would be held to a "strict accountability for the acts of its naval authorities." And on the same day he protested to Great Britain against the use of an American flag on a British vessel in the war zone.

Thus began the two years of correspondence between President Wilson and the German Government which culminated in America's entrance into the World War. During the first year and a half of that correspondence, the period which affected the campaign of 1916, it was apparent that our Government, under the leadership of Wilson, was trying, with a patience which seemed pettifogging to those who saw the hope of the world in Allied victory, to live peaceably and with the Christian virtues in the world infested with a paranoiac at large. Yet because there is bred in us the deep respect for those virtues which give us some small right to be called a Christian nation, America followed Wilson, sometimes in doubt, often grumbling, but in the end faithfully. It was in those days of note-writing that America came to realize the power that rested in their leader's words; not fully but slowly did that realization come. During the year 1915 and in the year 1916, in spite of the assaults of his enemies, the

American people began to understand the strength of the humble, the high potency of an ideal.

In June, 1915, Secretary Bryan resigned. Ellen Axson's judgment of him was verified. It became apparent in the spring of that year and early summer that Secretary Bryan's pacifism was tempered, not with the intellectual quality that made the Wilson pacifism strong, but with an emotional quality which would have surrendered our souls. The self-respect with which Wilson steeled his philosophy, the self-respect which is as much the attitude of your true democrat as self-forgetting, Bryan's pacifism lacked. It was abject because it was blind, and so, lacking respect, savored of cowardice. Bryan's departure strengthened the President.

In May, 1915, the Lusitania was sunk without warning and one hundred and twenty-four American lives were lost. President Wilson was stirred to his depths. Outwardly to the public he seemed calm. But the torpedo that sank the Lusitania seems to have hit Woodrow Wilson's whole foreign policy and all his visions of peace. Few persons knew how terribly he was agitated. For years in Washington, among the newspaper men, a story has been circulated of an early morning conference in the White House, known as the "Sunrise Conference." It was held in May, 1916, a year after the Lusitania went down. During that year, under the bedevilment of the German submarine programme, the banked fires of Wilson's wrath must have smouldered, in spite of all his fine talk of peace. Washington heard that at this conference the President was ready to put the country into war. It was a most disturbing story, this story of the Sunrise Conference. Four men were present, according to the story: Congressman Claude Kitchin, Democratic House leader; Congressman Henry D. Flood, of the House Foreign Relations Committee; Speaker Champ Clark, of the House; and the President. Clark died, then Flood, then Kitchin. What actually happened at that Sunrise Conference is one of the mysteries of the War. Here is the story as Gilson Gardner knew it:

"As the story was told to me, this early morning conference at the White House was attended by Representatives Clark, Flood, and Kitchin. It was at this conference that President Wilson announced his intention to put the United States into war and to do so immediately. Clark, Flood, and Kitchin were shocked at Wilson's announcement and declared that it was impossible; that the people did not want this country put into war, and that any effort on Wilson's part to force such a result would be met by them with a very bitter fight. Wilson threatened, and said that any man standing in the way would be politically destroyed if he started to carry out his purpose. There were heated words, and the conference broke up with a declaration by these leaders that they would resist the President to the utmost in any such effort."

Then, one by one, those Democratic leaders died. Just before the death of Claude Kitchin, Gilson Gardner, as set down above, of Washington, wrote him a letter in which he set forth the story that the reporters knew, and asked Kitchin to verify the truth of the story. Kitchin's letter to Gardner, in reply to Gardner's statement setting forth the commonly accepted story of the conference, is given below:

SCOTLAND NECK, N.C.
December 22, 1921

MY DEAR MR. GARDNER:

. . . I will return to Washington, I hope, sometime in January, and will then go over the whole matter with you to which your letter refers.

You know both Clark and Flood are dead, the only ones present with me. It is unfortunate that we then did not get together and write out our recollections of the conference, as the last time I saw Clark and Flood together we promised to do, and each take a signed copy by the three. I am sure, however, that there are some members of Congress who will remember our talking the matter over with them the day the conference took place, and also the conference the afternoon before between the President, Senator Kern, Democratic leader in the Senate, Senator Stone, Chairman Foreign Affairs of Senate, and Flood, Chairman Foreign Affairs of the House, to which I was invited by Kern, Stone, and Flood, but was then busily engaged in another important matter before the House and so excused under existing circumstances. I do not believe it wise to talk now.

The conference the day before, referred to above, was the cause of Clark, Flood, and I making an engagement with the President early the following morning at 7.30 or 8 — very early to prevent newspaper men and others seeing us or knowing of the conference. . . .

Yours very truly
(Signed) CLAUDE KITCHIN

Kitchin died before he saw Gilson Gardner again. So on this letter hangs the only confirmation of the story. But it seems to indicate rather clearly how near America was to war in May, 1916. The memorandum which he read to these Congressmen represented Wilson's indignation rather than his judgment. The Democratic leaders were thinking in terms of a Democratic Congress. They, and not Wilson, seem to have kept us out of war in May, 1916. Yet it is characteristic of Woodrow Wilson that he stood manfully against the uproar and contumely hurled at him by the war party in America during that spring of 1916; let men call him coward and pettifogger, and said not one word in his own defense, released no whit of the truth which would have shielded him from the scorn and abuse of his enemies.

Another thing, this episode would seem to put a most human face on Wilson as a man who felt his way, coming against dead walls, turning, backing, hesitating, but always trying to move forward toward the light. However deeply he was shaken and unsettled by the Lusitania incident, he seems to have righted himself quickly. Outwardly he gave no sign of his inward wrath. But, at any rate, three days after the sinking of the Lusitania we find the President in Philadelphia addressing an audience of newly naturalized citizens. There he was preaching the pacifist doctrine which had engaged him for over two years. It was at Philadelphia that he used the famous phrase which astounded his countrymen:

> There is such a thing as a man being too proud to fight.

Tumulty and others tried to get the sentence out of the address. They realized what the President could not, being obsessed with his idea of the power of reason, that the sentence following, which qualified that phrase "too proud to fight," would not be read into the text. He had said:

> There is such a thing as a nation being so right that it does not need to convince others by force that it is right.

That was the smashing argument which he had intended to force home upon the submarine murderers of Germany. He had declared a few weeks before that his interest in neutrality was not a petty desire to keep out of trouble, and that:

> There is something so much greater to do than to fight. . . . There is a distinction waiting for this nation that no other nation ever has got, that is, the distinction of absolute self-control and self-mastery.

There is the philosophy of Jesus pushed to its ultimate in the practical affairs of a weak world wallowing in the slough of materialism. Brave words were they before a cowardly deed. Probably no such high dramatization of the philosophy of Jesus had been set before the world since He left it.

Yet so wroth was America at the sinking of the Lusitania that for a time, while the clamor rose and passions burned, the strength, the audacity, and the beauty of Wilson's heroism passed almost unnoticed.

It is hard to realize, in a time of peace, far removed from the threat of war, how the sinking of the Lusitania aroused America. Every agency of wrath let out its rage. Newspapers, politicians, the pulpit, the organized forms of public sentiment, clubs, unions, associations, suddenly became organs of vituperation chiefly directed at Germany, then, after the Philadelphia speech, somewhat aimed at the

President for what they called his supine attitude. Then, indeed, was the White House the vortex of a mighty storm. How Wilson avoided the terrible currents that surged about him, how he kept himself serene, how he held his course, proved the steel of his spirit. He was in that time the Woodrow sublimated. Yet that we may not seem to be bowing down to a stone idol, it may be well to remember that even he did not come to his final rigidity alone like a pre-visioning god, but only through circumstance.

It was like Wilson to stand unflinching before the contumely of his enemies, not telling the country that his party leaders and not he had tempered the note to Germany. He was then a lone man in the White House. Not even the death of Ellen Axson the year before cleft him so completely from the world as did that Philadelphia speech three days after the supreme challenge from the high priests of Baal on the Irish Sea. But the man who had walked for thirty years hand-in-hand with Ellen Axson, who from his father and his mother's fathers had received the heritage of an abiding faith which his life's companionship welded into the motive power of a noble soul, rose in those days to the stature of a world figure which shall epitomize the best aspirations of his times. Later, he was armored for action by the devotion of Edith Bolling, his wife. She kept him bodily strong by every wifely care. She gave him gay companionship in a terrible hour. She furnished him with every pleasant relaxation that a troubled mind could take. No thought of her suffering, no burden of her grief at the untoward times, laid a finger's weight upon the President. With all her light and love Ellen Axson, with her serious mind and heart that bled so easily, so freely, could not have stood beside her mate in those days of the war as helpfully, as strongly, as Edith Bolling stood.

If the fates were prescient, they were kind to him. He was going into a battle the like of which few warriors ever entered. Six years of it stretched before him; six years of turmoil, terror, strife, jealousy, strain, defection, intrigue; apparent failure like a pack of hounds lay waiting on his path and leaped upon his faith, yet did not drag it down even at the last.

It probably was months, possibly years, after the Lusitania went down, that the Nation began to realize what manner of man the War had developed as their leader. Certainly his partisan Democrats did not understand him. The man who wrote the slogan, "He kept us out of war," understood him least of all. In Wiison's correspondence with the Imperial German Government which followed the sinking of the Lusitania, it is evident to-day, reading these notes in the light of all that Wilson tried to do during the closing months of the War, and at Paris, with the Covenant of the League of Nations, that keeping us out of war was the least of his endeavors. He was trying to set forth in a righteous attitude, in time of war, the spirit of the Christian philosophy as it was exemplified by the Protestant faith of John Calvin.

> America [he said] asks nothing for herself except what she has a right to ask for humanity itself.

This was, in international terms, only a translation of the keynote of the liberal, altruistic philosophy of the day; a philosophy which before 1914 was coming deeply and surely into the hearts of the leadership of Europe as well as of America. How that leadership changed under the stress of war, how it failed the world, is one of humanity's great tragedies. But it is no wonder that the heart of a liberal America, which had seen Wilson's liberal leadership in domestic affairs justified by the works of the Congress which he led for nearly four years, and then had seen, even if it did not realize fully what it saw, his liberal spirit dramatized in the great world drama, followed him in the election.

Late in 1915, it was apparent to President Wilson, who perhaps was reluctant to see it, that America should prepare for her defense. He seems to have decided that neutrality was soon to end. Former President Roosevelt and his friends had been rather more than mildly audible in their demand for preparedness. Whether or not they forced the preparedness issue upon him, no one can say. That they did have great influence with a large section of the American public no one can deny; and that Wilson was as sensitive to public opinion as an honest President might be and as accurate in his judgment of it as a sensitive man in the White House could be, there can be no doubt. But it is no part of the philosophy of Christianity to let evil triumph unmolested, to stand by defenseless when a righteous cause needs material strength. It was in November, 1915, when President Wilson, speaking before the Manhattan Club of New York City, gave out his first definite intention to stand for a policy of national defense. The Manhattan Club is a Democratic Club in New York City; and New York City, of all American communities, lay the most open and defenseless to alien attack. The Eastern seaboard was also defenseless. It was, too, one of the American strongholds of those materialists who in peace and war had furnished the sinews of the opposition to Wilson. They were not greatly to blame; they saw this philosophy of altruism, which the President had been preaching for a year and a half, baring our breasts to an enemy whose coming would be invited by his posture of pacifism. And Wilson's friends in the East recognized that whatever might be the attitude in the West, where the problem of defense was geographically a minor problem, in the East the President was losing ground. So, when he came to the Manhattan Club to talk to his partisan friends, he found a cold audience, not knowing what his pronouncement would be. He sat at the table before a thousand people, obviously affable to those near him, but apparently not constrained. Care had chiseled down the face of the Princeton professor of the nineties, and the years in the White House had changed even the proud, happy features of the Governor of New Jersey to a certain sphinx-like reserve. Grief and worry had not brightened his face. The forehead, the eyes, the sensitive nose, still held their nobility. But the hammer and chisel of time and care had cut away the soft lines from his jaw. It revealed a certain carnal coarseness that shocked a stranger. Yet that coarseness was only a pretense. An honest study of his life, shrinking at nothing, has revealed no justification for the implication of that heavy jaw. He sat there, carrying in his mind a speech which was in its way to reveal the passing of another milestone in his course. No anxiety was apparent; he was captain of all his physical and spiritual resources. He rose to speak amid cheers which were more for his office than for the man.

But it became evident as he talked that he was entering upon a new phase of our position in the world drama. He unfolded his new position without emotion, as one who read a specification in a contract. What Roosevelt would have declared amid a whirlwind of enthusiasm, Wilson set forth clearly, definitely, with a certain maddening righteous punctility that took the enthusiasm from his auditors, whose agreement with him should have made men leap to their feet with acclaim. It was a characteristic Wilsonian occasion, this first declaration of the President that he was ready to go forward on a programme to maintain our national defense. He answered the question of the times, as to "how far we are prepared to maintain ourselves against any interference with our national action or development," by answering that we were ready for whatever augmented military power was needed for the defense of our citizens and our territory, for the defense of the ideals of the American people. This defense, he declared, was to be "for constant and legitimate uses in times of international peace." He declared that it had been the policy time out of mind "to look to the Navy as the first and chief line of defense." But he did declare himself for a programme looking toward a larger measure of preparedness, making it clear that it was for our ideals rather than for our material interests that he had taken this step.

His address received something more than the response of a perfunctory applause, but not much more. The Democrats were satisfied with half a loaf, and the liberals of the country, even the Rooseveltian liberals, were glad it was as sound a loaf as it was. Yet from that speech dated the beginning of our entrance into the World War. It was a year and a half before our formal entrance. The whole campaign of 1916 lay ahead of us. The paper for the posters which proclaimed "He kept us out of war" was still in trees growing in the forest.

America certainly did not realize how much it cost the President to declare his programme then. For he had hoped that America would be the peaceful mediator that should end the War. He surrendered none of his faith; the sublimity of his vision was not tarnished by the knowledge which was coming to him that America would have to give herself in the struggle for its realization. But that knowledge surely did come to him in bitterness and pain.

In the meantime he wrestled with Congress for his domestic programme and pushed most of it through in that final year before the campaign. He was learning the game of politics. His years of academic training stood him in good stead. His mid-fifties found his brain supple, tenacious, capable of great strain, ready to carry every command of his mind, quickly, surely, faithfully, into intelligent action. His brain was a first-class brain, whatever his mind may have been. And in those days his mind, even though it was chiefly used in welding words, rose to its highest power, achieved its greatest usefulness, for those words in those hours had all the force of deeds.[1]

Yet to appreciate Wilson best, one must get down to earth. We are not dealing with a marble statue, but with a flesh-and-blood man. In those days, when his high purpose reflected a noble faith, when he was starting out on that long up-reaching journey which led him, because of his unflinching faith, to what

[1] Those closing days of Wilson's first Administration marked the gathering of a new group about him. Probably the dominant man in that group was Newton Baker, his Secretary of War. Baker was a militant mid-Western liberal, philosophically a pacifist, politically a Democratic adherent of the left wing in his party. As Secretary of War he deeply offended certain military men of America and of the world by his obvious loathing of the business of war. He conducted that business with as much effectiveness and celerity as the circumstances surrounding our entrance into the war would permit. But his unconcealed loathing for "the gentle art of murdering" gave his enemies deep offense. Another liberal spirit that came into the Wilson councils was Justice Louis D. Brandeis. Brandeis had a first-class mind. He was an uncompromising liberal, and a loyal friend with whom the President never broke. William Gibbs McAdoo, a New York promoter, whom Wilson named as Secretary of the Treasury, and who, early in the Wilson Administration, had married the President's daughter, was another liberal, who thought in economic rather than in social terms, and whose advice Wilson turned to in those last years of his first term and in the first years of his second term.

may become a place among the immortals, he was never more than a man. He snubbed politicians whom he did not understand; was not above cutting his old associate President Hibben of Princeton on the station platform, when President Hibben had invited President Wilson to use Prospect when he came home to vote; avoided telling McCombs the truth about his incapacity for public service, using Tumulty as a bumper; and, having picked his old friend and ally George Record for a place upon the Federal Trade Commission, and having given out his name, withdrew it brutally because it offended a conservative Democrat. No Sunday-school character is this Woodrow Wilson. Often he seems vain, sometimes irritable; alternately, proudly aloof and infinitely patient with friend or foe without distinction. The uncompromising spirit of the Woodrows often guided him in his highest moments, but their hermit habits, while sometimes they spoiled his manners, never broke the quality that made him great, the faith which was the mentor of his soul.

CHAPTER XVI

HOW THE MAGICIAN WON THE WAR

It was President Wilson's friends and not he who stressed the phrase, "He kept us out of war," in the campaign of 1916. The President talked in that campaign not so much of foreign affairs as of domestic issues, and of the record of his achievement as a liberal President. He knew well how slender was the hope of keeping America out of the World War. So he was chary of the boast that he had kept us out of war. With all his might, indeed, he was making a diplomatic position for the United States at home and abroad so strong that our entrance, when it came, would be in a righteous cause. Early in May, 1914, three months before war actually opened in Europe, the President sent Colonel House on a semi-official errand to try to convince the Governments of Germany, France, and Great Britain of the danger in the situation, and to ask them to take preliminary steps to form some tribunal or conference table where the coming misunderstanding, inevitable to Europe as it seemed that summer, might be considered, arbitrated, and settled without war. Colonel House, indeed, for nearly seven years, before the

War, during the War, and after the Armistice, was traveling between the capitals of Europe and Washington as the President's representative; eagerly urging upon the responsible rulers of England and the Continent the principles of international amity as the President was proclaiming them, and trying to establish these principles as the basis for a working agreement in the interests of a peaceful world.

Until war actually came, the President and his friends hoped that they might keep America out of the brawl; but in 1916 the hope was slight. The ruthless encroachments of Germany upon the lives of American citizens, an encroachment unbelievably blind in the light of all that happened as a result of it, finally forced the President to abandon even the thread of hope.

The tenor of his notes to Germany before November, 1916, was patient beyond belief. Perhaps his patience was founded upon the hope that the United States might be the great conciliator of the world peace without America's actual entrance into the War. The President had his pride. If he could have avoided war for America and brought about a peace without victory, at which he hinted; if he could have become the mediator of a sound and permanent world peace, his name would have been safe in history. And if that ambition was in his heart, it was a pardonable one, and none should gainsay it to him. As the third year of the War began, Wilson became a magnified figure in the world; somewhat because we were the largest civilized group outside of the conflict; but chiefly, probably, because Wilson took world leadership through his notes to Germany and by his patient pacifist philosophy; the only hopeful philosophy for sick humanity amid the carnage.

The world was full of pacifists, of course, during the War; but at the end of a long chain of fortuitous circumstances reaching back, Heaven only knows how far into the past, there sat in the highest place of the most important neutral nation in the world a pacifist who was a skilled debater. We must remember how Tommy Wilson, of Princeton and of Johns Hopkins, excelled as a debater; what extraordinary talent he had. We must then recall his passage at arms with the Princeton alumni, with the forces of organized wealth, in which he won; and winning, lost. Also, we must not forget the momentous debate of the election of 1912, in which he went out against the sturdy Roosevelt. And as one year of the Great War piled on another, and as America was slowly and tragically being drawn into the vortex of war during three terrible years, let us recollect, as our chiefest pride, the fact that our President, as a debater, was clarifying the issues of that War —

perhaps actually creating a new issue by his very insistence upon them — in his notes to the Imperial German Government. He was, as the months went by, making it clearer and clearer to the world beyond our borders how the issue stood. But even more important than his influence abroad was his slowly growing power at home. He was uniting America while he converted the world. The propagandists of the Allies could not clarify that issue. Clemenceau, George, Orlando — perhaps because they were so near to the combat — could not define its meaning in terms that would convince the world of the righteousness of the cause against the Central Powers. This Wilson did. His talent as a debater was his armor. The everlasting series of notes which he wrote and wrote and wrote, when impatient critics were demanding deeds and not words, were, after all, more than guns and ships and the provender of war, the real munitions that broke the German front. He was hypnotizing the world!

In that magnificent debate, Olympian in its grandeur, probably the most vital interchange of contesting ideas that the world has ever seen, we find this Celtic statesman at his best. His mind was fitted by its very limitations for its task. No great philosopher was he; the restrictions, qualifications, niceties of statement that would have crowded in upon a first-class mind, would have robbed his issue of its force and turned it beyond the comprehension of the common mind. But Wilson, from his Irish heart, matched minds with the common people of the world. He was given Divine grace to see, as the world could not see, the fundamental issues of the Great War. When he was framing his Lusitania note, Frank Cobb, chief editorial writer of the "New York World," was with him. Cobb had supported his candidacy for President in 1912; had been Wilson's close and affectionate friend during all his presidential career. Often Wilson sent for Cobb, and that day Wilson spent nearly an hour talking to Cobb, and what he said comes to something like this; wise, prophetic, and beautifully clear and simple:[1]

I do not know whether the German Government intends to keep faith with the United States or not. It is my personal opinion that Germany has no such intention, but I am less concerned about the ultimate intentions of Germany than about the attitude of the American people, who are already divided into three groups; those who are strongly pro-German, those who are strongly pro-Ally, and the vast majority who expect me to find a way to keep the United States out of war. I do not want war, yet I do not know that I can keep the country out of the War. That depends on Germany, and I have no control over Germany. But I intend to handle this situation in such a manner that every American citizen will know that the United States

[1] From *Cobb of the World.* New York.

Government has done everything it could to prevent war. Then if war comes, we shall have a united country, and with a united country there need be no fear about the result.

Here is the whole policy, the gist of the long debate that preceded our entrance into the War.

The campaign of 1916 seemed to lubricate Wilson's mental processes. With the momentum of the campaign in his soul, he began that series of utterances upon our foreign policy which rallied the American people as a united nation, forming around Wilson a spiritual phalanx which went out upon the crusade to save the world for democracy. December 16, 1916, the President transmitted to the Entente Allies the German offer to negotiate peace, an offer made December 12th. December 18th the President suggested to the nations at war that they state their aims in simple terms, so that the people of the world might understand them. This was a diplomatic master-stroke. It enraged the Germans. At first the Allies were puzzled; then they rose to the occasion and for the first time made a statement sufficiently clear, high, and broad to warrant America's coöperation with them. December 26th the Germans characteristically replied to the President's note, setting forth no statement of terms, but proposing a conference of belligerents. January 11th again

Germany wrote, trying to clarify her war aims, but her reply was cluttered with material things. The Germans, January 13th, returned a supplemental reply, amplifying the terms on which a durable peace might be obtained. In it they suggested international coöperation to preserve the peace of the world. January 22d, the President laid before the Senate his famous document containing what may be called the foundation of peace. Probably no greater state paper has been handed by king or premier to a legislative body in modern times than this message to Congress on January 22, 1917. In it we find a hundred winged sentences that go to the heart of civilized international relations. As a piece of writing the style is clear and strong, with few adjectives to weight it. He said his say in short simple words, homely common words, Lincolnian in their Saxon strength. Of course it brought us one step nearer to war, but it brought the world also many steps, a long way forward in the path of permanent peace.

I am proposing, as it were, that the nations should, with one accord, adopt the doctrine of President Monroe as the doctrine of the world; that no nation should seek to extend its polity over any other nation or people, but that every people should be left free to determine its own polity, its own way of development, unhindered, unthreatened, unafraid, the little along with the great and powerful.

I am proposing that all nations henceforth avoid entangling alliances which would draw them into competitions of power, catch them in a net of intrigue and selfish rivalry, and disturb their own affairs with influences intruded from without. There is no entangling alliance in a concert of power. When all unite to act in the same sense and with the same purpose, all act in the common interest and are free to live their own lives under a common protection.

I am proposing government by the consent of the governed; that freedom of the seas which, in international conference after conference, representatives of the United States have urged with the eloquence of those who are the convinced disciples of liberty; and that moderation of armaments which makes of armies and navies a power for order merely, not an instrument of aggression or of selfish violence.

These are American principles, American policies. We could stand for no others. And they are also the principles and policies of forward-looking men and women everywhere, and of every modern nation, of every enlightened community. They are the principles of mankind, and must prevail.

The reply of Germany to that tocsin of peace was the announcement of the renewal of the submarine warfare within a large war zone; force meeting reason. It shocked the world, and it enraged the United States. February 3d, the United States severed diplomatic relations with Germany and the President set forth the issues of our special controversy with Germany so exactly, so dispassionately, so convincingly, that even the German-Americans were silenced. February 26, 1917, the President again came to Congress with a message this time asking for armed neutrality. It was a straightforward business document with little eloquence and many practical suggestions for American national conduct.

He took the oath of office for his second term Sunday, March 4, 1917, in private, and Monday, March 5th, the oath was renewed in public before a crowd in front of the Capitol. Amplifiers were used for the first time to carry his voice across the plaza to the thousands assembled there.

Woodrow Wilson that day loomed the largest figure in the civilized world. Four years in office had not broken him, but they had changed him greatly. His face was lean, his body straight and strong. A commanding resonance had come into his fine tenor voice. One cannot be President of the United States four years and feel constantly in one's conscious moments the responsibility of the place, the consciousness that one hundred million people have him and his personality always in the back of their minds, without some change in his psychological attitude toward life. This feeling of leadership, of responsibility, of what might be called publicity of one's daily life and inner thoughts, weighs upon a man until it makes him something different from the private citizen who went into the office without these conscious burdens upon his soul. We must remember what manner of man he was: the Celt, the dreamer, the word-worker; the man of books and theories, the man of vision and hypotheses. We develop with the years, unfold what we are in the soil of circumstance, and we must not forget that in the kernel of this man was little Tommy Wilson, the child, writing the log of the Avenger instead of wrestling with the barn-loft gang in his alley; little Tommy Wilson seated alone, aloof, as the soldiers pass; little Tommy Wilson in the grove back of the manse playing with the elf folk and the fairies. Behold now the grown up, the hypnotist, the world wizard! This high dream of peace, that he fabricked upon the anvil of a three years' debate with the contenders for a feudal world in the agony of its death struggle, was perhaps the embryo plan of a new order entering the womb of time to be born in another and brighter day; even as the blood of the Irish and the environment of America planted in Tommy Wilson's soul the lovely things which his childhood knew.

He appeared there, that first day of his new term, before the people, exalted, happy; pleasure reflecting from his gaunt face, out of his bright eyes and out of a consecrated soul, bewitched by his own spell. He was on a rising tide that day. Much that followed in the four years ahead of him took him to higher places and greater estates, but in that day there before his people entering upon his new term, Woodrow Wilson saw the largest hour that ever came to him at home.

March 12th,[1] the American Government put armed guards upon all American vessels sailing through the war zone. Those were hard days for the Allies; their low tide. America was coming in, but slowly. The Russian Czar had abdicated. On March 22d, the United States recognized the new revolutionary government of Russia — the Kerensky Government. Closer and closer to America came the necessity of war. Probably even to the last the President dreaded the declaration, postponed it, hoping against hope that it might not come. The first phase of his resounding debate with the German Imperial Government had about closed. The last night in March he felt definitely that the end of peace was at hand. He was restless in his bed, got up, went out on the south veranda of the White House, took his little typewriter with him. Mrs. Wilson heard him, and quietly went to the kitchen, put a bowl of milk and crackers by his side and left him. There in the early morning he wrote his war note.

[1] The dates, facts, and many of the conclusions in this chapter and the immediately preceding ones may be found in Robinson and West's *The Foreign Policy of Woodrow Wilson* (New York, The Macmillan Company, 1918), and this acknowledgment is gratefully given.

All day it was with him, and he considered it carefully, perhaps changing it here and there as men do who hold an important manuscript with them during many hours of crisis. He sent for his friend, Frank Cobb, of the "World." Cobb was delayed in coming. At one o'clock in the morning, Cobb found the President in his office. Here is Cobb's story:[1]

I'd never seen him so worn down. He looked as if he hadn't slept, and he said he hadn't. He said he probably was going before Congress the next day to ask a declaration of war, and he'd never been so uncertain about anything in his life as about that decision. For nights, he said, he'd been lying awake going over the whole situation; over the provocation given by Germany, over the probable feeling in the United States, over the consequences to the settlement and to the world at large if we entered the mêlée.

He tapped some sheets before him and said that he had written a message and expected to go before Congress with it as it stood. He said he couldn't see any alternative; that he had tried every way he knew to avoid war. "I think I know what war means," he said, and he added that if there were any possibility of avoiding war he wanted to try it. "What else can I do?" he asked. "Is there anything else I can do?"

I told him his hand had been forced by Germany; that so far as I could see we couldn't keep out.

"Yes," he said, "but do you know what that means?" He said war would overturn the world we had known; that so long as we remained out there was a preponderance of neutrality, but that if we joined with the Allies the world would be off the peace basis and on a war basis.

[1] From *Cobb of the World*. New York.

"It would mean that we should lose our heads along with the rest and stop weighing right and wrong. It would mean that a majority of people in this hemisphere would go war-mad, quit thinking, and devote their energies to destruction." The President said a declaration of war would mean that Germany would be beaten and so badly beaten that there would be a dictated peace, a victorious peace.

"It means," he said, "an attempt to reconstruct a peace-time civilization with war standards, and at the end of the war there will be no bystanders with sufficient power to influence the terms. There won't be any peace standards left to work with. There will be only war standards."

The President said that such a basis was what the Allies thought they wanted, and that they would have their way in the very thing America had hoped against and struggled against. W. W. was uncanny that night. He had the whole panorama in his mind. He went on to say that so far as he knew he had considered every loophole of escape, and as fast as they were discovered Germany deliberately blocked them with some new outrage.

Then he began to talk about the consequences to the United States. He had no illusions about the fashion in which we were likely to fight the war.

He said when a war got going it was just war and there weren't two kinds of it. It required illiberalism at home to reinforce the men at the front. We couldn't fight Germany and maintain the ideals of government that ali thinking men shared. He said we would try it, but it would be too much for us.

"Once lead this people into war," he said, "and they'll forget there ever was such a thing as tolerance. To fight, you must be brutal and ruthless, and the spirit of ruthless brutality will enter into the very fiber of our national life, infecting Congress, the courts, the policeman on the beat, the man in the street." Conformity would be the only virtue, said the President, and every man who refused to conform would have to pay the penalty.

He thought the Constitution would not survive it; that free speech and the right of assembly would go. He said a nation couldn't put its strength into a war and keep its head level; it never had been done.

"If there is any alternative, for God's sake, let's take it!" he exclaimed. Well, I couldn't see any, and I told him so.

The President didn't have illusions about how he was going to come out of it, either. He'd rather have done anything else than head a military machine. All his instincts were against it. He foresaw too clearly the probable influence of a declaration of war on his own fortunes; the adulation certain to follow the certain victory, the derision and attack which would come with the deflation of excessive hopes and in the presence of world responsibility. But if he had it to do over again, he would take the same course. It was just a choice of evils.

The next day Woodrow Wilson appeared before Congress and read his War Message. It was a gorgeous spectacle. America rarely has seen such pomp — the Congress, the Court, the Army, the Navy, the diplomats — tall hats, gold braid, and much tinsel. So the new phase of the debate with Germany began.

To the actual administrative business of conducting the War, President Wilson gave his whole physical strength. There was good Woodrow executive ability in him, but it was the kind of executive ability which does too much personally and trusts too little to others. Wilson always was in danger of becoming a stamp-licking, office-sweeping executive. During the War he might appear any day at the War Department, a stern, unsmiling Woodrow, scaring the daylights out of the desk men as he passed along; standing over this man a moment, looking critically at things the grim man understood but poorly; passing across the room to another and frightening him into chills; and so on through the department, trailing terror in his wake. The merry heart that made the Wilson countenance glad to his friends did not shine in his face often in public places in those war days. He was a quiet, hard-working Woodrow, punctual until it hurt, exacting, often cruel, and sometimes futile, even fatuous in his deadly desire to do the exact and proper thing in harrowing circumstances. Congress obeyed him with almost manikin response to his wishes. And when the President demanded the Selective Service Act to raise ten million troops if they were needed, Congress gave it to him with but a spasm of protest. He selected General Pershing and gave him unbroken support. The country would have been glad to see Colonel Roosevelt go overseas in command of troops.

Colonel Roosevelt, in an almost undignified passion to serve, all but begged for the chance. The cold face that Woodrow Wilson turned to West at Princeton met Roosevelt's plea in Washington. General Wood trained a division and was ready to go overseas. He was turned back almost at the dock with cruel discourtesy. Probably the activity of General Wood in the establishment of training camps in 1915, before the President was ready to reveal his preparedness policy and to enter upon a preparedness campaign in his debates with the Kaiser, furnished the needed excuse in the Woodrow heart for the ruthless sacking of General Wood. Later the President told the editor of the "Springfield Republican" that he had a request from General Pershing that General Wood be kept in America. Wilson gathered around him men of the soft approach, gentle-voiced men who knew much and massaged it into the Wilson consciousness with honeyed words rather than with battering emphasis. But the President conducted the War. His methods, his advisers, the whole atmosphere of Washington during the War was an offense to those whose ways were more direct, whose temperament was more Prussian, whose impatience often blurred their judgment. Colonel Roosevelt, representing a profoundly opposite type from the President, felt it his duty to lead the attack upon the

President's conduct of the War. So a great clamor arose in the land. That there was waste, no one can question; war is waste. That there was dishonesty is but a quibble. For when a nation gives itself to wholesale murder, it must not forget that peculation is the necessary complement of carnage. Behind the caravan of war, wherein we had millions in arms, of course came the camp followers, the plunderers, the panderers, and the commercial harlots with their blandishing intrigues. It was horrible. But war is hell, and when one goes to war one meets horror. Seeing some of these horrors, realizing them all, it is no wonder that the Woodrow in the President's chair turned a fierce and unlovely face to the world.

But another President also sat there, the son of Joseph Ruggles Wilson, who was conducting a greater war, a more invincible combat in the lanes above the battle. Woodrow Wilson, the administrator, the head of the Army and Navy, put into battle millions of men, and treasure beyond the dream of avarice. During the nineteen months of the War, those men and that treasure, hurtling out of the catapult of our physical fortress, crashed into the German forces terrifically. Probably no conqueror in the world, not Philip of Macedon, not Cæsar, not Genghis Khan, not Napoleon, ever in so short a time assembled so much death-dealing force against an enemy. Wilson, meeting force with force, was an Ajax hurling thunderbolts. And yet, what he did with force will crumble. If only force had conquered the Kaiser, he and his kind could return again. But the conflict in the upper zone, the weapons of the spirit, the thunderbolts of reason, the shafts of resistless logic, Wilson's will for a more abundant life on this planet, his vision of a new order, his call to a nobler civilization, the Olympian debate which he began April 2, 1917, and continued for three years until he was stricken — that is a part of the conquest of this war which leaves him a world conquerer, the only one whose fortifications will not turn to dust.

From day to day, from week to week, this great Celt, agile, unshaken, resourceful, even felicitous with a Titanic joy in his job, sat in the White House at the head of an army, accoutered with pen and ink and paper, books, libraries, laboratories, typewriters, telephones, clicking telegraph machines, world-reaching radios. He had commissioned Colonel Edward M. House as a sort of sub rosa generalissimo, and under House, President Wilson had conscripted a thousand brains, those brains which he and Colonel House considered the best brains. As commander-in-chief of that army, Wilson was gathering data from all over the world. He knew his history, of course; he knew something of political science in theory. He summoned men who knew more than he. He sent messengers all over the globe scouting, reporting, interpreting. Digested for him daily were tons of facts compressed into a few short truths. College professors, reporters, editors, jurists, a cloud of men interested in things of the mind brought to Joseph Wilson's son their treasure. While Janet Woodrow's son made war with a powerful right hand, Joseph Wilson's son made peace under the benediction of John Calvin. In his heart he knew that God rules; that men who are essentially noble are working in some great mystery toward some splendid hidden goal. He felt with an almost mad passion this truth about God and man. So all the force of the spirit which he could command from America, he set to work. Every day, briefed before him, he read the newspaper opinion of the world, of Germany, of Austria, of the Allies, of the Asiatic and Scandinavian neutrals alike — all opinions. It came to him predigested through many synthetic spiritual processes until he had the essence. Scores and scores of men, trained men, truth-loving men, with fact-finding antennæ, hurried over the earth to gather its spiritual harvest for Joseph Wilson's son. He took it, absorbed it, gave it out in many ways; in letters, in speeches, in public documents, all with one purpose, one terrific spiritual desire, to meet the will of the Prussians, "the will to conquer," and to break that will in shame. What Wilson said was winged across the world as were the words of no other man who ever trod this planet. No accident was this great voice. He set it up himself. The cable, the wireless, every physical machine that would spread his words, Wilson erected and used. The magic of the Arabian Nights was primitive compared with the work of this Yankee genie.

The President's magic worked most wonderfully in America. Every night the American people stepped from reality into the high visions of his noble world. A new psychology bound them; new moralities held them. To give was more blessed than to receive. Millions worked for the common good with no thought of reward except the joy of service. It was as though America had been suddenly shot forward a thousand years into some Utopia. Those who lagged in the world of reality, who felt the sense of hysteria about the new order, who failed to give spontaneously of their money to the Liberty Loan, of their food to the soldiers, of their goods, time, and chattels to the Red Cross, felt the sting of public opinion upon them. This was the conjured world of the President. More or less his conjuring affected the human race, but in America, during nearly twenty months, the master wizard never lost his power. He created a world as it must be when his major dream is realized. What a transformation it was in thought and motive that caught the American people out of themselves into the new order! Germany heard him as plainly and quickly as Connecticut. Under Pershing, the physical forces of America were smashing into Germany's lines. Under Wilson, the spiritual forces of America were smashing the German morale, breaking the iron Prussian purpose. Tommy Wilson, the prize debater of Princeton, agile, quick to see the adversary's fault, and with a thousand magnifying eyes and ears in every corner of the world, sat in his office, like a high priest in his temple, making his great magic. Is it any wonder, looking back upon his own career from the start, seeing how exactly he had been given by circumstance and heredity the necessary training, inclination, talent, genius for the work of that hour, he should have believed in his calling and election, the foreordination and predestination of him and his office and his work? Nothing strengthens a man's faith in God as do his own felicitous experiences. The Devil knew this when he tempted Job.

Nineteen-seventeen passed. The Fourteen Points,[1] which were the charter of a new order, were proclaimed. In them in embryo was the soul of the best aspiration of the League of Nations. They provided

[1] See Appendix B.

for justice to small nations, self-determination of peoples held in bondage, the freedom of the seas, arbitration before war, and open covenants. They smote the spirit of Germany like a cleaving sword. These Fourteen Points, by the way, were Wilson's, largely by absorption and adoption, assembled from a dozen sources. Colonel House, the generalissimo of the spirit, like a sleepless Ariel, was gathering from the hearts of men, through his messengers, scores of pregnant suggestions that were born in the details of the fight.

Nineteen-eighteen came. The Bolshevists took Russia out of the war. Wilson probably fumbled there. He could have stopped that *débâcle*, but Russia was a friend who questioned his imperious will, and so became an enemy. The harsh words which Wilson sent to Russia in her fall were costly to the Allies. It was his first minor blunder; the first time he let his spirit, his happy Irish spirit, be guided by the dour Scot within him. But he went on living in his world of high visions, saying noble things where they were needed, with telling emphasis, every hour hammering upon the souls of men in the states of the Central Powers.[1] Airplanes scattered his

[1] We may trace briefly one of these threads of diplomacy which the President was forever sending out through undiplomatic sources, by considering a mission of George D. Herron, who met Professor Heinrich Lammasch, the last Prime Minister of Austria-Hungary, at the

speeches, which were more destructive to Hindenburg's line than Foch's famous seventy-fives. And

château of Mr. Meuhlon near Berne, Switzerland, February 3, 1918. They had met to consider Austria's withdrawal from the War under the sanction of President Wilson, prefaced by an imperial decree constituting the different nationalities of the Empire into a United States of Austria under a presidential monarchy. They met as unofficial persons, each acting deliberately and under official direction. Professor Lammasch felt that the Empire was with him. It was to consider the transformation of Austria-Hungary from a monarchy to a democracy; how it could be brought about to end the War in a moral rather than a military victory, and how the United States of Austria might be made a member of a society of nations which at that time President Wilson, even before the Armistice, had it in his mind to ask. Both the British and the French Governments had discovered beforehand that the meeting was to take place. They knew nothing of the purport of the discussion. Professor Lammasch was a devoted preacher of the Wilson principles and the Wilson doctrine of a peace without victory. He had written a German introduction to a collection of Wilson's speeches published in Leipzig. It was part of his diplomatic policy to build what he called a golden bridge between Austria and the United States of America. He proposed that President Wilson should make a public address to recognize Count Czernin's address to Wilson upon the subject of peace, as indicative of Austria's readiness for peace. Then the Austrian Emperor was to respond to the President's speech in a letter to the Pope giving it to the press, expressing a desire for the reintegration of the people within the bounds of the Austrian Empire; addressing the settlement of all geographical questions to a Society of Nations, which was then more or less discussed and hoped for by the Central Powers.

The whole day long they talked and each was convinced of the possibility of the golden bridge. Mr. Herron cabled his report of the conversation, and suggested a direct contact between the President and the Emperor without diplomatic conveyance. But alas! The heart of man on this planet was not ready for that high enterprise. A few souls there were in lonely places who could have walked the bridge; but only a few. So it vanished as a dream, as one of the many dreams that Wilson dreamed and other great leaders of the War on both sides dreamed. The golden bridge faded into unreality. Czernin discovered, through his agent, something of what had taken place. He hurried, suspicious, to Berlin. Berlin served an ultimatum on Vienna.

in the summer of 1918, the world suddenly realized what a battle line he had formed there above the trenches in the hearts and aspirations of the world. Below came Saint-Mihiel and Château-Thierry and the Allied push. With nothing behind it, with all the morale and courage sapped by Wilson's attack, and — let us never forget this — with famine planted in the German populace by the British Navy, the German line began to slow up, to stop, to fall back, and finally incontinently to retreat. And humanity applauded, not Foch so much for his guns and his drums and his clattering sabers, as Wilson who, men said, had won the battle of the upper air.

Then at the zenith of Wilson's power, the Devil grinned. Wilson wrote a letter asking America for a partisan Democratic Congress. He was treading the upper spiritual zones of idealism when he wrote it, probably self-hypnotized by his own bright vision. Certainly he was tired and absent-minded. His National Democratic Committeemen asked for the letter. His imagination was dull in the lower levels

Kaiser Carl wavered, then failed. The letter to the Pope was not written and the War went on. Probably George D. Herron had more to do than any one else with the preliminary negotiations which ended in taking the seat of government of the League of Nations to Geneva. He was a person whom the President trusted. In the Hoover War Memorial Library at Leland Stanford University, which is to be sealed for a period of twenty-five years, will be found several documents which will indicate how closely Mr. Herron had the President's confidence in those days.

of partisan policies. He slipped. America turned savagely upon its hero who had shown a human weakness, and returned a Congress against him.[1]

The Armistice followed the next week. Wilson's shafts crumbled the line behind the line, and the Kaiser fled. It was the greatest victory that had ever come out of any war; not the victory of a conqueror by arms and bleeding men, but the victory of one who had overcome his foe by persuading the civilian population to surrender. If the material world has added new terrors to burn and break and crush the human body, the same world has shown us a new engine of conquest: the words of a righteous man spoken in the passion of a great exhortation.

[1] A fuller explanation of this episode may be found in a letter from former Postmaster General Albert S. Burleson beginning on page 512 of the Appendix.

CHAPTER XVII

UNCLE SAM DISGUISES AS A PHILOSOPHER

FIGHTING in the Great War ceased on November 11, 1918. It ceased not entirely because the German soldiers were defeated, but somewhat because they were deserted by the German people, whose morale had decayed. It was Wilson's victory as much as Foch's. But the British Navy also should be given its full third of credit for the victory. The Fourteen Points were incomplete, without the fifteenth, which was famine destroying interior Germany. The German people undoubtedly believed, when they refused to back their military leaders, that the surrender would not be to Foch, but to Wilson and the Fourteen Points, which guaranteed all that any civilized nation could ask of its warring neighbors. But the German people also surrendered to the Fifteenth Point, the famine; and the British Navy produced the famine. Whatever may have been in the hearts of the European leaders, military and civil, when Foch accepted the surrender of the German generals in the Armistice, Wilson expected, when the peace terms were made, that they would be made so that the new order of things international, which he had been preaching for more than three years, might be written into the treaty and made a part of the realities of the peace at the end of the hostilities. His good faith never has been questioned.

Wilson's mistake, which was natural enough, was too much confidence in his ability to talk away the realities of the War. During the three years of debate, and particularly during the climactic two years before the Armistice, he had substituted the Wilsonian hypothesis for those realities. Briefly, that hypothesis was this: that the War was a noble attempt upon the part of the democratic peoples of the world, the English-speaking democracies, the French, the Italians, the Belgians, and alas, later he included the Japanese, to overwhelm the wicked rulers of the Central Powers who sought to spread over the world a government of autocracy. He had not quite the courage to say plutocracy, though in his heart he doubtless meant it. That shrinking was the weak link in his chain. For three years he preached this hypothesis with all the grace, strength, and ardor of his Celtic heart. If he had been given a little more strength, a little more flexibility and resilience after the War, he might have embedded his hypothesis of a democratic world deeply enough in the hearts of civilized men, by his process of hypnosis, to make it persist as the reality. But he could thrust it no farther into life than he had thrust it. So when deadly daily routine took men from their war madness, the realities of life returned.

The realities of the Great War were, briefly, these: Germany and the Central Powers had been preparing for war for at least three decades. England had been watching their preparations carefully, jealously, answering the German challenge of land armaments with naval armaments. England was better prepared than Germany on the sea, the Germans better ready for the war on land. France and Russia were in an alliance. England and France were in an alliance. It amounted to a triple alliance against Germany.

The struggle for commercial supremacy was back of these alliances; back of this terrible preparation for war. At the last, in 1914, Austria was insolent to Serbia; Russia arrogant to Austria. The German military crowd, which was, of course, the commercial crowd, eager for the fray, egged on Austria; and France did not restrain Russia for fear of losing the Russian Alliance. In England, the same crowd that threw Germany into the War hailed England's entrance with joy. The British Navy and the British commercial classes who dominated the British Foreign Office could have stopped the War, but did not. Russia mobilized; Germany attacked France, invaded Belgium, and, when it was too late to stop the War, Great Britain suddenly sprang into the fight. Democracy had no champion in those days. It began as a war for commercial power. War motives were shot through with the greed of junkerdom in every European capital. Captains of business and finance superimposed their will upon the will of kings. Three years later, Wilson brought America in to overthrow the kings. Thrones tottered when he touched the war machine. But the thrones had been undermined by the will of business. Kings were puppets.

Wilson junked the marionettes. He did not put a hand on those who pulled the strings. Whether he failed to see them, or whether he feared them, no one knows. His eloquence, the tremendous glow of his Calvinistic faith in the glory of God and the goodness of men, which would have created a millennium if it could have been realized in common life, exalted the common people with a deep hypnotic purpose.

But when he went to Europe, he found that his hypnosis had not changed permanently their motives. The old nationalism with its greeds and envies still was latent in the blood of Europe. He then was faced with the realities of the War. Treaties, understandings, agreements, obligations among the nations — the wires which had pulled the poor scrapped puppets still were running across the world, moving events, peoples, races, as though the puppets had not been snipped off. Into that entanglement the spectacled knight of democracy rode his white horse.

The world may be many years — indeed, many decades, possibly many centuries — coming to the high point of spiritual consecration that it reached the night of the Armistice, November 11, 1918. Then actually, among the common people of the world, came peace in the human heart toward all men of good will. The hates, the envies of nations, the lust to kill, all the passions of war that had been released by the War, were subdued that night; but the realities of the War came with the dawn.

The peoples of the world had not developed leaders who could make the dream stick in their common daily life. The statesmen of the world and their masters betrayed the hope of the world. If they had wished to do so, they might have held and maintained much of the dream that rose in the hearts of the people. Instead, the leaders of all the nations began preaching hate, clamoring for revenge, intriguing for their own power, and idly bartering away the precious heritage of blood which the soldiers thought they were buying for the race. The fall of Lucifer was no more terrible as he went back to hell than that of disillusioned humanity as it returned empty-handed to the old world; blind to its vision, hopeless, cynical, pitiless, greedy, suspicious, cruel, hugging all the ancient human vices to breasts where once men held a precious faith. Wilson in America, after the Armistice, must have seen with amazement what Lloyd George was doing to England in the campaign of 1918, in which he appeared as a firebrand scattering hate across England; what Clemenceau was doing to France; what Orlando and Sonnino were doing to Italy; what the Prussian junkers were doing to Germany.

Possibly that spectacle moved him to go to Europe. He knew of the secret treaties which brought Italy and Japan into the War and which bound the Allies to a programme of loot and reprisal. Letters are extant from Balfour which seem to prove that Wilson knew of these treaties. Colonel House explained to the press in December, 1918, in discussing his chief's presence in Europe, that the President knew of the secret treaties. The treaties were published in 1918, and were of general circulation in America and of common knowledge. And because of them, the President must have been moved to go to Paris with the Peace Commission to undo, if he could, in the Peace Conference, the work of those treaties.

Before Wilson went to Europe, while he was making up his list of advisers, the Devil, who had sneered at the Wilsonian righteousness, grinned again as he saw Wilson's mind at work upon that Peace Commission. The President was cut to the quick by the rejection of his party at the polls. Being crossed, as he felt unjustly, even maliciously, his imperious will would have none of his adversaries. His friends, Colonel House, former Attorney-General Gregory, and others, urged upon him the wisdom of taking with him to Paris certain leading Republicans; men who had opposed his cause, but whose support was necessary in America if his cause should win. It was the fundamental and fatal weakness of Woodrow Wilson that, constituted as he was, he trusted his own powers, his "first-class mind." He did not see that he must convince his adversaries. He had dreamed of a world too noble for its inhabitants; so naturally he set out upon a task too high for his own mortal achievement. His Peace Commission carried no political weight with it either in America or Europe. It was not that Wilson was greedy for credit. He was never that. But he was balefully distrustful of those who bitterly opposed him. Lodge, Taft, Root, Roosevelt, Republican leaders who would have followed him in Paris and in America, who would have strengthened him, he could not work with, and refused to consider. He thought for a time of taking certain members of the Supreme Court, probably his own appointees, certainly members of his own party, but Chief Justice White asked the President not to disturb the Court. After that it made little difference what particular group of his own friends and adherents he took with him. He was discredited politically at home, by the election, and he emphasized that discredit by puerilely refusing to recognize those who had defeated him. Tommy Wilson threw down his bat and left the field, taking with him such followers as felt the injustice that had been meted out to him. If Tommy had only learned to stand and fight and fail and fight again, what a world — but things being as they are, the consequence of things will not be as they should be!

The President went to Europe on his first peace mission, December, 1918, on the George Washington. He named as high commissioners Secretary of State Lansing, Henry White, former Ambassador to France, Colonel Edward M. House, and General Tasker H. Bliss. Also he had with him a shipful of scientists of one sort and another whose knowledge might be needed in playing Providence to the map of Europe. They were for the most part college men, professors; generally men with their doctor's degrees, young men in their mid-thirties or early forties, who had achieved distinction in the academic world, or who had attracted Colonel House during the War while he was scouting around the earth with his army of intellectual reporters covering the state of the world. On the George Washington, the President's attitude was particularly happy. There he was back in his own world communing with people who really knew things, who arrived at decisions over ground as he covered it. No intuitive guesses, no political hunches, no forming opinions at third-hand, did he find in this group. So he took them to his heart. Many times while they were at sea he gathered with them and talked with them and listened to them in conference. He was full of quip and wit and fantasy; an intellectual satyr amid his academic fauns!

"Show me," he cried one day to his herd assembled in the salon — "Show me the right and I will fight for it."

Applause followed, and the world seemed whizzing into its next millennium. But this group of academicians appalled Congress. No Congressman had recommended any member of the Peace Commission for office. And Congress, wearying of its consternation, grew sick. Also a large number of Democratic members of Congress, that fine December day when the President was spiritually pirouetting among his collegiate wood-nymphs, had been incontinently defeated by the President's inept demand for a Democratic Congress. So, as he sailed, he sailed, an altruistic Captain Kidd to raid the wicked shores of materialism of its loot and plunder, Congress whetted its knife on its boot for the President, saying nothing, but feeling deeply. And we must not forget, even if he did, that the United States Senate had the final say to ratify or to reject any treaty that he would make.

An odd galleon was that which landed at Brest in early December, 1918, when the George Washington anchored. Down the gangplank walked this Yankee knight errant followed by a desperate crew of college professors in horn-rimmed glasses, carrying textbooks, encyclopædias, maps, charts, graphs, statistics, and all sorts of literary crowbars with which to pry up the boundaries of Europe and move them around in the interests of justice, as seen through the Fourteen Points. Of course, these invaders were trying to implant an ideal. At bottom the ideal was an attempt to institutionalize the Golden Rule — a big job. Precious little khaki and brass buttons were seen on the horde of invaders that poured down the gangplank, and no sabers rattled to terrify Europe when these conquerors came. Yet it was the "Avenger of the South Seas" — this Wilson ship — a dream realized.

The President sent most of his army of experts and advisers to Paris. He began touring Europe. He had come without explaining his mission. It was his reticent way to let the mission explain itself. Yet if he had said to the American people, "This war was fought to end war through the establishment of a council of nations, and that I may be sure that the covenant of the council is wisely drawn, I am going to Europe," American opinion would have been undivided. But he said no such thing. He took five amiable gentlemen, of some literary, military, and diplomatic distinction, with him as high commissioners, vouchsafed no explanation for his own presence, walked down the gangplank, and began a tour of Europe. His tour was to strengthen public opinion in Europe for his covenant so that public opinion might influence the Premiers of Europe. But that also he left to the imagination of America. And many of his fellow citizens thought he was gallivanting about Europe feeding his own vanity. They could see no reason for his tour, and so distrusted him. He loved the American people, but he often treated them to an uncandor which seemed like contempt.

Perhaps to have explained all that he intended would have seemed to him like heroizing himself, and that he would never do. The tour of Europe lasted until nearly mid-January. He spoke in the larger cities of France, England, Belgium, and Italy. His speeches were brilliant, dynamic, convincing. He was at his best form. But he was in Europe and did not know the European idiom, did not know his way around in European politics. The thing we commonly know as Europe is a geographical location. Europe is vastly more than a place on the map. It is a plane of thought, a spiritual attitude, a civilization profoundly different from our civilization. Thousands of years of tradition are woven into the consciousness of the European mind. "We are ruled by our dead," gibed Clemenceau. The European begins his mental process with almost a different premise from our premise. Our American passion for posterity is like the European respect for ancestry! Long bitter experience has taught Europe to face the rear, to look back for motives, to suspect all things, to fear all things, to covet all things, to take all things not nailed down or red-hot! To Europe America was — and still is — the dollar worshiper.

It is not clear to Europe even now why Americans came into the War; but Europe knows well that we had an ulterior motive. Perhaps it was to grab colonies. No? Well, then, to protect our credits. No? Well, surely to sit in the seats of the mighty. No? But we must not pretend that we came over as a fairy prince to help the oppressed. Europe long since smothered her fairies, and as for princes—"Put not your trust in princes." So the ruling classes of Europe, those controlling the actual Governments of Europe, mistrusted President Wilson, and greeted him with a leering and suspicious eye when he crossed the sea to sit in the Peace Conference.

But the presence of Wilson in Europe revived the fading hopes of its people. How they rallied about him! What vast crowds gathered under his banner! Their own statesmen had dashed their hopes and crushed them with the old political bludgeons and cudgels of a day which they hoped had been forgotten, but which unfortunately the people themselves had not quite the will to forget. Like children the masses of Europe flocked around Wilson. Probably never, since the days of Peter the Hermit, had Europe so blindly, so affectionately, so eagerly followed one leader.

It was a beautiful thing that he said in the church at Carlisle, England, the town where his mother was born (Janet Woodrow of the curls), typical of the idealism that was in his heart in those hours:

It is with unaffected reluctance that I inject myself into this service. I remember my grandfather very well, and remembering him, I can see how he would not approve. I remember what he required of me and remember the stern lesson of duty he spoke. And I remember painfully about things he expected me to know and I did not know.

There has come a change of times when laymen like myself are permitted to speak in congregation. There is another reason why I am reluctant to speak.

The feelings excited in me to-day are really too intimate and too deep to permit of public expression. The memories that have come of the mother who was born here are very affecting. Her quiet character, her sense of duty, and her dislike of ostentation have come back to me with increasing force as these years of duty have accumulated. Yet, perhaps it is appropriate that in a place of worship I should acknowledge my indebtedness to her and her remarkable father, because, after all, what the world now is seeking to do is to return to the paths of duty, to turn from the savagery of interests to the dignity of the performance of right.

I believe as this war has drawn nations temporarily together in a combination of physical force, we shall now be drawn together in a combination of moral force that is irresistible. It is moral force as much as physical force that has defeated the effort to subdue the world. Words have cut as deep as swords.

The knowledge that wrong has been attempted has aroused the nations. They have gone out like men for a crusade. No other cause could have drawn so many of the nations together. They knew an outlaw was abroad and that the outlaw proposed unspeakable things.

It is from quiet places like this all over the world that the forces are accumulated that presently will overpower any attempt to accomplish evil on a great scale. It is like the rivulet that gathers into the river and the river that goes to the sea. So there comes out of communities like these streams that fertilize the conscience of men, and it is the conscience of the world we now mean to place upon the throne which others tried to usurp

Mrs. Wilson, who went with her husband and always appeared with him in public, perhaps gave the cast of gayety and happy courage to his face; for we see him passing for hours, days, and weeks through deep banks of cheering humanity with her beside him, smiling, almost blithe again, all but the Irish play-boy of an earlier epoch in his life. At Milan one Sunday night he appeared at the opera — and a Presbyterian elder, too — and threw kisses and kisses at the crowd that threw kisses back at him; threw them back at him over the heads of the rulers of Europe, threw them back at him as the hermit crusader who should rescue the Holy Sepulchre and restore the Holy Grail.

In the meantime, Colonel House knew the truth. Toddling about Europe, a serene Yankee mandarin, soft-voiced, sweet-faced, and gentle, yet never fooled by the tall prattle of stupid or selfish men, Colonel House knew that the day had passed when Wilson could salvage much of his dream out of the European cataclysm. Yet the Colonel's courage was not broken, and he set to work to serve his friend with a will. Probably he had his vanity. He had done unusual things; unusual things were possible still for him. He knew the personnel of the great figures in Europe as no other American knew them. Moreover, he still was generalissimo of his army of trained genii. Facts came to his hand when he rubbed his wishing ring, and truth, separated from the facts like gold from ore, always was at his hand ready for his chief.

Just here it is necessary to define the American idea which President Wilson brought with him — the vision which he would have realized. For, after all, our President was not important as a man, but as a representative of an ideal in connection with the story of the Peace Conference. As a man always he was remote, sometimes vague, and never very interesting in Paris. But the ideal he took there was dynamic, and he cherished it and impersonated it well. It was the ideal of faith; faith in humanity, faith in the moral government of the universe, faith in the power of the spiritual forces of life to triumph over the material powers that be. He believed that reason, being the will of God, would prevail in international affairs if a reasoning place could be set up for international usage. Hence he stood for a League of Nations as a divinely appointed institution.

In presenting his ideal to Europe, with its age-long habit of doubt, doubt grounded in cynicism, it was as though grown men should suddenly turn up in a solemn conclave telling fairy tales. Responsible rulers in Europe could hardly keep their faces straight. Monsieur Clemenceau chortled in his glee.

"God," said Clemenceau, "gave us his Ten Commandments, and we broke them. Wilson gave us his Fourteen Points — we shall see." And again: "My friend President Wilson is a man of *noble candeur*" — *noble candeur* is a French idiom, which means stupid simplicity!

The Italian statesmen gave the signal for a demonstration to the President in Italy almost bacchanalian in its fervor! And, winking a merry eye at him, pointed to Fiume! President Wilson ignored these covert affronts, if he saw them, and passed on, telling his gorgeous fairy story about the goodness of men and the powers of God.

"And the common people heard him gladly." So he tried to appeal to the common people of Europe over their actual Governments; he spoke most directly and most simply, but withal not quite candidly, about the things which America hoped for as the outcome of the War. His uncandor lay in the fact that he did not tell the people what dangerous ideals he was preaching, how revolutionary was his plain language of high aspiration, and, most grievously of all, he was uncandid in withholding from the masses the knowledge of how utterly his ideals were at variance with the ideals of the statesmen of Europe, and with the plans of the Governments of Europe. Perhaps he did not really know what heresy he was spreading. For alas! though he talked like a revolutionary in December and early January on his grand tour, often circumstances made him act in the spring like an orthodox horse-trading Presbyterian elder, when he had to compromise himself like a gentleman to win even the remnant he could get of his vision. But he did sow the seeds of spiritual revolution in the hearts of the common people of Europe, and there is reason to feel that some of it fell on good ground.

It was terrific, this creed of the peace from good will as opposed to the peace by force. And that was the essential fairy story that America brought to Europe; that was the American ideal. Obviously it was not peculiarly President Wilson's creed. In America, at the core of our hearts, we all carry this hope. For we have no traditions back of us to make us doubt; we have only youth with its boundless faith. We are the new world.

So much for the stage setting. Now for our gallant hero. After his parade through Europe, he came to Paris to meet his experts. He rose from the cloud of his American satellites, like one of Raphael's cherubs suddenly stretching his legs in the seventh inning, to look at the glories below.

He rode nearly always with Mrs. Wilson, who affected purple, a dark wine purple, and who looked with him very much the figure of a smart, middle-aged American woman, about her own business, which was the care and feeding of a President.

Closer to him physically than were the experts in horn-rimmed spectacles came certain heads of important commissions and committees in the Allied organization. These men many times found their wisdom unheeded by the President. Still closer to him were his fellow peace commissioners. Even they were not always in his confidence, and each of them has pointed out to his friends important obnoxious features in the treaty which were there because the President acted in disagreement with the judgment of even his fellow commissioners.

He settled down in Paris in mid-January after his triumphal tour was finished. So far as the outward man was concerned, he was static. But behind the doors of the little White House in Paris great changes came into his life and heart. The anguish of compromise scaled off much of his complacency, and there were days in the late spring when he walked to his spiritual Golgotha. But outside the door, along the street, before the eyes of Europe, he remained always an amusing figure to the powers that were — the governing classes of Europe, the men holding the manikin wires — a mild-spoken academic gentleman in glasses, with always a faint odor of the sanctuary in his conventional black coat, with nicely creased trousers; sallying forth with a few well-chosen remarks on the good of the order to remake the fortunes of mankind.

Yet he had something else in his kit and accouterment; something which gave him vast power. That was the Yankee of it; we are dreamers, but we do not talk in our sleep. We are tremendously practical. The President, with his amiable speeches and his noble aspirations, had in his portfolio the promissory note of the Allies for eight or ten billion dollars. Also he had the surplus food needed to feed a starving world. All of which made more curious and interesting the picture of this elderly professor with his gentle inveterate grin roaming through the forums of Europe, disguised as a philosopher, but in effect half green-grocer and half banker! Surely Uncle Sam never before cut so wide a swath!

And Wilson never removed entirely his disguise. Always he seemed to desire to appear as a philosopher. When he had finished his tour of Europe, when he had roused the base desire for higher things in the breasts of the masses, inspiring a pathetic Messianic hope which — sorry the day! — never could be realized this side of Jordan, he sat down at the Peace-Conference table as a philosopher.

CHAPTER XVIII

THE PATH OF GLORY ENDS

THERE at the Peace Conference he faced a serious combination. The four major Powers instinctively were arrayed against him, with only Great Britain's statesmen — and not all of them — understanding him. In addition to the responsible governors of the four major Powers, he sat with the representatives of the little nations, who, though they believed in Wilson as Santa Claus, were none the less dubious, none the less hungry, always European. This also must not be forgotten — that the President was playing one kind of a game, the Allies another. And it was not a difference in moral turpitude; it was a difference in stakes. They desired certain concrete things. Occasionally these concrete things overlapped. But they never differed in kind. Europe's diplomats sat at the table, playing for boundaries, for economic advantages, for military guaranties, for balances of power. They played the pre-War game. One must keep that in mind. For the President's appeal did not reach the men who sat with him in the Conference. It reached only public opinion, and, though European Governments are much more

Copyright by Underwood & Underwood, New York

LLOYD GEORGE, CLEMENCEAU, AND WILSON

flexible than ours, their public opinion does not seem to be so powerful as ours; and the fine phrases of the peripatetic philosopher, with his basketful of groceries and his walletful of I O U's, did not reach those in the Conference — save and except always certain of the English, probably Lord Robert Cecil and Mr. Balfour. But even they did not soften the British feeling that the Peace Conference was ordained to dole out material rewards for the virtuous act of winning the War. So all the nations, little and big, at the Conference desired material things, and America was playing for things spiritual.

But our player sat in the game and played a lone hand. He played with no one at his shoulder to check him. Time and again he had come out of the Council of Ten or out of the meeting of the Four or of the Five, realizing afterward and freely admitting in private that he had agreed to something or disagreed with something too hastily. Yet he was of the temperament that must play a lone hand. His relations with men were cordial, but never fraternal; he attracted followers rather than friends; he had experts, but he tolerated no partners. He could ask advice, but no one in the sacred circle of his acquaintance had the royal right to call him a fool and live. So he sat and played his lone hand in a game whose cards he knew but slightly; whose players, banded against him, he never could meet as cronies; and whose ill-gotten gains he despised.

Yet he played a great game, and posterity may call it a successful game. If only he could have put dramatic art into the game as well as head, he might have swept the table — or better, kicked it over!

Early in the session of the Council of Ten the President saw that valuable time was passing foolishly. In addition to the Ten were their secretaries and experts and assistants. And Lloyd George, being an orator, could not help assuming the oratorical manner. He talked too much. Every one talked too much, made speeches instead of getting down to business. The temptation was too great, with thirty-five or forty people sitting around as audience.

Wilson, himself, wasted much time in a punctilious desire to be over-courteous to the little nations. As presiding officer, he let them babble. Hence the Council of Ten was cut down to the Big Five. Then oratory vanished, and the Conference speeded up; but also then, unfortunately, President Wilson met his greatest defeats. In the Council of Ten always some one was near who might possibly advise him. But in the small group Wilson, pushing matters forward, sometimes went ahead ruthlessly, and his advisers, once in the matter of an island in the sea, once in the matter of a Near-Eastern settlement, sat silently aghast as he bartered away things which they knew were dear to him, in ignorance of the play on the board. He would have deemed it bad manners if they had stopped him, and they let it go. So his temperament handicapped him. His mistake was in not demanding absolute publicity for all meetings. Therein lay safety for the thing he desired. It could stand the light. And the things the others desired, if they were wrong, could not stand the light. But he believed in the white light of publicity chiefly for the other fellow. Woodrow Wilson did not function under it.

The President was the only one of the Prime Ministers who refused to meet the newspaper correspondents of his own country regularly and personally. Once he came before the American correspondents in late February. Some one betrayed his confidence; he never appeared again. Probably this shrinking from reporters was at bottom a lack of physical strength. But partly his shrinking was distaste for the rough-and-tumble that sometimes came at newspaper conferences; always good-natured, but still a mental boxing match. He let his excuses keep him from reporters. So his cause was hurt at home because it was not interpreted from his own angle; not that his Commissioners were stupid; not that Colonel House, who talked to a small group of reporters every day, was uninformed. But no man can speak second-hand to the press and speak clearly. The conferences with the other Commissioners than Colonel House were dreary affairs. Sixty reporters, representing American newspapers, assembled every morning in a salon at the Hôtel Crillon, where the American Peace Commission was housed. There, standing in a semi-circle around one of the Commissioners, for instance, Mr. Lansing, in a cutaway, heavily braided, ensconced in gray trousers, a dark tie, and glasses, the reporters asked vital questions and got futile answers. Perhaps the next day General Bliss, of the Commission, talked to the reporters. They asked, and he shook a good-natured head, and often told them frankly that he did not know. Henry White, of the Commission, whose memory led back to the days of the Paris Commune in the seventies, sometimes stepped out of the little group into the semi-circle, facing the hungry, barking pack of news hounds, and as a gentle diversion told them stories about the Empress Eugénie, and the last Napoleon, and the barricades. And one day, by way of furnishing "spot" news from the Commission, Mr. Henry White loaded the sixty reporters up in Seeing-Paris busses and took them about the town, showing to them the old houses of the old figures of an ancient epoch when he, young and handsome, was a tea gladiator in the early days of the French Republic. Once, early in January, before the Conference had really opened, when the Powers were skirmishing in committees on rules and order of business, the reporters, gathered in the lobby before the salon at the Crillon, were waiting for the Commissioners to appear, something as the lions waited for the early Christians in the Colosseum. Up came Evans, of the "Chicago News," a godless young man, and brushed by the group of news-gatherers. He stopped. Some one asked:

"Are you going into the Conference?"

"Oh, yes, I suppose so long as the performance in the main tent is not ready, we might as well go in to the side-show and gaze for a while at the ossified men."

Such was the newspaper opinion of the President's advisers. And he himself, rather than they, made that newspaper opinion by his treatment of them. Once Mr. Henry White, chairman of a committee of the Conference on boundaries and waterways, or something of the sort, stood before the reporters proud and happy with at last a news item. It effected Dantzic in some way. He gave it out. Half a dozen of the reporters knew that his story was incorrect. His committee had adjourned at five o'clock the afternoon before. Then the President and the

Premiers had taken his report, changed it entirely, and given out the news of their change. And our President did not think it was worth while to notify his Commissioner of the action of the Premiers; letting him go ahead and give to the newspaper men a mistaken statement. Fancy how the Hôtel Crillon would have shivered if Root, or Taft, or Roosevelt, or Hughes had been treated so scornfully. Which explains rather clearly why the President did not take Root, or Taft, or Roosevelt, or Hughes with him to the Conference. He could do no team-work with men who put passion in their self-respect.

In considering the attitude of the President to the newspapers, we must take account of the difference between the European and American press. The European press, at least the Continental press, differs as deeply from the American press as Europe differs from America. The American press supposed, when President Wilson in his Fourteen Points spoke of an open covenant openly arrived at, that he meant that the Peace Conference would be an open conference. But in Paris a closed conference was announced, to the consternation of the fifty or sixty American reporters representing all phases of American journalism; the dailies, the weeklies, the magazines, the Socialist press, the foreign-language press, and the reactionary journals. These men, meeting every morning with the members of the American Peace Commission, began to feel that they were getting no real news. Other nations were giving out their ideas of a League of Nations more or less officially. America — for that one thing as her reward for entering the war — was leading the world for a League of Nations, but for what kind of a league, no one could say.[1] The newspaper men, for

[1] The final text of the Covenant of the League of Nations as it appears in the Treaty of Versailles is best described by its preamble, which declares that the high contracting parties agree to the Covenant "in order to promote international coöperation, to achieve international peace, and security,

by the acceptance of obligations not to resort to war;
by the prescription of open, just and honorable relations between nations;
by the firm establishment of the understandings of international law as the actual rule of conduct among Governments; and
by the maintenance of justice and a scrupulous respect for all treaty obligations in the dealings of organized peoples with one another."

The membership in the League is to be composed of self-governing states, dominions, and certain colonies, and further admission is to be agreed to by two thirds of the Assembly. Action of the League shall be effected through an assembly constituting the representatives of the members of the League, who meet at stated intervals; and a council constituted of the representatives of the principal Allied and Associated Powers, together with representatives of four other members of the League to be selected from time to time by the Assembly. The Council also meets from time to time, but at least once a year. A permanent seat for the Secretariat is established at Geneva.

And under Article 10, "The members of the League undertake to respect and preserve as against external aggression the territorial integrity and existing political independence of all members of the League. In case of any such aggression or in case of any threat or danger of such aggression, the Council shall advise upon the means by which the obligation shall be fulfilled."

Members agree to submit disputes likely to lead to rupture either to the most part eager to support the American position, were not permitted to know even semi-officially what the American position was.

It is not surprising that under this state of facts they began to lose confidence in American leadership. They grew restive, though not hostile. One fine

arbitration or to inquiry by the Council, and agree not to go to war until three months after the award.

Article 13 is an agreement to submit disputes as to the interpretation of the Treaty and international law, and as to the existence of any fact tending to constitute a breach, or as to the extent and nature of the reparation of a breach, all to arbitration.

Article 14 provides for a permanent court of international justice.

Article 15 provides for the method of settlement of disputes by the Council, publicity of facts and acceptance or rejection of awards.

Article 16 provides that, if a member of the League should go to war in disregard of the three preceding articles, the other members of the League shall sever trade and financial relations with the offending member.

Article 17 provides for settlement of disputes between members of the League and non-members.

Article 18 provides that treaties or international engagements shall be registered with the Secretariat.

Articles 19 and 20 provide for the abrogation of undesirable treaties.

Article 21 excepts the Monroe Doctrine from possible undesirable treaties.

Article 22 provides for the colonies held under the League and the mandates to various members of the League which shall govern those colonies.

Article 23 provides that the members of the League agree to secure and maintain fair and humane conditions of labor for men, women, and children; to treat the native inhabitants justly, and to turn over to the League general supervision of the agreement with regard to the traffic in women and children, opium and dangerous drugs, and arms and munitions.

Article 24 provides for the establishment of certain international bureaus under the direction of the League.

And Article 25 has to do with the work of the Red Cross.

morning it was officially announced from the Peace Conference that the proceedings of the Conference were to be secret, and that no Government would be free to discuss with any newspaper men any subject not mentioned in the daily bone-dry *communiqué* of the Conference. The American newspaper men saw that this policy of secrecy was the rope with which to hang the President's League of Nations — whatever it might turn out to be. They realized that if our Government bound itself not to discuss with the press subjects not mentioned in the daily *communiqué*, the President thereby had lost his chance to appeal to the idealism of humanity as against the organized nationalism of the world in its actual Governments. So the American newspaper men blew up, went Bolshevik, and met in formal conference of protest. They gathered about them the newspaper men of France, England, and Italy, and the other Allied countries.

And then and there came another great disillusionment to the Americans. For they found that, instead of a unanimous demand from the press of the world for an open discussion, for the freedom of the press from censorship in Allied countries, and for the right to attend the Conference, the foreign press had quite another attitude. The nationalistic attitude of the foreign Governments was reflected in the foreign press. The Italian press had to be convinced; England was in doubt; France was resolutely against publicity. Italy and England and the press of the smaller nations, after debating the question from seven in the evening until three in the morning, finally joined the Americans in a demand for entrance to the Conference, for the lifting of the censorship, and for a verbatim report of the doings of the Peace Conference. France to the end stood out for secrecy. There was no trace of "*noble candeur*" in the French attitude. It was sophisticated to a degree! For French national aims, from the viewpoint of the French Government, which controls a certain element of the French press by unabashed government subsidy, depended not upon public discussion so much as upon diplomacy. It was good poker, and not the cards on the table, upon which the French press seemed to feel that France's case depended in the Peace Conference. The American reporters of the Peace Conference were the star reporters from scores of American newspaper offices; newspapers wherein "passing the buck" and "knocking the boss" is a fine art. They were not without guile. Yet when they saw the French baldly and almost indecently expose their methods and purposes, the American newspaper men were shocked into righteous anger. They rose in their wrath. It was that wrath which forced the first opening of the Peace Conference. Upon the opening of the Conference to the reporters, the success of the President's policy depended. This may be a long digression, but it throws a necessary illumination into the European situation with which President Wilson had to deal. Knowing this newspaper situation, we may more concretely understand the aspirations of the Allies in the Peace Conference; the things which our President had to meet.

It may be well to remember also that those aspirations rose chiefly from the geography of the case. England was a fan center, a spider in a web. From her radiated great trade routes, vast commercial enterprises, world-long threads of financial power touching lands poles apart. Great Britain demanded two things — territory and ships to reach them. France, with forty millions of people and a decreasing birth-rate, lying next to Germany with seventy millions of people and an increasing birth-rate, required one thing — safety; a guaranty that she might go on living as a nation. Italy, without coal and iron, but with man power almost unlimited, needed raw materials, trade regulations, eastern harbors, protection against encroachment from the north. Japan, expanding in population by the millions, with an awakening national consciousness, with a dream of domination in the Pacific, but without raw materials of industry, must have sea power — "Shoes — and ships — and sealing wax . . . cabbages — and kings." And each of the little nations about the board had its own little material problem, chiefly centered in the right to breathe. Across this tangle of material interests ran the secret treaties of 1915–16, and probably some sort of understanding between the British and the French just before we got into the War, or shortly afterward. Lloyd George seemed to be referring to it in utterances during the Conference, and, before the Conference opened, Monsieur Clemenceau spoke confidently about it. Doubtless the President knew of it.[1]

[1] The reader always must bear in mind this important fact: that the power of the secret treaties in Europe was no stronger than the fear of Lenin. This fear of communism was the deep, disturbing shadow under which Europe worked out its reconstruction through the Peace Commission in the year 1919. There abode in the Conference always three figures dramatizing three ideals: Clemenceau, representing the old order, the idea of a plutocratic control of Europe under definite alliances, treaties, guarantees, and balances of power; Wilson, representing a democratic control of the world under an open covenant, without special privileges to any nation, that capitalism might be maintained as a going concern in Christendom, modified only by such evolutionary changes as liberal majorities in the various lands from time to time might establish; and finally Lenin, personifying the spirit of communism. The plutocracy of Clemenceau under the old order would distribute economic goods by the right of might with scant consideration for justice. The Wilson scheme would distribute economic goods so that a man might get what he earned and must earn what he got. The Lenin plan would distribute goods according to need. And the threat of such a plan was potential dynamite to Western civilization. It was between these two grinding forces — a political plutocracy maintained under secret treaties by militarism on the one hand, and on the other the chaos of communism, a new, strange, and. in its passing phases, a bloody order — that Wilson worked in Paris

The President had his way for the most part during the first five weeks of the Conference, before he returned to America to settle up the loose ends of congressional affairs. He was able to introduce the mandatory system of administering the German colonies, against the protest of Australia. He was able to quiet the demands of France for territorial occupation of the Saar Valley. Fiume he kept off the boards. He fretted much in those days about the inter-Allied commissions, commissions that purchased and distributed food, ships, and the raw materials needed to keep civilization going. Wilson would have abandoned most of them. But gradually he came to see the economic basis of peace rather than the military basis, and wisely changed front on that notion. He and the British led in an attempt to formulate a Russian policy that should be non-military, and which the French quietly strangled. In those days he considered that it might be possible to divide Asia Minor into mandatories which would guarantee gradual self-government to the torn and distraught people of those lands. But chiefly he was interested in his League of Nations.

The League of Nations in the very beginning, before the Armistice, as early as 1916, was a British conception. The British put to work upon it a well-known pacifist judge, Lord Parmoor. Lord Robert

Cecil wrote to Colonel House about it; the Colonel wrote to the President. Each set down his own notion of the thing. They compared notes, locked up their two drafts until after the Armistice, and no one knows just what was in the President's mind when he sailed for Europe in December, whether he had his ideas clearly thought out or whether — to use a phrase of his own — he was merely "thinking without language."

The French had their draft and their conception of a League of Nations when the President arrived. Their conception was that the League should be a superstate with a superarmy and a superstaff which should always be ready to scare the superdaylights out of Germany if she began mobilizing on the French frontier. The British draft was read to the newspaper correspondents early in January. Its chief feature was that of progressive disarmament. Italy had a draft, but it never figured in publicity.

In the meantime no one knew what America wanted in the way of a League of Nations.[1] No

[1] This broad statement must be modified by the qualifying one that, in 1918, after Lord Robert Cecil had written to Colonel House suggesting the idea of a League of Nations, the Colonel wrote the first Covenant of the League, in July of that year, sending it to the President that he might answer a report, called the Phillimore Report, which had been sent to him by British friends of peace, acting with authority of high British officials. Colonel House, being asked by Wilson for House's memoranda, suggested by the Cecil letter, wrote an entire Covenant instead of a memorandum, and for the first time used the

American Peace Commissioner could remotely guess. In mid-January the President sat down at his typewriter and pounded out a draft. He passed it round to a few friends, to a few foreign statesmen; and the work of drafting the League Covenant began. It began in Colonel House's room, 315, at the Hôtel Crillon. The President and Colonel House represented America in the drafting committee, with a few experts always at hand to guide them. Lord Robert Cecil and Mr. Balfour took more interest than any other British statesmen in the work of the draft, and M. Léon Bourgeois — not a member of the French Peace Commission — was delegated to represent France. The Japanese modestly asked for race equality; were gently refused, and sweetly acquiesced, biding their time. The Italians also passed. Thirty hours

phrase "A Covenant for the League of Nations." In Europe, when the sub-committee on the League met to formulate a draft for the League under the instructions of the Peace Conference, they found the drafts for associations of nations by the English, the French, and the Italians. Wilson and House, taking these drafts, grafted them upon the House covenant, making something of a composite, but largely retaining the House covenant. Later this composite covenant was whipped into legal shape by Sir Cecil Hurst, Legal Advisor to the British Foreign Office, and David Hunter Miller, the American Legal Advisor at the Conference. This draft was used, when the commission met, as a basis for discussion, and the final Covenant was formed upon that. But this exact statement of the growth of the Covenant should in no way detract from the fact that President Wilson, with his own typewriter, prepared many of the vital clauses of the Covenant, and that his vision, his energy, and his indomitable spirit made the Covenant a reality.

at different times of the day and night for three or four weeks were consumed in forming that first draft of the Covenant. Ten hours were taken to add the amendments. In mid-February, 1917, Woodrow Wilson left for America with the Covenant of the League of Nations completed.

That day when Wilson read the Covenant to the open Conference was the greatest show day of his life. How the Wilson who wrote the biography of George Washington must have pranced in his heart as he viewed that gorgeous scene; his own big moment in the second act, the climactic pageant of a long life of happy and sometimes not unromantic tableaux. Because it marks an apex in his career, it may be well to pause here for a page or two and look at him and the stage upon which he stood in his day of glory.

His day of glory was typically Wilsonian. That is to say, toned down, understated, gray, shadowless, misty with a certain luminosity characteristic of a February day in Paris. In mid-afternoon lights flicker in the Place de la Concorde; honking carriages like great birds of passage flit in and out of the hazy mist. Inside a gray government building across the Seine from the Place de la Concorde is a large room, perhaps sixty by forty feet in area — a high-walled room, stiff, formal, French to the last tip of the gilded tail on the gilded flea on the gray wing of the putty-colored angels that jump out from the perfectly proportioned walls. Gray, putty-colored cupids and gray apprentice angels crawling out of the design hover dangerously, with their little pot-bellies filled with the diplomatic east wind, over a group of sober gentlemen, mostly bald or gray, wearing black three-buttoned cutaway coats, white vests, and pin-striped trousers. They are seated in gilded chairs upon a bright-red carpet — seated around a U-shaped, green-baize-covered table, two or three score of them, middle-aged, middle-class, dominated by a keen-eyed, yellow-skinned, bald little old man in gloves — always in gloves — the peace delegates and Clemenceau. The four walls, the cornices, and the ceiling are smeared with gilded wreaths, gilded leaves, and gilded flowers. Golden incrustations rise to the ceiling in a veritable chaos of ornate golden flopping of palm leaves and gilt gewgaws about a large gold clock, a clock which really keeps time; and from the clock the hall takes its name — the Hall of the Clock; a fussily over-decorated room, in the manner of the ancient French monarchs. "Plymouth Hall," gibed a reporter from Michigan in high sarcasm as he looked into this gilded interior. Above the gilded clock is the figure of a putty-colored lady scantily draped, which may represent France or Liberty, or any mistress of the particular dissolute monarch who drafted the slave labor that carried out the architect's splendid designing. Around the figure twine more leaves, more flowers, more geometrical designs, all bright, all golden, all meaningless to-day, all telling the story of another civilization than this. Here in this Hall of the Clock would seem to be no place for two doddering schoolmasters like Clemenceau and Wilson. Here's a place for bewigged gentry in pink breeches, blue coats, yellow waistcoats, to disport themselves "to the lascivious pleasings of the lute." Nothing in this room speaks of democracy. It is regal sham and bombast, reminiscent of the vast cruel presumptions of those who used to grind the face of the poor in the name of King, God, and Country. The room, beautifully drawn to scale, done perfectly to represent the genius of a bygone age, should trumpet to these middle-aged, middle-class bald gentlemen, in proper afternoon regalia, a shrieking warning from the past. Everything the room stands for — feudal despotism, the doctrine of the Divine right of might, hereditary power, or whatever clap-trap man so vainly has tried to use to enslave his fellows — a weary God has thrown into the scrap-heap. Amid this rococo grandeur, beneath the bloated little apprentice angels and the putty-colored figure above the clock, sat the delegates to the Peace Conference around their green-baize-covered table; a drab splotch in the middle of the gorgeous room. Here and there an Oriental delegate, perhaps from India or Arabia, in his native garb adds a fleck of color to this dark border about the green baize. But behind this border was another fringe. Here sat and stood the military figures of the Allies in the Great War. Admirals, generals, nothing less than colonels, all in brilliant array; brown, gold, scarlet, blue, green, brighter gold, deeper scarlet. Here indeed were the little playmates of the pot-bellied angels and the putty-colored goddess, all come to life.

And a fine, brilliant scene they made of it, bordering the gray and bald old gentlemen about the green-baize board. At the head of the table sat the Americans, the British, and the French, and near them on either side the Italians and the Belgians. Among the Americans at the right hand of Clemenceau sat Woodrow Wilson. Down the whole length of the green-baize table, between the two prongs of the U, sat Mrs. Wilson. Beside her stood Admiral Grayson, who gleamed a full-panoplied Apollo on guard, with his hand on her chair of state. She was in her wine-colored purple cloth suit, with her purple hat and purple plume.

Without ceremony or introduction, the President

of the United States of America rose. He smiled across the room at Mrs. Wilson, and then with a short shrift of some prefatory formality began reading a document in his hand. He read slowly, in an even voice which carried throughout the room, and which the reporters outside, peering through open double doors and standing on a string of chairs and tables in an adjacent chamber, could hear perfectly. He read without emotion or emphasis. Here and there he stopped reading to explain some ambiguous line of the text or to amplify some thought, but his spoken words were as lifeless as his reading. Slowly, as he read, his hearers realized that they were getting some new declaration of independence as well as of international interdependence. The import of the thing grew. Two or three hundred newspaper men, standing on their chairs and on the tables, tiptoed to see the President's face as he read the words before him; words of tremendous import it seemed, for we were hearing for the first time the Covenant of the League of Nations as the President read it to the Peace Conference. He droned on with as little intonation as if he were reading a list of goods at a receiver's sale. The light outside in the gray mist faded. The lamps inside danced in crystal chandeliers. And he read on to the end with no climactic tone or timbre in his voice.

Then he began speaking. What he said was well said. It was spoken from the heart, only a few typewritten headings in his hand guiding him. He improvised his paragraphs, and the stenographers took them down. Almost with a studied casualness he took the dramatics out of the day and scene. He was setting the oratorical pace of the occasion, and setting it deadly low. When he finished, not even a flutter of applause greeted him. The translator followed. He also was repressed, and after him rose Lord Robert Cecil, who read his remarks with the same impersonal, detached attitude that Wilson affected. With the monotony of a buzz-saw eating its way through oak, the translator followed Cecil. Then M. Léon Bourgeois spoke, who men said was to make a dramatic protest against the failure of the League Covenant to provide for an international standing army for policing the world. He lit no oratorical fire. Then one speaker followed another, with nothing particular to say and no voice for saying it, all in a dull, heavy manner without climax or dramatic form, without blare of bugle or fanfare of trumpet. So the League of Nations was born.

It was a typical Wilsonian performance; a great thing done insignificantly. All the notables crowded about him stiffly, shaking manikin hands with him;

apparently congratulating him. But Mrs. Wilson, who had exchanged smiles with him as he spoke, smiled proudly when he finished, and her smiles were the only human thing of the occasion; the only indication in the hour that this man had done a big thing, who, by sheer force of will, from unwilling Governments had wrested a radical covenant of democracy. From the whole tone which he set for the day, a stranger, not understanding his words, might have thought he was bidding on a list of live stock at a country fair. No heat of debate was in the ceremony; nothing of the hour when the French threatened to block the whole scheme because France was left without an international standing army; nothing of the fervor of the time when Premier Hughes of Australia fought the international receivership of the colonies, nothing of the anger which flared through Italy when she thought she saw her control of the Dalmatian coast falling away; nothing of the uproar that followed the adoption of the resolution establishing the Supreme Economic Council, taking most of the war power from the soldiers and putting those powers upon a civilian board. Nothing was left in that day but the feeling of monotony which matched the gray outside and a knot of uninteresting modern men sitting uncomfortably around a green-baize board. Heaven help the poet who would sing of this day! And the painter who would paint it must color his brush in dishwater. But Wilson had set the stage with the magic of the Woodrows, exact, unimpassioned, clear, explicit, and intelligently dull. If only the Wilsons might have come into that scene, Joseph Ruggles, with his gay persiflage, with the prancing strut that followed "The harp that once through Tara's halls the soul of music shed," what a day it would have been! But the Wilson blood in those days of travail had been yielding in the President to the Woodrow toxin. And so, when it was over, without tears or cheers and without applause, the President slipped through the crowd in the room, joined Mrs. Wilson in a corridor, and they two hurried in their carriages to the railway station and sped away for Brest. It was the end of an epoch in Woodrow Wilson's life. It was his last public appearance as the ruler of the world. Ahead of him lay his trip to America and the disillusioned nation which he found there. Behind him lay all his glory.

CHAPTER XIX

PRESIDENT WILSON'S SECOND EUROPEAN VENTURE

RETURNING to America in February, 1919, President Wilson met his first angry crowd. During his campaigns in America for Governor and for President, his partisans largely surrounded him. Later, the respect due to the President had guarded him. But when he came back with the Covenant of the League of Nations, to present it and to explain it to his countrymen, he found a considerable minority of the American people opposed to it. The Irish in his crowds were boisterous, and sometimes insulting. The Germans were studiously, and sometimes vocally, impolite. Republican leaders were after votes. So Woodrow Wilson, who had faced hostility in men, as individuals, met his enemy *en masse;* a disagreeable encounter.

Yet upon the whole, his first return from Paris was a satisfactory adventure. He had presented his case for the first League and had presented it well. He had accepted certain amendments drafted by Republican leaders, guided chiefly by former Senator Root, Judge Taft, and Justice Hughes. For years

PRESIDENT WILSON ON HIS RETURN FROM FRANCE, 1919, READY TO GO ASHORE AT HOBOKEN

these three men had been interested in an organization known as the League to Enforce Peace; a propaganda organization concerned with promoting some sort of League such as that which Wilson had sponsored in Paris. The officers of the League to Enforce Peace had no definite covenant or constitution to propose, but were anxious to promote any kind of international council under specific rules which would provide for arbitration and discussion of international differences. In 1918, before the Armistice, when the League to Enforce Peace was about to have a national meeting, Wilson told one of its leaders that he feared the meeting would be malapropos. Probably he really feared that it would set forth some plan for peace and for the settlement which should follow the peace, and he did not wish any settlement or discussion of settlements to precede the plans which he might hold in his own mind. For at that time, in 1918, he had not formulated his ideas into a plan.

The leaders of the American League to Enforce Peace were glad enough to coöperate with the President when he returned from Paris the first time. They knew the Republican Senate; for generally speaking, they were Republicans themselves. And after some private discussion with these leaders and public discussion in Eastern cities of his covenant, the President made one of the major blunders of his life by going back to Europe for the second time. The pocketful of amendments to the Covenant, which came as the result of Republican conferences, Colonel House easily could have put through. Wilson's presence did not particularly facilitate the passage of the amendments. If he had stayed in America to meet the American opposition to the League, House in Europe would have had to surrender less on the treaty than Wilson surrendered. The European statesmen at the council table were influenced by the opposition to the League of Nations which the President had stirred up on his hurried trip to America in February. A round robin of Republican Senators, just sufficiently large to defeat the Covenant, had been sent to the President and published to the world in which the signers declared they would not accept the Covenant of the League of Nations "in its present form." That round robin always was in the minds of the statesmen of Europe, and it made the President's situation more and more difficult at the conference table.

When he returned to Paris, his real troubles in Europe began. Here possibly is where the President's first distrust of Colonel House arose. Colonel House met the President when he disembarked from the George Washington at Brest. During the trip across, wireless messages had come to the George Washington indicating a status in Paris which gave Wilson anxiety. He felt that our Commissioners were surrendering too much. When the presidential party was on the train, taking it from Brest to Paris, Colonel House and the President were closeted for nearly an hour. It is probable that then the President voiced his anxiety; and possibly he put some petulance into his voice, but not enough to alarm Colonel House. During eight years they had been dear, affectionate friends. On every trip on which the President had sent his friend as messenger across seas infested with submarines, he had been more than brotherly in his loving care of him. They had been through a dozen hot campaigns in Congress and out. They saw eye to eye along the bright vista which ended in the President's high vision.

But we must also back-stitch a little and take up some hanging threads to understand this coming break. Colonel House had taken with him to Paris a number of Texas friends, his wife's brother-in-law, and his son-in-law, the latter, acting as a private secretary, paying his own expenses. The reporters in Paris used to refer sportively to this group as the Austin delegation. A book had appeared in the autumn of 1918, called "The Real Colonel House," which naturally made the Colonel its hero. It was a good book of its sort, but it might easily have annoyed a man who wanted no supers on the stage when he was doing his big act.

In his book about President Wilson, David Lawrence declares that a short time after the President returned to Paris, Mrs. Wilson, always charged in her heart with guarding her husband and his interests, showed to House a London newspaper clipping which magnified the Colonel as the brains of the Peace Commission, or some foolish thing of the sort. There was nothing to do about it. Colonel House could not explain it nor answer it. It did not seem relevant to the work in hand, and Colonel House went on talking to Mrs. Wilson about other things. So much for the tittle-tattle of Paris. Larger matters loomed up.

Colonel House's talent in politics was as a compromiser. He could plane off the jagged ends of self-interest in two opposing planks and join them in a workmanlike fashion. The President, in Paris, was in no compromising mood. When he found that the Commission under the leadership of Colonel House had separated the Treaty of Peace from the Covenant of the League, and when he suspected that Colonel House had made certain concessions to France in the Saar Valley, and when he realized the import of certain compromises around Dantzic, the President was annoyed. But chiefly he was annoyed at the suggestion, coming strongly from the French, that the treaty and the covenant be separated. Balfour and House had opposed the separation, and the French seemed about to overbear the Americans and the English. The President, hearing of these compromises, blamed House, probably unjustly. They seem to have been the basis for the interview between Colonel House and Mrs. Wilson.

Whatever he may have inferred from his talk with Mrs. Wilson, Colonel House did not then realize that it was the beginning of the end. Colonel House in his relation with Wilson epitomized House's whole relation to men in politics. For Colonel House came up through politics. He tarried but a few hurried years in the academic world, so he felt with Wilson rather than thought with him. Probably at base, although House was a liberal to the core, and although he greatly liberalized Wilson's attitude during the Wilson first term, after all, House had Wilson's personal interest at heart more deeply than he had Wilson's policies, even though some of these policies came to Wilson through Colonel House himself. That is the way of politicians in their relations with one another. They are emotional, personal, concrete. The affection of Colonel House for Wilson made him a marvelous messenger.

Not long after the President's return to Paris, the Fiume episode came up, which will be expanded later, and then the Shantung compromise came. In each of these incidents, Colonel House, who was a master compromiser, tried his hand earnestly at resolving the differences between the President and the diplomats of Italy and of China into their lowest component parts.[1] A few days afterward, he received instructions asking him to go to London to take charge of some matter before the British Government. He went. In due time further instructions came which kept him in London. He was called to Paris to sign the treaty, parting with Wilson when he left for home June 28th. It was their last meeting.

When the President sat down at the peace table, after coming from home in March, the others about the board had their cards on the table. They knew his hand then; understood his game, valued his stakes. In his absence they had been trading among themselves. The French asked for a neutral republic in West Prussia, and the Allies wanted to give the Saar Valley outright to France. Fiume also was to go to Italy.

Joseph's coat was fairly well divided among the brethren when the President returned from America. And then he witnessed a curious thing. During

[1] House was the only commissioner who agreed with Wilson. The other commissioners wrote a letter of protest to the President which House refused to sign.

January the French press had sneered so openly at the President's aspirations that his friends wished to move the Conference from Paris. When the President returned in March, the French press covered him with encomiums. No adjective was too saccharine for their uses. Evidently the powers that controlled the French press thought they had President Wilson's game beaten, so far as it affected Europe, and that he would take the League of Nations and they would get their boundaries, and all would live happily ever after.

Here the President began to fight. He made alliance with the British and secured the League of Nations as a part of the treaty. He restricted French territorial aspirations in the Saar. He overturned the sterilized republic along the west bank of the Rhine, and did things to the arrangements about Dantzic. He changed his mood from the academic subjunctive to the presidential imperative.[1] His

[1] Raymond Fosdick, who was a Princeton student in the fall of 1904, when Roosevelt and Parker were running for the presidency, recalls an episode which may explain the Wilson temper. He says the students organized a Roosevelt Club, hired three or four old-fashioned horse busses, and decorated them with huge signs, "Vote for Roosevelt," and drew the busses in front of the chapel door election morning to gather the students as they came from chapel and give them a free ride over to the polling-place.

"I presume it was one of those delightfully idiotic ideas which constitute so large a place in the life of college students. Anyway, I was in charge of the busses.

"President Wilson was leading chapel that morning, and when he

disguise almost fell off. He nearly showed his groceries and his promissory notes. Then the French press became silent. And one bright spring morning in the meeting of the Big Five, just as the President was prepared to introduce one of the Root-Taft-Hughes amendments to the Covenant of the League of Nations, the one affecting the Monroe Doctrine, he discovered that it would not pass. He fumbled, withdrew his motion, and began to consider many things. They had him. He realized that, unless he could amend the League Covenant, it would be rejected in

came to the door at the close of the exercises and saw our gay arrangements for free transportation, his face took on the look of a thundercloud. Stepping over to me, he demanded to know who was responsible for the outrage. He said a number of things which in the confusion of the moment were mercifully not remembered, and he gave me three minutes to get the busses off the campus.

"Fourteen years later, in 1918, I accompanied Mr. Wilson on the George Washington to Europe after the signing of the Armistice, and one day during the voyage I reminded him of the incident. He was immensely amused, and laughed heartily at my description of it.

"'I remember it well,' he said, 'although I had forgotten that you were the culprit. But, Fosdick,' he continued, 'I don't recall being angry about it.'

"'Mr. President,' I said, 'in this one particular my recollection is infinitely better than yours. Your wrath was positively Gargantuan.'

"He threw back his head with a peal of laughter, and two or three times on the voyage after that he referred humorously to his capacity 'for Gargantuan wrath.' One day he said to me: 'If Clemenceau is recalcitrant, I'll try my Gargantuan wrath on him.'

"Two or three months later I met him in the Champs Élysées in Paris. He looked tired and drawn, but there was a twinkle in his eye. 'Fosdick,' he said, 'I've just been trying my Gargantuan wrath on this French crowd. I wish it worked on them as effectively as it did on you!'"

the United States Senate. Also our beloved Allies realized quite the same thing. That was the trouble!

He came to the parting of the ways. He could fight or trade. He could go home passionate with indignation, or he could stay and get the best possible bargain out of the Allies. It was inevitable that Woodrow Wilson would stay and try to patch up the situation. He was not a rebel. Of course he should have to come into the open to make his fight before all the world. He was as honest as daylight; but he just couldn't bear daylight. Drama irked him. He was a debater, not a gladiator. So he sat him down wearily to the long, miserable task of trading the substance of European demands for the shadow of American ideals. He was as much of a hero there in the room of the Council of Five, with the cards fairly well stacked against him and Lady Luck running away from him, patiently plodding hour by hour, day by day, week by week, month by month, plodding tediously through details of things which he loathed, that he might get the thing he hoped for — he was, indeed, as much of a hero as he would have been if he had sailed home with a gesture of defiance and scorn at the whole outfit, and had brought them to time by clamping down the lid of the grocery-box and calling in the outstanding notes. But alas, his fine heroism availed him nothing.

For a long time he sat patiently in the game, and saw the Conference going round in circles, arriving nowhere. One day he would convince Clemenceau about the justice of a certain course in the Saar Valley, only to find that the next day it had to be done all over again. So he called for his good ship, the George Washington, and made a feint of starting home.[1]

Then the Conference speeded up until it came to the Italian deadlock. Italy wanted to take the Dalmatian coast and hinterland. There Wilson really balked. Moreover, he had the support of Lloyd George and Clemenceau. He wrote a ringing note of protest. There is no doubt whatever that they read his Fiume note and approved it. Very likely they did not know the hour it was to appear. As a matter of fact the President heard that Baron Sonnino was about to leave and issue a note, and the President

[1] It may interest American readers, and it certainly will demonstrate the power which our British Allies held during the War, to know that when President Wilson sent a cable to the Secretary of War, asking that the George Washington be sent to Brest for him, the cable had to pass through the British Cable Office at London. There it was held for nearly forty-eight hours. The President in Paris gave out the statement that he had sent for the George Washington. It created a European sensation. By wireless the American reporters in Paris sent home references to the President's request for the George Washington. These references were met by denials of the fact at the Navy Department and by Mr. Tumulty. When Great Britain got ready to let the American Government communicate through London, the cable was delivered.

issued his note first. And for a few days there was a fine tempest in a teapot. George and Clemenceau were properly shocked, for public and diplomatic purposes. Yet, at the very moment when the Italians were fuming most gorgeously, they had on the President's desk for his approval a request for a loan for fifty million dollars with which to buy coal for their furnaces. Without the money they could not get the coal, and without the coal Italy might be in a revolution in a week. And Sonnino and Orlando knew, and every one in Paris knew, that the Italian journey to Rome was merely a ten days' leave. The Italian members of the Peace Conference committees — the member of the Economic Council, for instance — attended meetings, arranged for Italy's coal and food supply, and functioned blithely while their superiors were gone.

There can be no doubt that the President's blast against the Fiume annexation afforded him satisfaction. For weeks he had been edging along, giving up something every day, and getting precious little back. The Fiume protest released much steam. But the Italian protest made the Japanese compromise inevitable. And that broke the President's heart. The Japanese played their cards well. They knew — what every one about the Conference knew — that President Wilson would not give in to Orlando in the Italian demands for Fiume. The Japanese also knew that the Italians would leave the Conference with a potential threat, a threat which would be important only if some other nation left the Conference. So, most deliberately and with Oriental calm, Japan made it obvious that she would leave the Conference also if her aspirations in China were denied. There was the same basis for denying the Japanese aspirations that underlay the Italian denial. But to deny Japan would take her from the League of Nations and make it worth while for Italy really to stay out of the League. With Japan and Italy out, the League of Nations would fail. It was all good whist; but bad morals. The President evidently felt that if the League of Nations failed, there was no hope for the peace of the world and that our men had died in vain. To him it was plain that, if the League of Nations were formed, and if it became a vital force, it could protect the rights of China which Japan insisted upon taking from her. The Japanese Government claimed, under the secret treaties between Japan, Great Britain, and France in 1917, rights to special commercial privileges in Shantung: the right to construct, operate, and police a railroad which in effect seemed to amount to a Japanese invasion of the Chinese province of Shantung. The Japanese agreed to withdraw their police within five years and to accept a loan from inter-allied bankers, and to return Shantung to China upon certain stipulations. The settlement, as Ray Stannard Baker says, "made a great sensation." The Chinese at first were for withdrawing from the Conference, and they issued a number of public statements of protest and criticism, which, by the way, greatly undermined the President in America. And in the end they refused to sign the treaty at all.

Shantung was a moral surrender, and no one felt it more keenly than President Wilson. His silence when the Japanese took Shantung cost him days of restless unhappiness. He felt that the Japanese invasion was wicked. To concur in it shattered his self-respect. But the price was an agreement upon certain amendments which were necessary to go into the League of Nations. His body had been breaking under the strain. He laid off a few days in the early spring and afterward showed distinct signs of temper which were purely pathological. Once he snapped at Herbert Hoover when Hoover used the word "compromise." At another time it was Secretary Lansing. At still another time it was General Tasker Bliss who broke the short pie-crust of his good nature. That illness in the spring of 1919 was the beginning of the end that came six months later. Many of those who were near him felt that he never regained his poise and strength entirely after that illness. He had brought Dr. William Westerman from Wisconsin to Paris as an expert in Near-Eastern matters, and one day Westerman tried to explain to the President a mistake into which he had been drawn — the landing of the Greek troops at Smyrna, May 15, 1919 — which caused the loss of many lives, but still was not irreparable; Wilson spent three quarters of an hour lecturing to Dr. Westerman on the Near East, a topic which he discussed only superficially, but glibly. He seemed totally devoid of a sense of introspective humor. And when Westerman went away, he realized that the Near East was a lost cause. That was not the Wilson of 1916 and '17, nor the Wilson of the splendid debates with the Kaiser. In many ways he showed that the stress of Paris was hobbling his nimble mind. Indeed, his outstanding weakness was the result of his amazing mental quickness, which gave him a political sentimentality opposed to political realism and produced strongly the effect of mental arrogance in those weary, lonely days at Paris. Yet he was not arrogant; not at heart. It was his body, not his spirit, that was producing ugly symptoms. So when he had given his body for the cause that had dulled his brain, he gave his soul for that cause when he kept silent before the Shantung agreement. It is true that in the later years, under the lash of the public sentiment of the world and under the eye of the League of Nations, the Japanese have justified his bargain; they have done, to the surprise of their enemies, and to the honor of their friends, all that they said they would do. But when in the spring of 1919 men doubted this, Wilson's silence was the token that he had given his soul to the thing which had taken his body. And yet, by the very weight of the price, may men know how tremendous was his purpose.

The President, in handling his foreign policy, since August, 1914, had made thirteen major decisions—far-reaching for America and the world and important in his own career:

First, the decision to maintain neutrality and to act as mediator.

Second, his decision to permit the Japanese occupation of Siberia. That was his first break with his idealism. But the pressure was terrific; the whole world of the Allies was upon him when he yielded.

Third, in April, 1916, he seemed to have decided that neutrality should have an end which should put America with the Allies after the country had been thoroughly prepared by debate for our course. In one of his speeches at that period he uses the expression "the end of neutrality."

Fourth, his propaganda for freedom of the seas, contending first with Great Britain for property rights and then with Germany for human rights.

Fifth, his demand for peace without victory by which he expected a negotiated peace rather than a military peace. He might have come to this decision because he felt, being an historian, that any peace founded on force, the peace which the conqueror gives the conquered, is always a wicked peace.

Sixth, a shift from the "freedom of the seas" to a better slogan: "Making the world safe for democracy." In his dramatic debate with the world before him, the President being sensitive to his audience came to realize that back of him in the Middle West was a people not vitally affected by freedom of the seas, and to whom freedom of the seas was an academic question. But that group was tremendously sentimental, and when he changed his keynote from the freedom of the seas to making the world safe for democracy, instantly the West responded.

Seventh, his consent to the partition of Austria-Hungary, somewhat as the result of intrigue at Washington, Paris, Rome, and London, and of his personal friendship for President Masaryk, whom Wilson had known in his professorial days.

Eighth, his decision to go to Paris in December,

1918, the first time; a good decision. On that first trip he produced the Covenant of the League of Nations.

Ninth, his decision to return to Paris in March, 1919; a bad decision because at Paris Colonel House representing him could have bargained better as an agent than Wilson, himself, could bargain as a principal. Always the Colonel could have stood back and deplored the man in Washington who remained immovable. But when the "man in Washington" was seated in a chair across the table, the agent had small power and the chief had to compromise.

Tenth, his decision to keep the treaty and the covenant one document, which seemed at the time to be a good decision; for in the spring of 1919, when he made that decision, apparently America was for both the treaty and the covenant. But alas! The treaty was not completed, and later America, revolting at the treaty, rejected the covenant.

Eleventh, his decision to keep the treaty officially from the Senate when it was published in the newspapers was a bad decision. Precedent and custom warranted the decision, but good sense and good fellowship would have counseled against it. But the President never forgot that Congress had gone against him; so he was cold, suspicious, and hypercritical with Congress. Hence he withheld the treaty, and for the first time revealed a vindictive face to his countrymen.

Twelfth, his decision to refuse reservations and maintain the break with Colonel House, who was weakened by accepting during the President's absence, the division of the covenant and the treaty, and by his efforts to compromise the Shantung and Fiume proposals.

His thirteenth important decision was made in Paris, when he consented to compromise by specious interpretation of the Fourteen Points upon which Germany had surrendered. His trip through Europe had told him that he was the leader of the common people of the world. In those days nine tenths of the German people were looking to him for a miracle. Before he left for America the first time, he realized that in the Council of Ten the Fourteen Points were being ground to chaff. There were days in February when he was tempted to rise and say in effect to the Council of Ten:

"I came here upon the basis of our signed contract with Germany to make peace on the principles laid down by me in the Fourteen Points upon which Germany asked for an armistice. You gentlemen have no intention of keeping the contract, therefore I have nothing to do here and I shall return to Washington."

Not a European Government could have stood overnight against this attitude. George D. Herron, who had been Wilson's envoy in Austria during the latter part of the War, under whom negotiations were pending with Austria for a separate peace, saw Wilson several times in Paris, and appealed to him to withdraw from the Peace Conference. Herron is an earnest man, passionate and convincing when he talks. The President was greatly moved by Herron's appeal, and walked up and down the floor exclaiming in great agitation: "My God, I can never go through with it." Which was the exact truth. His splendid courage was welded for other tests. It had too fine an edge for hammering.

Yet he surely realized that, if he could go through with it, he would have won the peace which he desired. Time and again in Paris the great temptation to leave in protest at the knavery of it all came to the President; he dallied, hesitated, and finally denied the voice that might have saved the world.

Much of this runs ahead of our narrative. Yet it must be put down here, and the decisions good and bad put on one string, to get an idea of the course which he traveled in the five years from August, 1914, to August, 1919. In these decisions his foreign policy came to its dramatic peak, its highest moments. In these moments Wilson revealed all that was good and fine in him and all that was base and petty. In these decisions is the equation of the man. Here stand his forbears, pouring their blood into his life; the Woodrows, strongly intellectual, ruthlessly uncompromising; the Wilsons, Irish followers of noble visions, more or less pliable, aspiring to great things, rhetorical with splendid polemic talents, and Ann Adams, the Irish grandmother, with her implacable face, who turned from her own daughter even in death. She was pouring into his soul a strain of inheritance that may have been the more virulent because he tried to keep it decently suppressed. Upon these thirteen decisions shall rest his monument. And in the end those footings that were of the earth earthy shall fall away, and that which is of the spirit shall remain.

He fought on after the Chinese surrender, knowing that public sentiment at home was hardening against him, but confident that he had chosen wisely between the evils; never regretting his choice, but greatly saddened at the need for such a choice.

After he had put into the covenant the amendments suggested by the group associated with the League to Enforce Peace, certain members of the group cabled other suggested amendments, and the President balked. He could have secured them, but his suspicion was aroused. He felt and told his friends that if he accepted these, there would be others and others and still others interminably. And so he decided to go back to America and fight it out, even at the risk of losing those Republican allies who had worked with him upon the amendments when he had returned from Paris in February. This was probably at the bottom of his decision in Paris to reject the second set of so-called Root-Hughes-Taft reservations which they cabled to him.

When the treaty finally was ready with its provision for years of vassalage for Germany, and with the broad gesture of humiliation for the vanquished which France needed to wipe out the stain of 1870, Wilson accepted it because it held the League of Nations within it.

At the end of the Conference, he had to take a bad treaty. He would not present the amendments which might have made it possible for him to succeed with the United States Senate, perhaps because to secure those amendments he would have had to take further undesirable clauses in the treaty, and perhaps because he was suspicious of the good faith of those who presented the further amendments.

Whether he believed in the treaty or whether he knew its weaknesses, no one knows. It is unthinkable that he should have been blind to its faults. And it was unstatesmanlike that he should not have been candid with the American people about those faults. He chose to defend it entirely in order to get through its Siamese Twin, the Covenant of the League of Nations. The signatures of some of his own Commissioners to the treaty were secured under protest. The world was disillusioned with its faults. It would have been easy to lay the treaty and the covenant before the Senate as a bad lot, but the best he could do; but that would have been to confess weakness, to admit failure, something Wilson could not do. He was schooled in the counsel of perfection and could give his approval to nothing less than perfection. So he brought home the perfect treaty and the impeccable covenant, and laid them both before his countrymen as the work of God. But the United States Senate, which had to accept or reject the treaty and the covenant, even before the Senators began to consider the documents, had other and significant ideas about this perfect work of God.

This is not the heroic attitude. It was indeed a sad anticlimax to the high emprise which carried us into the War; yet it was the only result that a man of Wilson's reserve, of his hermit habit, could bring out of the clash between the ideals of the old world and of the new, between the realities of the War and his vision of the War. Another man, deeply emotional, capable of dramatizing a situation, of illuminating the dark tragedy of the struggle with a lively and lovable personality, perhaps might have done better; certainly he would have done differently. But history has no "ifs." The record is the record.

Yet this also should be in the record, and Americans always must read with pride that their President more than any other man is responsible for giving the world its first draft of a real League of Nations. If he had not come to Europe, the idea would have been abandoned. Clemenceau publicly declared in January that he was for the old-fashioned idea of the balance of power. The British understanding to which he referred seemed to imply that Great Britain also favored a balance of power. Italy and Japan had no other thought. The League of Nations, before President Wilson came to Europe, was a pacifist's dream — iridescent, but also evanescent. He made it real. For it he gave everything — even his good name. He sacrificed profoundly for the idea, and saved it to the world.

Time is long, and the deep aspirations of men will wait. But our American democracy may be honestly proud that it has raised up one who put into the hearts of all the world, because we set him high where he could speak to all the world, the aspiration of our hearts for the coming of a peace of good will among men of good will.

CHAPTER XX

HOW WILSON LOST THE PEACE

WOODROW WILSON lost the peace because it could not have been won; not the peace he visioned. Humanity was not ready for it. We Americans like to think that we were ready for it. In the sense that we were not bitten by the dogs of old nationalist enmities and suspicions, this is true. But we had our jingoes as well as did Europe. And our jingoes preferred the peace of the militarist to the peace of the conference table. So we joined the jingoes of Europe. The common people of the world were ready highly to aspire with Wilson. But they were not wise enough to choose leaders of his kind. Europe had scores of leaders. But Europe listened less patiently to these gentle leaders than they gave ear to Wilson. When it came to the surrender of their ancient prejudices, the peoples of Europe responded to their intriguing leaders, even as Americans responded to their irreconcilables. This must be said always in the defense of President Wilson's apparent failure in the struggle for a peace based upon reason rather than upon force. His peace implied more good will in the heart of the white race than two thousand years of Christian philosophy had been able to put there.

Yet, when that is said in extenuation of President Wilson's temporary futility, we must not withhold the fact that he might have attained much more of his ideal if he himself had been able to exercise the very good will and comradery which the world lacked and which in all conscience he should have had. In Europe he followed grudgingly the advice of Colonel House, and wrote a letter inviting the Foreign Relations Committee of the United States Senate to dine at the White House on his return and hear his exposition of the treaty and the covenant; chiefly the covenant. A majority of the committee was Republican. And a majority of the Republican members was instinctively against the treaty, partly because of training, temperament, or an environing constituency, and partly because of a profound personal dislike of the President. He knew it; the committeemen knew it. It was the Republicans who circulated the round robin in March, published just before his second sailing for Europe, which served notice on the world that the Senate would not accept the Covenant of the League of Nations "in its present form." That round robin the President regarded as a challenge and an insult. It was characteristic of him to take insults personally and to give them impersonally. Rancor in him begot rancor in others. The rancor in the Republican members of Congress and in the Republican majority in the Foreign Relations Committee was the direct result of his own blundering in asking for a partisan Congress. His blundering did not chasten him. It enraged him.

He formally laid the treaty before the United States Senate at the meeting of the Foreign Relations Committee at the White House in June, 1919. That meeting, which should have been a time and a place for conciliation and concession, became only a slaughter-house of what small good will there was between the President and his senatorial enemies. He handled himself badly, as he always did in the presence of his adversaries. His single-track mind was inadequate to carry his anger and his intelligence. He became confused as he did in the presence of the unfriendly trustees at Princeton. He told them there in Princeton that he had never seen the West brochure advertising the proposed Graduate School, when as a matter of fact he prepared the preface and probably read the proof on the book. He told the Senate Committee that he had never seen the secret treaties, when as a matter of fact there is documentary evidence to the contrary. He was not lying in either case. He was confused before what he regarded as injustice, thwarted in what he considered the execution of a Divine purpose. He could not throw down his bat and leave the field; he had to stand, agitated, hectored, ireful. And his single-track mind did not carry his memory straight. His cause did not sustain him. That it was attacked unjustly by pettifogging or by ignorance aroused and unleashed all the devils of malice which he commonly kept chained in his heart. And while they barked out in biting sarcasm and impotent rage, his cause disintegrated into a quarrel. As a debater at long range, with his books at hand and all his impedimenta of war around him, he was a valiant knight. As a speaker dealing with great principles, before the masses, he had no equal in his time. Roosevelt was nearer his equal than any other contemporary. But at close quarters Roosevelt's sense of humor, his capacity to stand beside himself and grin at his own antics, thereby correcting them, was his saving grace. That grace comes to a man only when he has served a boy's apprenticeship in the jungle combats of his race; an apprenticeship which Tommy Wilson skipped. So in personal quarrels Woodrow Wilson failed. In his contest for the ratification of the treaty which would have entered America into the League of Nations, President Wilson had to follow the curve of his life, even as Roosevelt had to follow his curve when he met the friends of Taft in Chicago. Wilson's intolerance for opposition often made him raze a great cause into a private quarrel; Roosevelt had some Titanic sense of drama which enabled him to dignify a petty quarrel into a great cause.

When the Senate Foreign Relations Committee left the White House that June night in 1919, the President knew that he was facing the conflict of his life. He wrote Colonel House a rather formal letter to tell him that the meeting had turned out as the President had feared and expected it would; perhaps even as he secretly hoped it would; such was his lust for battling when it was once unleashed. Always in the Senate from the beginning to the end, a majority — not always the constitutional two thirds, but always a working majority — existed for the League of Nations with certain mild reservations suggested by those who held the middle ground. This majority was made up of Wilsonian Democrats and Republicans who believed in the ideals of peace which the President had expounded during the War. But the President made it plain in midsummer of 1919 that he would accept no amendments or reservations to the Covenant of the League of Nations.

That was the President's last great blunder. On his part he felt bound in honor to his associates around the conference table at Paris to bring America into the League without reservations. Possibly — though maybe even that inference is unfair — he had his pride in sending back the Covenant of the League of Nations as he and they had agreed upon it. Whatever was his motive, his experience should have taught him to distrust his combative instincts. He was not in form to go into the arena with the beasts at Ephesus. He had been suffering from a progressive decay of his spiritual strength — probably the reflex of a physical weakness which was approaching rapidly. The first surrender of his idealism when he consented to the Japanese occupation of Siberia caused some loss of his quick sense of justice. His surrender to the politicians of the National Committee and of the Congressional Committee in the autumn of 1918, when they asked for the letter requesting a Democratic Congress, showed that either his physical resistance or his spiritual sense was weakening. His failure to surround himself with men of his own political size and mental stature when he went to Paris indicated again either a physical shrinking from strangers or an insensibility to his moral obligations. His return to Paris, after he had lived six weeks in the low environment of the Conference, and knew how futile were his high weapons of reason and altruism against his adversaries, denoted a growing bluntness of his once acute prescience. His surrender upon the

Shantung proposal, though it cost him agony, did not leave him strength to renounce the whole miserable business and come home.

And when he got home, he was not the man who challenged the Kaiser in 1915 and routed him and the Devil and all his works in 1918.

The story of Woodrow Wilson's physical disintegration some day may be written and understood in the light of all he aspired: how in those summer days of 1919, the Philistines laid hold upon him, "put out his eyes, and brought him down to Gaza; and he did grind there in the prison house." And Samson "wist not that the Lord was departed from him."

He fretted through the summer of 1919, losing ground. Senator after Senator deserted the covenant. No gay persiflage, no cheerful and engaging stories came from the White House indicating that the President was willing to regard the contest as one in which give-and-take may prevail. The charm of Woodrow Wilson, which made him the most popular professor in Princeton, the charm which he showed to the people of New Jersey in his first campaign, the bright and engaging manner which he maintained in the campaign of 1912, the rollicking Irish spirit that had taken the United States and put it behind him in a contest with the plutocracy during the first years of his first term — that was gone. For all that the people knew, in 1919 there might have been no Irish blood in Woodrow Wilson. He was grim. The high purpose, which had held him through all the years in a divinely beautiful faith, became by some alchemy of his grimness translated into obstinacy, into mean and petty stubbornness, in the popular eyes. The people had, curiously enough, from him and the Senators, each giving it out equally, a sense of quarrel rather than of cause. Colonel House came home from Europe sick in body, taken off the steamer on a stretcher, but vigorous enough in mind.

In August, 1919, the President, discouraged with defections in his own party in the Senate, and stung by the gibes of the Republicans, decided to go to the American people, making what he called "the appeal to Cæsar." Physically he was failing. His doctors advised against the trip. He was restless and irritable, but burning with his passion to convince the people. He believed that he could do with the United States in peace what he had done with the world in war. But he forgot that the disillusion which was the natural reaction of any war had changed the attitude of the people toward the idealism with which he would have conjured. The liberals of America who had been Wilson's strength saw in the Treaty of Versailles a reversion to the old type of European diplomacy. It was shot through with the rapine of defenseless peoples, permeated with the greed of victorious nations for power and spoil of war. It was green with jealousies and purple with revenge, that treaty, and it stood as a great material shadow between Wilson and the idealism which he would have preached to the people. Under its shadow they were cynical. He failed to find the quick and stimulating response which he had hoped to encounter when he went to the people.

Probably even then they were not convinced against him. In his audiences were thousands of Democrats who traditionally followed their leader; also thousands of Republicans still holding in their hearts some remnant of the ideals which urged them into the crusade which made the War in America an adventure in idealism; perhaps unreal, perhaps tawdry, certainly discouraging at times in its bigotry, but still withal a beautiful adventure. But as a beautiful adventure it was fading into the past. Wilson could not make magic with his words as he made it but a year before. The man, the subject, the occasion, had shrunken. So after a few days' journey out of Washington, he became bitter. He magnified the evidence in the popular mind that he was taking a quarrel, not a cause, to the people, by his words at St. Louis, by his vituperation in the Northwest, by his scolding everywhere. When he came to Denver, he was sleeping for only a few hours, possibly a few minutes, every night. His digestion was working badly. Even then his doctor counseled him to turn back, or to slow down and rest a few days. But his will was stronger than his flesh, and he went on. A train hurrying across the continent pestered by a thousand intruders, always thrusting the sense of time and action into one's consciousness, is no place for a man with broken nerves to restore his equilibrium. This train, which carried the President through the country, carried with him several carloads of reporters and all sorts of publicity devices. He might as well have lived in a glass cage in the dome of the Capitol so far as serenity, security, and privacy were concerned. Every hour turned the screws of his nerves tighter and tighter.

In Los Angeles he found a note from Mary Hulbert, and he and Mrs. Wilson went to see her. She told him what she had written to him some time before, that the whispering campaign which had connected their names so cruelly in 1916 had resulted, during the War, when spies were busy with nothing to do, in a thousand annoyances to her, invasion of her privacy by agents from the Federal Department of Justice of his own administration; that yellow newspapers had haunted and hounded her, and that she was troubled and needed his help. Naturally what she said shocked him, and he was in no condition to stand any shock. Also he found her with her money gone, her son ill, and trouble beating upon her. The butterfly of Bermuda, gay and beautiful, with the quick and lovely mind, the agile, sprite-like soul, the gracious and charming heart, was all chilled, saddened, beset with fear — the butterfly in autumn. Her plight would have smitten a harder heart than his. So he left Los Angeles puzzled and worried, with no resilience in his mind or spirit, and no reserve in his body to reinforce his tired nerves.

Turning eastward, he found himself one night at Pueblo crying in his speech. Tumulty had been advising against the impatient attitude which had crept into his speeches; the irritation which the President had manifested with the willful "pygmy men" of the Senate, and Tumulty had advised putting a little emotion into the speeches. "More of the sob-stuff, Governor," quoth Joe.

Wilson's tears, which came in his speech in Pueblo almost in a flood, showed upon what a thin texture of resistance he was walking. The night after the Pueblo speech he could not sleep. In the evening, east of Pueblo, they stopped the train, and the President and Mrs. Wilson walked for a time upon a dusty, white country road. His temperature rose. As he slept under a narcotic, his mouth drooled. His body testified in many ways to an impending crash. His next engagement was at Wichita, Kansas. Admiral Grayson, his doctor, and Mrs. Wilson ordered him to cancel it. The train stopped on a siding near Wichita, and then rode around the town. The reporters learned the truth; that the President was unable to rise to the daily struggle with his engagements. The train turned eastward, and swiftly with drawn blinds, hardly stopping except to change engines, hurried across the continent. In two days the train came into Washington.

Probably he had had some premonitory warning that an apoplectic stroke was pending. But courageously he stepped out of the car, courageously walked down the long platform into the station, and bravely took his carriage for the White House, greeting the people who gathered along the way in his old manner. But his face was haggard, his hands moved heavily, his eyes were overbright, and his smile was set and ghastly. They put him to bed, where he rested badly. He saw no one except Mrs. Wilson, Admiral Grayson, the doctors whom Admiral Grayson had summoned, and occasionally Tumulty. So he lay for days, and then in late September came the thing which had been sending its warnings.

A stroke, affecting his left side, fell upon him one morning, and another messenger of evil came to

Woodrow Wilson. They had been crowding thick and fast, these messengers of evil tidings, since the first one came when Ellen Axson died. And now they left him stripped naked to his enemies. Gone was his glory, his power, his very strength. And he sat among the potsherds even as Job. Pain racked him, and he cried out against it because his nerves were aflame. A dozen years before, while the Roosevelt children were playing on the south White House lawn, their balls began breaking windows in its lower levels. Dr. Rixey and young Dr. Grayson put bars there to save the glass. For the first time men noticed these bars, and then, possibly because the President was in pain and it could not be concealed, and because of the natural predilection of the human mind to imagine vain things, and the human tongue to translate imaginings into lies, men said that these bars held a mad President, and the Senate began to buzz. The pain fell away from him, but left him weak. The treaty still was pending. The broken man in the White House had to see it slipping farther and farther away.

It was then that Colonel House turned to him. The correspondence between him and the President had slowed down during the spring and summer. "Affectionately yours" had become "Sincerely" at the close of the letters. As autumn opened, the

Colonel, regaining his strength, felt coming with it a keen desire to help his friend. He knew what was happening at the White House. He saw, from a perspective which the President could not gain, how easily the whole problem of the treaty and the covenant might be solved, the tangled affair unsnarled. He realized no serious reason why he should not hurry to his friend's side. So he wrote a letter to the President in the old manner of affection and fellowship. He sent it to former Attorney-General Gregory and asked Mr. Gregory to hand it to Mrs. Wilson.

In the letter he made it plain that he desired to come to Washington to help; that he had certain fairly definite plans which he would like to try by which he hoped to get a favorable vote on the treaty and the covenant. He did not set forth his plans, but the letter breathed a fine chivalric spirit and came clearly from an unselfish and fraternal heart. He waited five days, then ten. No answer came. He wrote another letter, not quite so glowing with affection, but happy, cheerful, and hopeful, again offering to come. Again a week passed, two weeks, a month, and no answer came. The letters never were acknowledged.

It may be of some passing interest to set down the plan which Colonel House had in view, but which he did not disclose in his letters. The plan provided for a message to the Senate declaring in effect that the President was under obligations to his fellow counselors in Paris to present the treaty as it was, without amendment; that he could accept no amendment, but calling attention to the fact that the Senate of its own motion could do what it would with the treaty and the covenant, accept it, reject it, or amend it; and that the Senate's conclusions would be returned to the constituted European authorities for their action. Then Colonel House felt that it would be wise for the President to resign in order to remove any vague suggestion or remote contention that his own personal fortunes were tied with the treaty; using his illness as an excuse for resigning, leaving the whole matter to Vice-President Marshall. Colonel House believed that this attitude would entirely end the quarrel and restore the Cause. He felt that at the same time, by its self-effacement, the resignation would endear the President in his illness to the United States and ennoble him before the world. The plan was never submitted to the President. And neither by message nor by any indirection of word or deed did he ever hear from his friend again. House had reached the scrap-heap!

It was the Woodrow who lay on that sick-bed during that long autumn, refusing hint of compromise.

Once two Senators, Senator Fall and Senator Hitchcock, called upon an official mission. The mission was to inquire into the sanity of the President. Whatever else might have been wrong with Woodrow Wilson, his mind was clear. Senator Fall was of the Republican persuasion, and later made a sad exit from politics. He was convinced that the President was crazy. Hitchcock was a Democrat and a friend, and knew the truth. When they called first, Mrs. Wilson and Admiral Grayson hesitated about letting them into the sick-room. But Senator Fall made it very clear, and Senator Hitchcock corroborated him, that many members of the Senate believed the President's mind had failed and they were expected to come back with the truth. When this situation was presented to the President, for a moment he was furious, and then the humor of it got him, and he asked Admiral Grayson to bring them in. For half an hour they saw upon the bed, with his face twisted and his left side limp, a sick man and weak. But they had from Wilson thirty minutes of the gayest, blithest, sanest talk they had heard in months. He must have made a mighty effort to rise as he did. He gibed Fall about trying to get a war with Mexico to protect his local interests. He played gayly with Hitchcock in talk about the reservations, and generally embroidered the occasion with persiflage and repartee. No doubt was left in the senatorial minds when these men returned to their colleagues.

Nevertheless, after the stroke which fell in October, the world practically was shut off from Woodrow Wilson. All his life he had been afflicted with a mild Narcissus complex, desiring to see himself in everything, his views, his faith, the facts as he knew them. This complex did not hold him completely, but it stood in the wings of his consciousness always too ready to act. And when the public was shut away from him, he knew nothing of the truth about public sentiment in the country. It was as though the curtain had fallen upon him with the roar of applause which greeted his speech at Pueblo always reverberating in his heart.

When he decided to reject any reservations to the treaty, his ears were full of that applause. He thought it represented public sentiment. His devoted wife, who was surrounding him with every physical comfort and every spiritual easement, was not trained in public affairs. She was almost as isolated as he. Admiral Grayson had no access to the truth about public opinion, no means of interpreting the facts, no great interest in the clamor outside the sick-room. Tumulty saw his chief rarely, with Mrs. Wilson standing at the head of the bed to shake her head when Tumulty broached a subject that might irritate the President. It was easier for those about him to hold to his face the mirror of his own conception of public opinion than to irritate him with the story of a gradual, inevitable change in the American attitude to the League of Nations. It was a statesman's job to convince Woodrow Wilson that the jingoism which follows war had alienated the people from the generous pacifist President of Princeton. And the only statesman who could have told him, he had put away when he banished House. The autumn of 1919 deepened into winter, and his friends outside saw with fear and consternation that the President was determined stubbornly to face the incoming Congress with an immovable determination that the treaty should stand or fall as it was. But he called no counsel about him and saw few visitors. Moreover, he was desperately sick, sick in mind and perhaps in heart. Each day he could consider a few letters, but only a few. Lansing was dismissed. The President did not even sign or formulate the letter of dismissal; merely consented to it. He had appointed Lansing in the kindness of his heart with no special political reason and without much consideration. The President knew he would be his own Secretary of State as he had been under Bryan, and to him letting Lansing go was much like changing doormen in the State Department, a casual thing. The few decisions which were checked up to him every day by Mrs. Wilson or Admiral Grayson, he made quickly and, under the circumstances, well, but he had no strength for more. One day, in the spring of 1920, Senator Hitchcock came to him to discuss obliquely and tentatively, as he must, the situation in the Senate. Hitchcock was the Democratic leader in charge of the treaty and the Covenant of the League of Nations. He saw the face of a broken man, withered and weary, on the pillow. The old exuberance was gone, even in semblance. Hitchcock explained as gently as he could that some concessions might tempt the Republican Senators to accept the treaty; elaborating deftly, without wearying the sick man, just what concessions Hitchcock thought should be made. Then he said:

"Mr. President, perhaps the time has come to extend to Lodge and his followers the olive branch in the interests of an equitable settlement."

The sick man closed his eyes, shut his mouth, and was silent for a moment. Then he replied in the deadly voice which closed the episode:

"Let Lodge extend the olive branch."

The winter wore away. Democratic leadership in Congress had not been fostered under Wilson. He was the Premier, the legislative leader as well as the President. He was, indeed, more Premier than President, and devoted more energy and keener interest to Congress than he did to his executive work, which often irked him. So his party in Congress, and particularly in the Senate, was without strong leadership. When the fight upon the treaty and the covenant came, no friendly hand was at the wheel. The treaty and the covenant drifted on the rocks. It was apparent in the early winter of 1919 and '20 that, unless the President accepted the mild reservations urged by the Republicans, the covenant would be defeated. A strong group of his friends, some of them men who had stood by him during his Princeton days, all of them men who had been with him during his whole political career, signed a letter asking him to accept these reservations. He refused. In March, 1920, the covenant was defeated, but it was merely a parliamentary defeat. There were votes and to spare for the covenant with the reservations. On the final vote, fifteen irreconcilable Republicans voted "no" on the covenant, and twenty-four Wilson Democrats, who were for the covenant, but objected to the reservations. Twenty-three Democrats stood for the covenant with reservations and thirty-four Republicans stood for the covenant with reservations. A word from Wilson would have united these forty-seven Democrats and thirty-four

Republicans, thus producing the constitutional majority necessary to adopt the amended covenant. It was a strange freak of Wilsonian leadership that allowed the covenant to be defeated by twenty-four votes of his own adherents.

In the White House, during the spring and summer of 1920, the President, who was gradually regaining his strength, saw the failure of the treaty with consternation. He felt that it was a plot of wicked men and not the natural result of a leaderless party following the ruthless will of a shattered President. Those were days of self-searching and self-questioning with Wilson; terrible days, full of remorse, full of recrimination, but never without the sustenance of a great faith. Job sitting among the potsherds was still able to cry out in exultation: "I know that my Redeemer liveth." He did not realize how far the country and the world had been carried by the currents of hate and suspicion and fear that hurried humanity away from his ideals.

The Democratic National Convention assembled in San Francisco. He felt that he might have a complimentary nomination, which he would, of course, refuse. It was not seriously considered. He sent to the convention a plank calling for a modification of the Volstead Act to provide for light wines and beer. It was ignored; not even presented. William Gibbs

McAdoo, former Secretary of the Treasury, and son-in-law of the President, could have been nominated for the presidency if Wilson had said the word. All one day the friends of McAdoo, who was the leading candidate before the convention, besieged the White House with long-distance telephones across the continent and telegrams asking for some word from Wilson, not in public, but in private, that would take the New York delegation to McAdoo. No word came. The White House was sealed. As it had been picketed against Colonel House, so it was closed to the appeal of McAdoo's friends. No one knew why.

In the autumn, the President's general health was better. His left side never recovered; he could not stand erect upon his withered leg. Sometimes he went out for a drive, and the people saw a prematurely old, gray man, with a lean, almost wizened face; a bright-eyed old man smiling automatically, trying to hide the left side of his face. His public appearances were rare. A few friends were admitted at the White House, but they knew he was not able to discuss large matters seriously. So even then he did not know the truth about public sentiment in his country. It came with crushing force in the election returns of 1920. The President had assumed as a matter of course that the country at the election of

1920 would rebuke his enemies by electing a Democratic President and a Democratic Congress who would immediately adopt the treaty and the covenant as President Wilson had presented them to his country. The defeat of Cox, the Democratic presidential candidate, and the return of a Republican Congress, fell upon Wilson as a thunderbolt. But it did not break his courage; it did not weaken his faith. Never for one hour did he doubt the ultimate success of his cause.

"You can't fight God!" he cried to his visitors — Job's comforters who came to him in his affliction.

"We are winning, Cecil, we are winning; hold fast, don't compromise," he said to Lord Robert Cecil, who came to see him in those dark hours.

To Ray Stannard Baker, his devoted friend and wise interpreter, he said: "We're right, Baker, we're right; that's enough; don't fear the outcome, we're right."

And if he put his curse upon Lodge in those days and upon the fifteen irreconcilables in the Senate, they were the good, round curses of a man who knew the joy of a quenchless hatred. His left cheek was withered by the stroke of fate, but he never turned the other cheek

He was able to go to his office in the White House

in those latter days of his administration and to do a little work.

March the fourth, 1921, they helped him painfully down the steps of the White House into the carriage with Senator Harding, the President-elect. The two chatted gayly as they rode through the throng to the Capitol, where the inauguration was to take place. The Senator told the President a funny story about elephants, and he told the Senator another story or two that he had heard or read in a book, and they came to the Capitol. He had a number of bills to sign. He went to the President's room near the Senate Chamber. Senator Knox came to the room and invited Wilson to come to the Chamber to witness the inauguration of the Vice-President. The Chamber was on a level a few steps higher than the President's room. He explained to Senator Knox that he could not get up the steps, and added, with a feint at gayety: "The Senate has thrown me down; but I don't want to fall down!" Senator Lodge appeared to notify the President that the Senate was ready to adjourn. Woodrow Wilson gazed at thin air as Lodge spoke. No hint of gayety touched his voice as he replied, turning away and addressing thin air: "I have no further communication to make" — and stumbled away on his cane.

He did not stay for the inauguration, but hurried

away from the Capitol in a closed carriage. Where he was recognized in the crowd he was cheered, but the crowd was not his crowd, the cheers must have been perfunctory. But in the street before his new home when he drove to it with Mrs. Wilson, a great multitude of his friends assembled to greet him. All day long these faithful followers stood before the new house. But it was not an ovation for a coming man; it was hail and farewell for a passing hero.

And so ended the path of glory which Tommy Wilson saw far ahead; which Woodrow, his legatee and successor, trod so proudly, so valiantly, carrying a high vision in his noble soul.

If it were not for the world's tragedies, men would lose their faith!

CHAPTER XXI

WAITING FOR THE CURTAIN

THE WILSONS went from the White House to their new home in "S" Street, a rather good house on a rather good street in Northwest Washington. There for nearly three years Woodrow Wilson and Edith Bolling, his wife, lived as private citizens of the Republic. The good taste which marked Woodrow Wilson all his life for a gentleman, stood him in good stead in those days. For of all the positions in this country which strain one's tact and intelligence, the position of an ex-President of the United States is most difficult. To lag superfluous on the stage and yet not interrupt the other player's lines nor get in the way of the action about one, and still to hold one's interest and self-respect in untoward circumstances, is a difficult assignment. Yet the Wilsons met their public problems with simple, kind-hearted directness. Of course, to a large minority, perhaps to a majority of Americans, Wilson was a hero when he left the White House. His party for the most part still honored his name and respected his passing leadership. And millions outside his party revered the ideals for which he stood so bravely during his public career. From time to time, upon holidays and in public ceremonies, demonstrations for him occurred upon the streets of Washington and before his home in "S" Street. He received these tokens of public affection with a courteous grace which neither emphasized nor minimized their importance. In his public appearances, broken though he was with his left side paralyzed, he seemed to revert in character back to those gracious golden days in his thirties and forties when as a young Princeton professor he caught and held the hearts of the boys — the most popular man on the campus.

Within the walls of his home probably he was not so happy as he seemed outside. The weight of his affliction must have been a terrible burden to him. He knew well that his "first-class mind" was not up to its old agility and strength. Miss Ida M. Tarbell, who for ten years had been his good friend and supporter, called once or twice to see him; once to urge him into some sort of literary enterprise — a "Primer of Democracy" or something of the sort — and he let her know very gently and sweetly that he did not dare to try it. Once he wrote a short article for the "Atlantic Monthly" and sent it unsolicited. It lacked the distinction which he knew it would have had in another time. He never wrote again. His nervous strength limited him to one or two callers a day. With those he was cordial and seemed almost gay at times. James Kerney brought his gay Irish presence to the house in "S" Street and the two "micks" chuckled over the turns of the Trenton game. They recalled Joe Tumulty and his festive ways. And when Kerney had gone, Wilson wrote a letter suggesting Joe as a candidate for United States Senator — so vivid did the color of the other days come back.

To his older and dearer friends he liked to talk of his father, the Reverend Joseph Ruggles Wilson, and the hard, sound Presbyterian doctrine that came to him out of the home in the South. If his nerves, his brain, and his mind were worn by the ten years' struggle through which he had come, his intrepid soul still stood defiant in its militant faith. The self-questioning and doubt which those three years of waiting brought to him never shook the fundamentals of his life's belief in God and man. With Ray Stannard Baker and with the Bishop of the Cathedral at Washington, he liked to speculate somewhat in the old Princetonian way about religion. He was no fundamentalist. His own salvation did not concern him — that was settled with his calling and election; but the social salvation of humanity, through an approach to just relations among men, deeply moved and interested him. Near him was a Bible with well-thumbed passages which refreshed his soul. In his room Edith Bolling had kept all the mementoes he had cherished, of the old life in Princeton. There were two photographs of Ellen Axson, and her paintings adorned the house. One of the many times when Stockton Axson came for a while to chat and gas, something as they used to sit in the golden afternoons in the Princeton days when the old Doctor had been with them, Axson glanced up at a landscape on the wall:

"I don't seem to remember whose work that is."

And his host said: "Why, that is Ellen's."

"I didn't realize," said her brother, "how professional her work had become."

"It is professional," nodded Woodrow Wilson proudly, and they fell to talking of the days at Lyme, Connecticut. Stockton Axson and Woodrow Wilson spent many hours conjuring up the old familiar scenes as they sat in the "S" Street house.

The world outside whirled on. The ideals for which he had given his strength apparently were trampled underfoot amid sneers and contumely. Those surface bubbles — popular jokes — were made of things sacred to him. Politicians, who read superficial signs, thought it smart to jeer at ideals which he had ennobled. He had to live to see everything that he had held high and holy reviled by the governing majority of his country. It was a bitter curse that fate put upon him. The sores of Job could not have burned with greater agony than did this spiritual humiliation of Woodrow Wilson burn in his heart in those days of 1921, '22, and '23. But those days with their infamy passed over him as a breath of wind that did not flicker the even-flaming candle of his devotion and faith. How well those long-consecrated generations of Calvinism had poured their iron faith into every chamber of his soul! Voiceless to refute the day's sophistries and the calumnies of the passing hour that covered his ideals with ignominy, powerless to stop noisy currents which, others thought, were sweeping over his life's work, he moved through his little routine of the day serene and, in so far as a man broken, impotent, and down may be happy in the midst of alarms, his spirit flaunted its gay banner and knew no inner grief. America had never seen before so inspiring a spectacle, so triumphant a climax to a bitter tragedy.

Every physical care and comfort surrounded him. He often went to Keith's Theater when the bill changed, and two strong doormen gently helped him to his seat. The bright vaudeville cheered him, and he never missed the twinkle of a pretty pair of heels. He kept an allowance going to old Dave Bryant, of

Wilmington, that had continued through the years; not much, but something to remind old Dave of the better days. During the White House years this allowance had never ceased, and sometimes an overcoat or a suit went with it for which Dave had occasionally refused a king's ransom from curiosity hunters. And in the last days his mind may have been on Dave and the Wilmington scenes.

Edith Bolling Wilson could make him smile to the last hour of his conscious life by the buoyancy of her presence. Her arms were almost literally about him as he went down through those last weeks slowly into the valley of the shadow.

For six months he had been growing weaker. Armistice Day, 1923, a crowd gathered uptown in Dupont Circle. Joe Tumulty had hired a "scratch" band, and Victor Murdock headed a procession that walked out to "S" Street. It was not the élite of Washington, nor the elect of the Government, but the simple people, department clerks, young boys and girls, a few straggling colored people on the edge of the crowd, which was not in marching order, but swept along the street, some on the sidewalks, some in the center of the pavement. Near the head of the procession was an old man who looked like Uncle Sam, a kindly, familiar old gentleman who lent his presence to any town procession no matter what its

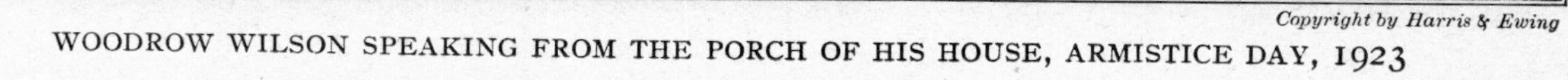

Copyright by Harris & Ewing

WOODROW WILSON SPEAKING FROM THE PORCH OF HIS HOUSE, ARMISTICE DAY, 1923

import. As the crowd came nearer to "S" Street, came closer to Wilson's home, the people of the faubourg, some of the Really Best People, joined it. The ex-service men in the crowd were placed at the head of the procession. Respectfully it gathered about the door of the Wilson house on "S" Street. When the band had ceased playing, the expectant eyes of the crowd saw an old man come out leaning heavily upon his cane. Supporting him stood Senator Carter Glass, of Virginia, who read a prepared introductory address. The old man beside the Senator lifted his face, and they saw the kindly smile that Wilson was wont to bestow upon the populace in his happier days, the last gleam of the lamp from the hall of the Irish Kings. Amid the cheers were tears in the eyes that saw the waning smile. He asked about the young men in front of the door, learned they were ex-service men, and then his eyes filled up. Wilson began to speak, apparently thinking that the whole crowd was of ex-service men. He recited his speech carefully in a voice unexpectedly clear. Then he paused.

Around the doorway were gathered a number of his old friends. The windows about him were filled with former associates. Senator Swanson, of Virginia, not to be out of the picture with his colleague, Senator Glass, supporting the President, was conspicuously leaning over the sash. When the ex-President paused, he said: "That's all I can do." The crowd broke into sturdy, supporting cheers. He seemed to have finished. The police were busy whacking camera-men — dragging a snap-shooter from an elm tree opposite. The band seized the silence. They were about to break away when he began again. The band had to be squelched. Then he finished his speech. It was not a particularly notable utterance. It had none of the old fire, none of the appealing fervor that the War President had kindled, but it held high and unshaken the torch of his faith. He smiled again, waved his free hand, and so turned almost jauntily from the crowd forever, to face the messenger who had been calling him through his declining years.

CHAPTER XXII

REVIEWING A DOZEN YEARS

If one fixes the date of Woodrow Wilson's entrance into politics at September 15, 1910, when he was nominated for Governor of New Jersey, we may say that he lived in American politics for thirteen years and four months. Thirteen was his favorite number; his lucky number. It was one of his few Irish superstitions to fondle the number thirteen in his life. In 1913 he became President. There were thirteen letters to his name, Woodrow Wilson. His automobile in Paris had a number which added up and made thirteen. He counted Friday the thirteenth a day of double luck. Thirteen years in public life is the shortest career that any American President has had. And when one realizes that eight of those thirteen years were passed in the White House, and nearly three of them as an ex-President, one comprehends dramatically how swiftly he rose in those two years which took him as a college president and landed him in the presidential race of a major party in a successful contest for the presidency. Nothing like it in our history before had been recorded.

The years that he spent in the house in "S"

Street, in Washington, as an ex-President, were lonely years in spite of the occasional parades, processions, and pilgrimages that used to gather about his door. Conclaves of the lowly always, never affected with pomp and circumstance, were these all but impromptu gatherings that came to pay homage to him. Yet, during those years in "S" Street he was still in politics, still walked, a powerful figure, through this world. His cause did not languish with his body. In every important political convention, legislature, congress, parliament, or high conference, Wilson sat in spirit. When the United States, by what seemed like a rebuking majority, elected Harding over Cox, Wilson's enemies were gleeful. For, said they, "this ends the League of Nations." President Harding, in an official utterance, excoriated the League of Nations. President Coolidge wrote in his first message: "The League of Nations is a closed incident." The United States maintained an elaborate fiction that it was not associating with the League of Nations. Yet Woodrow Wilson sat by and saw his country coöperating with the League, and saw it take world leadership, coöperative with the League at every necessary point. The spirit of Wilson lived through all this clamor and rejoicing at the passing of the Woodrow spirit. While the body slowly lost its vigor and the mind its power in the house in "S" Street, the Wilson spirit remained untouched by time. Few men have risen to power so quickly as Wilson. Probably no man has ever lived in the flesh, helpless and all but physically dead, to see his own immortality. That was one of the major blessings which the high gods showered on this man as a reward for his good service. This blessing sustained his faith to the last.

But, of course, in those lonely, questioning hours in the house in "S" Street, when, in spite of an occasional flare-up of ambition in which he thought, perhaps, he might return to politics, or might go back to be a college president, and then in the depths of his heart knew better, there must have been hours when he called a vain roll and heard the responding voices of dear friends call "absent." Dr. Hibben, of Princeton, was one of those who answered "absent." Colonel House, whom he had addressed many times in letters, "My dearest friend," answered "absent." Mary Hulbert Peck, who had given him such joy with her nimble wit and beautiful, elusive spirit, answered "absent." John Bellamy, of the piny woods — "absent." Did Woodrow Wilson ask himself why, and did he realize how often he had said of a passing acquaintance, some possible candidate for his consideration, "I picked his brains"? Maybe likewise he picked men's hearts. Maybe he got at the best of them, learned their tricks and their manners, saw their secret ways which delighted him for a time and then bored him. Perhaps it was not his temper after all, nor his stern Scotch standards of conduct that alienated his friends. Perhaps deeply inside of him, when he knew that a friend no longer eluded him and so no longer delighted him, his impatience, an outer sentinel of his heart, closed the door.

There came a time, before he left the White House, when he was brusque with Tumulty and seemed to take no joy of him. After he left the White House, Tumulty sometimes called at "S" Street, for he was a faithful soul, one of your loyal Irish who may blunder, but never betray. After a visit in "S" Street, one day, Tumulty went to a public dinner and delivered some irrelevant and innocuous message which might possibly have committed the ex-President to the presidential candidacy of Cox, who had been defeated in 1920 so ingloriously. Whereupon, in due course, yet not before Tumulty had pleaded and tried to stay the blow,[1] Wilson gave such a bitter, cruel lashing, by public letter, to Tumulty that all Wilson's friends were ashamed beyond words. Then Tumulty was upon the "absent" roll!

[1] See Correspondence in the Appendix.

One day in March, 1924, the writer of these lines sat in Tumulty's office and asked him about that episode. And Tumulty, replying, spoke for ten minutes or so, and what he said takes us back so far and so vividly into the thirteen years and four months of Woodrow Wilson's public career, that Tumulty's words may well be set down here just as they came, in the vernacular of his heart. To the question about the Cox episode, he answered:

Well, now, you see — well, I am going to tell you the whole story because, you see, it is hard to get it unless you know certain things. In 1909, I am a police court lawyer down in Jersey City — maybe a little better, but mostly that — and my father, he is pretty well-to-do, but there are five of us boys, and we have to get out for ourselves. And Little Bob Davis for one reason or another — maybe pop, I guess it was pop as a matter of fact — well, anyway, Little Bob Davis came to me and said: "Joe, I'm going to nominate you for the legislature."

And I was mighty proud, and, anyway, I had been reading Tom Lawson's articles about the terrible things the New Jersey laws were doing to people outside of New Jersey, so I was glad enough to get in and fight some of them. And one day I was going along the street and I saw a policeman beating the brains out of a man — him lying there unconscious and the cop leaning over beating him, and the women were all crowded around yelling, "Oh, my God!" every time he gave the poor bleeding head a whack and the men turning their heads away, and I jump in and say:

"Here, you damn brute, you can't do that."

And he says: "Shut up, or I'll beat you!"

And I say: "No, you won't!"

And he says: "Yes, I will!"

And I turned to the crowd and said: "Now, all of you are witnesses to what this fellow is doing. I want you all to show up in police court to-morrow morning, when I file a complaint against this officer."

And I passed my card around in the crowd and said: "I am Joseph P. Tumulty," and went away.

Well, that night I got home for supper and my wife hears a knock, and she is carrying Mary then, our oldest girl. And she says:

"It's a police captain." And was frightened.

And I say: "It's all right." And I went in the parlor where he was, and he says: "You're Joseph P. Tumulty?"

And I say: "Yes."

And he says: "Now, I hear you had a little misunderstanding with an officer."

I say: "Yes, he was beating up a poor devil."

And he says: "Yes. And I hear you're going to make complaint to-morrow morning."

And I say: "Yes."

And he says: "Now, I wouldn't do that; the officer is all right. He's a good man and a friend of mine, and all the boys like him, and you don't want to do that."

And I say: "Why?"

And he says: "Oh, you don't want to do that. If I was you I would forget it."

And I say: "No, I won't forget it. I'm coming down there to get him."

And he says: "You are, are you, young feller?"

And I say: "Yes!"

And he says: "You want to go to the legislature, don't you?"

And I say: "Yes."

And he says: "Well, we'll see that you don't."

And I say: "You will, will you?"

And he says: "You're damn right we will." And squinted his eyes at me and went out.

So about two months after that the convention was held, and pop had all his friends there to see me nominated, and just as we were going upstairs at the hall, why, Little Bob Davis comes alongside of me going up the steps, and says:

"Joe, I don't believe I can nominate you. You've had some row with the police and they're fighting you, and I ain't any too strong this year to take on any more fights than I have to."

And I say: "That's all right."

And he says: "You ain't sore, are you?"

And I remembered what pop always said, to take your medicine and wait, and I said:

"No — sure I'm not sore."

And he shook hands, and I said: "Next year's a year, anyway."

And he laughed, and I felt pretty bad for pop and all his friends up there in the gallery, but I didn't say anything, and went to my delegation. And there was a recess along in an hour or so, and I ran into Bob Davis again, and he grinned and says:

"Joe, you're sure you're not sore?"

And I say: "Sure! Why should I be sore?"

And I say: "I was right, and I know damn well if you knew —"

Well, to go back — that next morning after the police captain came to my house, I went down to police court, and there was that man with his head all wrapped up bigger'n a washtub, and he went square back on me and not a witness showed up. The police had fixed it.

And I say: "Bob, if you knew why I got in this row with the police, you'd nominate me, anyway."

And he laughed, and so I stood there and told him the whole story, and he said:

"Well, you're not sore, are you?"

And I say again: "Why, sure I'm not sore."

And he stopped and sucked his teeth a minute, and says:

"Well, I'm damned if I don't take a chance on you."

And so they nominated me, and I went all over the district telling that Tom Lawson story and all about the way they used the fellow-servant and contributory negligence to rob the injured workmen, and I won.

Well, when I got to the legislature I talked and worked and got my bill through the House, and Everett Colby was in the Senate and he got his bill through the Senate, and he comes to me and says:

"Joe, you got a bill and I got a bill for the same thing, and maybe your bill is a little better than mine, but the way things are lined up the politics of it is to get my bill through."

And I say: "Sure, what do I care? You go ahead and call it the Colby law."

And we did, and so I got to be interested in the Progressive movement and got aboard the Wilson bandwagon. And I'm a Roman Catholic, but Wilson liked me, and I guess Colonel House and Jim Kerney and the boys stood for me. Anyway, Wilson sent for me and offered to make me his private secretary, and I joined, though why I should I don't know, for the babies were coming right along and I was making $7500, and he could only give me $3500; but, anyway, I wanted to show him, a Presbyterian, how Roman Catholics could play the game, so I went along and we went through the New Jersey fight and I went with him to Washington, and you don't get the idea about him. He was the tenderest hearted man I ever knew; just like a baby. Now to show you; one time — my wife has had all these babies and finally had to have an operation; that was in Washington.

And the Governor says one day: "How is Mrs. Tumulty getting along?"

And I told him about her and about the operation, and he says: "Now, I've got a friend — he's the best surgeon in the country, and you go to him and he'll treat you right."

And I said: "All right."

And the operation was a success. And one day, oh, maybe six months after, he asked me how his friend treated me. And I said: "Oh, all right. He's going to sue me for twenty-five hundred dollars because I can only pay him a hundred dollars a month."

And he says: "Twenty-five hundred dollars!"

And I say: "Twenty-five hundred dollars."

And he put his head in his hands and his elbows on the desk and said: "Oh, my God! Is there no such thing as friendship?"

And he touched a button and sent for his personal stenographer, and in three minutes he had a check for twenty-five hundred dollars made out and made me take it. But I says no, and when he insisted, I took it and tore it up. For while I was only making thirty-five hundred dollars, I could have got pop to raise the money easy enough, but a man doesn't want to go to his father for things like that with four other brothers. Well, that's just to show you what kind of a man he was and how we got on.

Well, when his first wife got sick — she loved me, that woman did. And I was in to see her a great deal. And she used to call me one of her own boys. And he was awfully worried and used to write notes — well, you remember how I gave it out that he wrote that great note to Carranza sitting on the side of her bed. Well, that stretched it a little, but he did write notes there, and

I was with her and I lost one of the best friends I ever had.

Well, then he married Mrs. Galt. Now, remember that his first wife was my dearest friend, and she said she loved me like one of her own boys, and I felt pretty bad, and I talked a good deal to Grayson about how I felt. And one day, about a week after the wedding, I picked up the Philadelphia Public Ledger with a story of how Cary Grayson had made the match.

After that, some more things began to happen. When we'd all go away on official trips, my name would not be on the list. It happened a lot of times, and one day we were going down to New York, and the Governor said: "You're coming to New York with us?"

And I said: "I don't know."

And when he went out, Charley Shwen, his personal stenographer, said: "Now's your time to meet it and fight it out."

And I told him I would go. So I went, and when they got off the train and into the carriages — Colonel House met them — they all were loaded into the carriages and poor Tumulty was left on the platform. I grabbed a taxi and went uptown and called up pop, and said I was coming over to see him. And when I got there he says:

"The President has been calling for you, Joe."

And I say: "Has he?"

And he says: "Yes, he wants you to call him up at Colonel House's."

I say: "Does he?"

And pretty soon he called up again and says:

"What become of you, Joe?"

And I say: "I saw I wasn't expected, so I came over here."

And he says: "Well, you were and you're going to the game with us, aren't you?"

And I say: "I'm not, and what's more we may as well understand it right now. You can't treat me this way, and I can resign right now if you want me to."

And he laughed and said: "Well, anyway, you're coming to the game with us this afternoon?"

And I say: "No, I ain't."

And he says: "Why?"

And I say: "You know."

And he says: "Well, if you don't go, I don't."

And I say: "Of course, if you feel that way."

So I went, and that afternoon Colonel House comes around and says:

"You're going to the theater with us this evening, aren't you, Tumulty?"

And I say: "No, Colonel. I got a real friend who bought me some tickets and I'm going with him."

And the President says: "Here's a pretty spirited Irishman, House."

So I went with my friend.

Well, that's the way it went. Then the President got sick and no one saw him. Oh, I came in once in a while and saw him when he was in the White House, but not much. When he got out of bed, of course it was different. Well, it came on to the last day, and the third of March. He sent me a beautiful letter — there it is in that frame on the wall — nominating me to that job and a good one — ten thousand dollars a year or something like it. Well, that night along walks old Billy Wilson — the squarest member of his Cabinet — past my house with his hands behind him, a poor broken old man with his wife dead — and you remember that poem he wrote about her like "My Old Dutch" — it was when she was dying, and his money was all gone and he had no job. He was just a miner, and he and she were married when he was a miner, and I said to my wife: "Look at him! Why should we have this fine job? We're young, and I can make it all right. I'll go into law" — though you notice I didn't get any of those big retainers — not a one, not a crooked dollar ever came into my shop. And I took for a partner a boy who used to caddy for me out on the links. Well, for a week I had been interested in an old man out in Nebraska who had to go to jail for a federal offense. He had a crippled daughter — and they were the sweetest family I ever saw, and a son that just idolized him. And I thought it would be just like pop going to jail, and so I said:

"All right, I'll help you; only you must not have a lawyer."

And I tried to get the pardon, but could not, and I found one day after I'd failed they gave a friend of mine a fee of ten thousand dollars and I made him give it back — every cent of it, and show me the receipt before I would make one more try. Well, that last day — March fourth about an hour before the inauguration — I came into the office. He was sitting alone and he says:

"Well, Joe —"

And I said: "Well, Governor!"

And he says: "Well, Joe, you've served me faithfully through it all."

And I said: "Well, Governor, I'm glad to hear you say so."

And I went on: "I am a Roman Catholic and I wanted to make a record so that men would say, well, here's how Roman Catholics play square hands with the Presbyterians." [1]

And he touched my hand, and I said:

"Governor, my wife and I talked over the office that you've offered us and we can't take it."

And I told him about seeing old Billy Wilson pass the window, and says:

[1] In the conversation it was evident that Mr. Tumulty had pride in the way his church was proving the unfairness of the attacks against it by his own conduct, which certainly had been splendid.

"Now, Governor, for me won't you sign this commission for him?"

And he smiled and said: "All right, Joe, all right."

Then I said: "Just one act more, Governor; let the curtain go down on an act of mercy — the last act an act of mercy. And I know, some way, when you need mercy the last act will be remembered for you!"

And I had the recommendation for the old man's pardon all made out and handed it to him. He looked at it and shook his head.

"No, Tumulty, no!" he says. "No, that's too much like the Morse case. That case has been reviewed."

"But," I said, "it's an act of mercy, and your last act, Governor, and there is something in the balance of things."

And I told him about that old man waiting outside for me — just like papa — with his son and crippled daughter, an old man seventy years old, and his eyes filled up and he says:

"No, Joe, the country needs to see the law vindicated. The country needs the spectacle of a stable, just, and righteous government more than that old man needs a pardon or I need an act of mercy."

So he took the paper and wrote "Disapproved" across it in the strongest hand he ever had written in months, and so he went out!

Well, to get to the point about the Cox dinner: I'm going to show you the correspondence between us in which I begged for a hearing.[1] But it did no good. Nothing could get to him. Well, when I heard he was sick the last time, I went to the house and stood on the sidewalk and finally slipped in the door. I went to Grayson and said:

"It seems to me that ten years' faithful service have

[1] See Appendix C.

earned me the right to go in and look once into his eyes, or maybe just pat his forehead before he goes."

And Grayson says: "Yes, Joe, you're right and he will be glad to see you, but he's asleep now."

And he promised and promised over and over to call me if there was any real danger before the end. But the end came too quickly and when it came poor Joe was on the sidewalk with the rest.

And at the funeral — not a word. Finally, McAdoo comes to town, and on the last day about noon calls me on the 'phone, and says:

"I'm going to see that you're invited."

And pretty soon Mrs. Grayson calls up and says of course Mrs. Tumulty and I are expected to the house for the funeral. And we go, and they let us in, and we come out afterward, and they call out the names for the carriages and I listen, and all the other names of friends and statesmen are called out there before the reporters, and then, after the names of two doormen from Keith's Theater, at the very end of the list comes poor Tumulty! And I got in and followed the hearse. [1]

Woodrow Wilson died Sunday, February 3, 1924. The end came in his sleep. Only his brother, Joseph, and his daughter, Margaret, at his bedside connected him with the old life which he led before he left Princeton. The other watchers were out of the new life that he had found when he quit the schoolroom.

[1] This is not a stenographic report of Mr. Tumulty's remarks. It was written without notes an hour or so after the interview by the author and naturally is full of human errors. Probably some words have been ascribed to Mr. Tumulty which are not in his vocabulary, but the spirit of the conversation is accurately transcribed.

Upon the sidewalk before his house and upon the pavement was a throng of watchers, the humble folk of Washington, chiefly. As the hours of his last illness became days and nights, they knelt in prayer — the common, praying people of the land. There they knelt through the long winter days, a voiceless crowd. When the doctors left the house, the watchers in the street, knowing that the end had come, rose and went away. It was as he would have staged it — the end; without demonstration, without passion even in grief, with its drama repressed, its very significance only implied, not quite in focus, gray, blurred, Wilsonian!

They gave him a state funeral, yet as simple as they could make it in the "S" Street house. As he lay in his coffin, a copy of Bouguereau's Madonna, a favorite picture done by Ellen Axson in the old Princeton days, smiled down upon him across those golden years and through the battle storms that followed, a favorite picture that recalled a happy time. At the funeral were gathered scores of the great who had supported him — some who had fought him, and a few of those who had loved him through the years. But some were missing. Colonel House's invitation miscarried.

They took him to an Episcopal Cathedral, where he lies outside the fold of his father's faith; there in the tabernacle of a creed in which kings and powerful persons go to rest. He is not of the royal blood. So lying in the shadow of an alien covenant, he seems shy, remote, aloof — a Woodrow to the last, even in death!

Out in Madison Square Garden in New York, standing among the throngs that heard the services was a little man in a fur-lined coat and a soft hat, who heard the prayers and the funeral service and the preacher's words from afar. He was Colonel Edward M. House, for ten years the dead man's dear friend and most trusted servant. Some quirk of fate, even across the dark portals, held him, would not let him relent, this grandson of Ann Adams, who vainly beat her soul out on "the iron gates of death!"

CHAPTER XXIII

THE ASSESSMENT

WOODROW WILSON'S place in the history of the world will not be determined by his character. The relation between character and fame is not of first importance. Many good men live and die unknown. Bad men sometimes pass over into the immortal few. The quality of a man's mind brings him only academic fame. Many stupid men mount the steps of the hall of fame and live there on heights to which their brilliant contemporaries never attain. Only a man's contemporaries are influenced in their assessment of his worth by his character and the quality of his mind. If the man is a large figure in contemporary life and has lived decently and intelligently, and has done some notable contemporaneous work, men say: "Here goes a famous man."

The world of this third decade of the twentieth century, seeing in Woodrow Wilson a man whose motives were pure, whose mind was strong, and who built his life into an ideal which may be institutionalized as an international government, declares that his fame is safe. But alas, for predictions which are fathered by our desires and mothered by our hopes, fame does not come when a man's fellow citizens summon it to him. Whether or not Wilson will live as a world figure depends, not so much upon what work he has done as upon what the chance of time and circumstance will do with his work. He must live or die in world fame bound up in the League of Nations. If that stands, he may tower beside it as the Washington of a World Federation. If the League of Nations crumbles, if in the inscrutable ways of Providence some other method is devised by men to institutionalize their yearnings for peace, then Wilson will become one of the host of good men who spent their zeal striving for futile things. That he put into his endeavor heroic qualities of faith, noble qualities of persuasion, and the hard work, through vigils long of a body which he sacrificed to his ideal as surely as Cranmer gave his body to be burned, will avail nothing when Fame makes her award.

On the other hand, if his vision becomes reality, then all the petty faults which men saw and fumed about will fall away from him. His strength will survive; his moral courage will stand out. The fire of his words will not be quenched, and the sword of his faith will flame at the gates of a new order. This much we may know of Woodrow Wilson surely: If Fame does come to him through the conjunction of time and chance working upon the genius of the race to preserve the structure which he previsioned in his hour of trial, Fame will find a man here — a clean, wise, courageous man — ready-made for heroic stature. Little will crumble from him in that day. He will remain as we know him who worked with him. And the man we saw in our pride of him need suffer little change as his poor finite clay turns to memorial bronze.

THE END

APPENDIX

APPENDIX

A

THE WAR MESSAGE

Read by the President before a Joint Session of the Senate and the House of Representatives April 2, 1917

Gentlemen of the Congress: I have called the Congress into extraordinary session because there are serious, very serious, choices of policy to be made, and made immediately, which it was neither right nor constitutionally permissible that I should assume the responsibility of making.

On the 3d of February last I officially laid before you the extraordinary announcement of the Imperial German Government that on and after the first day of February it was its purpose to put aside all restraints of law or of humanity and use its submarines to sink every vessel that sought to approach either the ports of Great Britain and Ireland or the western coasts of Europe or any of the ports controlled by the enemies of Germany within the Mediterranean. That had seemed to be the object of the German submarine warfare earlier in the war, but since April of last year the Imperial Government had somewhat restrained the commanders of its undersea craft, in conformity with its promise, then given to us, that passenger boats should not be sunk and that due warning would be given to all other vessels which its submarines might seek to destroy, when no resistance was offered or escape attempted, and care taken that their crews were given at least a fair chance to save their lives in their open boats. The precautions taken were meager and haphazard enough, as was proved in distressing instance after instance in the progress of the cruel and unmanly business, but a certain degree of restraint was observed.

The new policy has swept every restriction aside. Vessels of every kind, whatever their flag, their character, their cargo, their destination, their errand, have been ruthlessly sent to the bottom without warning and without thought of help or mercy for those on board, the vessels of friendly neutrals along with those of belligerents. Even hospital ships and ships carrying relief to the sorely bereaved and stricken people of Belgium, though the latter were provided with safe conduct through the proscribed areas by the German Government itself and were distinguished by unmistakable marks of identity, have been sunk with the same reckless lack of compassion or of principle.

I was for a little while unable to believe that such things would in fact be done by any Government that had hitherto subscribed to humane practices of civilized nations. International law had its origin in the attempt to set up some law which would be respected and observed upon the seas, where no nation has right of dominion and where lay the free highways of the world. By painful stage after stage has that law been built up, with meager enough results, indeed, after all was accomplished that could be accomplished, but always with a clear view, at least, of what the heart and conscience of mankind demanded.

This minimum of right the German Government has swept aside, under the plea of retaliation and necessity and because it had no weapons which it could use at sea except these, which it is impossible to employ, as it is employing them, without throwing to the wind all scruples of humanity or of respect for the understandings that were supposed to underlie the intercourse of the world.

I am not now thinking of the loss of property involved, immense and serious as that is, but only of the wanton and wholesale destruction of the lives of noncombatants, men, women, and children, engaged in pursuits which have always, even in the darkest periods of modern history, been deemed innocent and legitimate. Property can be paid for; the lives of peaceful and innocent people cannot be.

The present German submarine warfare against commerce is a warfare against mankind. It is a war against all nations. American ships have been sunk, American lives taken, in ways which it has stirred us very deeply to learn of, but the ships and people of other neutral and friendly nations have been sunk and overwhelmed in the waters in the same way. There has been no discrimination. The challenge is to all mankind. Each nation must decide for itself how it will meet it. The choice we make for ourselves must be made with a moderation of counsel and a temperateness of judgment befitting our character and our motives as a nation. We must put excited feeling away. Our motive will not be revenge or the victorious assertion of the physical might of the Nation, but only the vindication of right, of human right, of which we are only a single champion.

When I addressed the Congress on the 26th of February last I thought that it would suffice to assert our neutral right with arms, our right to use the seas against unlawful interference, our right to keep our people safe against unlawful violence. But armed neutrality, it now appears, is impracticable. Because submarines are in effect outlaws, when used as the German submarines have been used against merchant shipping, it is impossible to defend ships against their attacks, as the law of nations has assumed that merchantmen would defend themselves against privateers or cruisers, visible craft giving chase upon the open sea. It is common prudence in such circumstances, grim necessity, indeed, to endeavor to destroy them before they have shown their own intention. They must be dealt with upon sight, if dealt with at all.

The German Government denies the right of neutrals to use arms at all within the areas of the sea which it has proscribed, even in the defense of rights which no modern publicist has ever before questioned their right to defend. The intimation is conveyed that the armed guards which we have placed on our merchant ships will be treated as beyond the pale of law and subject to be dealt with as pirates would be. Armed neutrality is ineffectual enough at best; in such circumstances and in the face of such pretensions it is worse than ineffectual; it is likely only to produce what it was meant to prevent; it is practically certain to draw us into the war without either the rights or the effectiveness of belligerents. There is one choice we cannot make, we are incapable of making: we will not choose the path of submission and suffer the most sacred rights of our Nation and our people to be ignored or violated. The wrongs against which we now array ourselves are not common wrongs; they cut to the very roots of human life.

With a profound sense of the solemn and even tragical character of the step I am taking and of the grave responsibilities which it involves, but in unhesitating obedience to what I deem my constitutional duty, I advise that the Congress declare the recent course of the Imperial German Government to be in fact nothing less than war against the Government and people of the United States; that it formally accept the status of belligerent which has thus been thrust upon it; and that it take immediate steps not only to put the country in a more thorough state of defense, but also to exert all its power and employ all its resources to bring the Government of the German Empire to terms and end the war.

What this will involve is clear. It will involve the utmost practicable coöperation in counsel and action with the Governments now at war with Germany, and, as incident to that, the extension to those Governments of the most liberal financial credits, in order that our resources may so far as possible be added to theirs.

It will involve the organization and mobilization of all the material resources of the country to supply the materials of war and serve the incidental needs of the nation in the most abundant and yet the most economical and efficient way possible.

It will involve the immediate full equipment of the navy in all respects, but particularly in supplying it with the best means of dealing with the enemy's submarines.

It will involve the immediate addition to the armed forces of the United States, already provided for by law in case of war, of at least five hundred thousand men who should, in my opinion, be chosen upon the principle of universal liability to service, and also the authorization of subsequent additional increments of equal force so soon as they may be needed and can be handled in training.

It will involve also, of course, the granting of adequate credits to the Government, sustained, I hope, so far as they can equitably be sustained by the present generation, by well-conceived taxation.

I say sustained so far as may be equitable by taxation, because it seems to me that it would be most unwise to base the credits, which will now be necessary, entirely on money borrowed. It is our duty, I most respectfully urge, to protect our people, so far as we may, against the very serious hardships and evils which would be likely to arise out of the inflation which would be produced by vast loans.

In carrying out the measures by which these things are to be accomplished, we should keep constantly in mind the wisdom of interfering as little as possible in our own preparation and in the equipment of our own military forces with the duty — for it will be a very practical duty — of supplying the nations already at war with Germany with the materials which they can obtain only from us or by our assistance. They are in the field and we should help them in every way to be effective there.

I shall take the liberty of suggesting, through the several executive departments of the Government, for the consideration of your committees, measures for the accomplishment of the several objects I have mentioned. I hope that it will be your pleasure to deal with them as having been framed after very careful thought by the branch of the Government upon whom the responsibility of conducting the war and safe-guarding the Nation will most directly fall.

While we do these things, these deeply momentous things, let us be very clear, and make very clear to all the world, what our motives and our objects are. My own thought has not been driven from its habitual and normal course by the unhappy events of the last two months, and I do not believe that the thought of the Nation has been altered or clouded by them. I have exactly the same things in mind now that I had in mind when I addressed the Senate on the 22d of January last; the same that I had in mind when I addressed the Congress on the 3d of February and on the 26th of February. Our object now, as then, is to vindicate the principles of peace and justice in the life of the world as against selfish and autocratic power, and to set up among the really free and self-governed peoples of the world such a concert of purpose and of action as will henceforth insure the observance of those principles.

Neutrality is no longer feasible or desirable where the peace of the world is involved and the freedom of its peoples, and the menace to that peace and freedom lies in the existence of autocratic Governments, backed by organized force which is controlled wholly by their will, not by the will of their people. We have seen the last of neutrality in such circumstances. We are at the beginning of an age in which it will be insisted that the same standards of conduct and of responsibility for wrong done shall be observed among nations and their Governments that are observed among the individual citizens of civilized States.

We have no quarrel with the German people. We have no feeling toward them but one of sympathy and friendship. It was not upon their impulse that their Government acted in entering this war. It was not with their previous knowledge or approval. It was a war determined upon as wars used to be determined upon in the old, unhappy days, when peoples were nowhere consulted by their rulers and wars were provoked and waged in the interest of dynasties or of little groups of ambitious men who were accustomed to use their fellowmen as pawns and tools.

Self-governed nations do not fill their neighbor States with spies or set the course of intrigue to bring about some critical posture of affairs which will give them an opportunity to strike and make conquest. Such designs can be successfully worked out only under cover and where no one has the right to ask questions. Cunningly contrived plans of deception or aggression, carried, it may be, from generation to generation, can be worked out and kept from the light only within the privacy of courts or behind the carefully guarded confidences of a narrow and privileged class. They are happily impossible where public opinion commands and insists upon full information concerning all the Nation's affairs.

A steadfast concert for peace can never be maintained except by a partnership of democratic nations. No autocratic Government could be trusted to keep faith within it or observe its covenants. It must be a league of honor, a partnership of opinion. Intrigue would eat its vitals away; the plottings of inner circles who could plan what they would and render account to no one would be a corruption seated at its very heart. Only free peoples can hold their purpose and their honor steady to a common end and prefer the interests of mankind to any narrow interest of their own.

Does not every American feel that assurance has been added to our hope for the future peace of the world by the wonderful and heartening things that have been happening within the last few weeks in Russia? Russia was known by those who knew it best to have been always in fact democratic at heart, in all the vital habits of her thought, in all the intimate relationships of her people that spoke their natural instinct, their habitual attitude toward life. The autocracy that crowned the summit of her political structure, long as it had stood and terrible as was the reality of its power, was not in fact Russian in origin, character, or purpose; and now it has been shaken off and the great, generous Russian people have been added, in all their native majesty and might, to the forces that are fighting for freedom in the world, for justice, and for peace. Here is a fit partner for a league of honor.

One of the things that has served to convince us that the Prussian autocracy was not and could never be our friend is that from the very outset of the present war it has filled our unsuspecting communities, and even our offices of government, with spies and set criminal intrigues everywhere afoot against our National unity of counsel, our peace within and without, our industries and our commerce. Indeed, it is now evident that its spies were here even before the war began; and it is unhappily not a matter of conjecture, but a fact proved in our courts of justice, that the intrigues, which have more than once come perilously near to disturbing the peace and dislocating the industries of the country, have been carried on at the instigation, with the support, and even under the personal direction of official agents of the Imperial Government, accredited to the Government of the United States.

Even in checking these things and trying to extirpate them we have sought to put the most generous interpretation possible upon them because we knew that their source lay, not in any hostile feeling or purpose of the German people toward us (who were, no doubt, as ignorant of them as we ourselves were), but only in the selfish designs of a Government that did what it pleased and told its people nothing. But they have played their part in serving to convince us at last that the Government entertains no real friendship for us, and means to act against our peace and security at its convenience. That it means to stir up enemies against us at our very doors the intercepted note to the German Minister at Mexico City is eloquent evidence.

We are accepting this challenge of hostile purpose because we know that in such a Government, following such methods, we can never have a friend; and that in the presence of its organized power, always lying in wait to accomplish we know not what purpose, can be no assured security for the democratic Governments of the world. We are now about to accept the gage of battle with this natural foe to liberty and shall, if necessary, spend the whole force of the nation to check and nullify its pretensions and its power. We are glad, now that we see the facts with no veil of false pretense about them, to fight thus for the ultimate peace of the world and for the liberation of its peoples, the German people included; for the rights of nations, great and small, and the privilege of men everywhere to choose their way of life and of obedience. The world must be made safe for democracy. Its peace must be planted upon the tested foundations of political liberty.

We have no selfish ends to serve. We desire no conquest, no dominion. We seek no indemnities for ourselves, no material compensation for the sacrifices we shall freely make. We are but one of the champions of the rights of mankind. We shall be satisfied when those rights have been made as secure as the faith and the freedom of nations can make them.

Just because we fight without rancor and without selfish object, seeking nothing for ourselves but what we shall wish to share with all free peoples, we shall, I feel confident, conduct our operations as belligerents without passion and ourselves observe with proud punctilio the principles of right and of fair play we profess to be fighting for.

I have said nothing of the Governments allied with the Imperial Government of Germany because they have not made war upon us or challenged us to defend our right and our honor. The Austro-Hungarian Government has, indeed, avowed its unqualified endorsement and acceptance of the reckless and lawless submarine warfare, adopted now without disguise by the Imperial German Government, and it has therefore not been possible for this Government to receive Count Tarnowski, the Ambassador recently accredited to this Government by the Imperial and Royal Government of Austria-Hungary; but that Government has not actually engaged in warfare against citizens of the United States on the seas, and I take the liberty, for the present at least, of postponing a discussion of our relations with the authorities at Vienna. We enter this war only where we are clearly forced into it because there are no other means of defending our right.

It will be all the easier for us to conduct ourselves as belligerents in a high spirit of right and fairness because we act without animus, not with enmity toward a people or with the desire to bring any injury or disadvantage upon them, but only an armed opposition to an irresponsible Government which has thrown aside all considerations of humanity and of right and is running amuck.

We are, let me say again, the sincere friends of the German people, and shall desire nothing so much as the early reestablishment of intimate relations of mutual advantage between us, however hard it may be for them for the time being to believe that this is spoken from our hearts. We have borne with their present Government through all these bitter months because of that friendship, exercising a patience and forbearance which would otherwise have been impossible.

We shall happily still have an opportunity to prove that friendship in our daily attitude and actions toward the millions of men and women of German birth and native sympathy who live among us and share our life, and we shall be proud to prove it toward all who are in fact loyal to their neighbors and to the Government in the hour of test. They are most of them as true and loyal Americans as if they had never known any other fealty or allegiance. They will be prompt to stand with us in rebuking and restraining the few who may be of a different mind and purpose. If there should be disloyalty, it will be dealt with with a firm hand of stern repression; but, if it lifts its head at all, it will lift it only here and there and without countenance except from a lawless and malignant few.

It is a distressing and oppressive duty, gentlemen of the Congress, which I have performed in thus addressing you. There are, it may be, many months of fiery trial and sacrifice ahead of us. It is a fearful thing to lead this great, peaceful people into war, into the most terrible and disastrous of all wars, civilization itself seeming to be in the balance.

But the right is more precious than peace, and we shall fight for the things which we have always carried nearest our hearts — for democracy, for the right of those who submit to authority to have a voice in their own Governments, for the rights and liberties of small nations, for a universal dominion of right by such a concert of free peoples as shall bring peace and safety to all nations and make the world itself at last free.

To such a task we can dedicate our lives and our fortunes, everything that we are and everything that we have, with the pride of those who know that the day has come when America is privileged to spend her blood and her might for the principles that gave her birth and happiness and the peace which she has treasured.

God helping her, she can do no other.

B

THE FOURTEEN POINTS[1]

THE programme of the world's peace, therefore, is our programme; and that programme, the only possible programme, as we see it, is this:

1. Open covenants of peace, openly arrived at, after which there shall be no private international understandings of any kind, but diplomacy shall proceed always frankly and in the public view.

2. Absolute freedom of navigation upon the seas, outside territorial waters, alike in peace and in war, except as the seas may be closed in whole or in part by international action for the enforcement of international covenants.

3. The removal, so far as possible, of all economic barriers and the establishment of an equality of trade conditions among all the nations consenting to the peace and associating themselves for its maintenance.

4. Adequate guarantees given and taken that national armaments will be reduced to the lowest point consistent with domestic safety.

5. A free, open-minded, and absolutely impartial adjustment of all colonial claims, based upon a strict observance of the principle that in determining all such questions of sovereignty the interests of the populations concerned must have equal weight with the equitable claims of the government whose title is to be determined.

6. The evacuation of all Russian territory and such a settlement of all questions affecting Russia as will secure the best and freest coöperation of the other nations of the world in obtaining for her an unhampered and unembarrassed opportunity for the independent determination of her own political development and national policy and assure her of a sincere

[1] From the address of President Wilson delivered at a Joint Session of Congress on January 8, 1918.

welcome into the society of free nations under institutions of her own choosing; and, more than a welcome, assistance also of every kind that she may need and may herself desire. The treatment accorded Russia by her sister nations in the months to come will be the acid test of their good-will, of their comprehension of her needs as distinguished from their own interests, and of their intelligent and unselfish sympathy.

7. Belgium, the whole world will agree, must be evacuated and restored, without any attempt to limit the sovereignty which she enjoys in common with all other free nations. No other single act will serve as this will serve to restore confidence among the nations in the laws which they have themselves set and determined for the government of their relations with one another. Without this healing act the whole structure and validity of international law is forever impaired.

8. All French territory should be freed and the invaded portions restored, and the wrong done to France by Prussia in 1871 in the matter of Alsace-Lorraine, which has unsettled the peace of the world for nearly fifty years, should be righted, in order that peace may once more be made secure in the interest of all.

9. A readjustment of the frontiers of Italy should be effected along clearly recognizable lines of nationality.

10. The peoples of Austria-Hungary, whose place among the nations we wish to see safeguarded and assured, should be accorded the freest opportunity of autonomous development.

11. Rumania, Serbia, and Montenegro should be evacuated; occupied territories restored; Serbia accorded free and secure access to the Sea; and the relations of the several Balkan States to one another determined by friendly counsel along historically established lines of allegiance and nationality; and international guarantees of the political and economic independence and territorial integrity of the several Balkan States should be entered into.

12. The Turkish portions of the present Ottoman Empire should be assured a secure sovereignty, but the other nationalities which are now under Turkish rule should be assured an undoubted security of life and an absolutely unmolested opportunity of autonomous development, and the Dardanelles

should be permanently opened as a free passage to the ships and commerce of all nations under international guarantees.

13. An independent Polish State should be erected which should include the territories inhabited by indisputably Polish populations, which should be assured a free and secure access to the sea, and whose political and economic independence and territorial integrity should be guaranteed by international covenant.

14. A general association of nations must be formed under specific covenants for the purpose of affording mutual guarantees of political independence and territorial integrity to great and small states alike.

C

CORRESPONDENCE ON THE COX DINNER EPISODE

WASHINGTON, D.C.,
11 *April*, 1924

MY DEAR MR. WHITE:

I have been giving serious consideration to the request contained in your letter of March fifteenth, that I let you have a copy of the correspondence between former-President Wilson and myself with reference to the Cox episode. I have decided to let you have it to make whatever use of it you may see fit.

Sincerely yours

J. P. TUMULTY

MR. WILLIAM ALLEN WHITE
EMPORIA, KANSAS

The first letter from Mr. Wilson was dated April 10, 1922, the Monday after the banquet in question. In this letter the President indicated that he was pained to see in the press, in the reports of the Democratic dinner, a statement that a telegram was read alleged to be from the ex-President. He suggested that, so long as Tumulty was present, it was possible that Tumulty might know how the report of the message got into the proceedings. He suggested that he was going to probe the matter and, after asking Tumulty's help, closed with a hasty but clearly affectionate greeting.

To the letter Tumulty replied frankly. But before writing he issued a public statement to the press entirely absolving the President from responsibility for the message. The statement said specifically:

> The message read at the banquet came merely in a casual conversation with me at Mr. Wilson's home on Friday, last, when he remarked

that he would support any candidate who stood for justice for all. There was nothing unusual in this, and it was not significant in any way from a political standpoint. He sent no telegram. He simply gave a casual message to me in a casual manner. It had nothing to do with any individual or any particular political situation.

Tumulty's letter to Mr. Wilson follows:

WASHINGTON, D.C.,
12 *April*, 1922

.. I am very sorry, indeed, my dear Governor, that there has been any misunderstanding as a result of the message read at the banquet. In the newspaper dispatches, containing accounts of the dinner, it was erroneously stated that you had sent a telegram, and unwarranted significance was unfortunately given to it by reason of the presence at the banquet of Governor Cox of Ohio. There was no telegram read at the banquet purporting to come from you. I accept full responsibility for the message of greeting to the Democrats assembled — a message which was handed by me to Mr. Rush and which was read to those in attendance by Mrs. Montgomery Hare.

On Friday, last, when I visited you, after discussing the matter which brought me to your home, I expressed a desire to have you send a telegram to the President of the National Democratic Club. You replied that you could not see your way clear to do so, saying that it was your desire to maintain a policy of absolute silence. After discussing other matters, we again came to the subject of the banquet and my trip to New York to attend it, a fact that I apprised you of. I told you with what warmth any message from you, no matter how inconsequential or insignificant, would be greeted by your admirers there. As I stood up to go, you took hold of my arm and in substance said what was contained in the message read by Mrs. Hare. It is only fair to you to say that there was no express direction on your part that I should convey any message, but I think I was justified by every fair implication, from what you said to me, in conveying a word of greeting to the Democrats of New York. Of course, your remarks were casual. . . .

There was nothing significant in the message which you addressed, but unfortunately the newspapers "played it up," and placed what, in my opinion, was an unwarranted interpretation upon it.

No one regrets this more deeply than do I, and that any act of mine should cause you the least uneasiness is of the deepest concern to me. While I am responsible for the delivery of this message, I think you will hold me blameless for the unjust interpretations put upon it.

Cordially and sincerely yours

JOSEPH P. TUMULTY

Apparently this did not satisfy Mr. Wilson, for Mr. Tumulty sends him another letter the next day, which reads:

WASHINGTON, D.C.,
13 *April*, 1922

. . . My memory is very clear on every detail of our discussion of Friday last. I recall, for instance, that we discussed the present plight of America by reason of our failure to enter the League of Nations, and when you asked me how I thought America felt about it, I said that there was only one thing that symbolized the grief of America and that was the statue of "Grief," by Saint-Gaudens, in Rock Creek Cemetery. You took issue with me on this, and, pointing to a statue on the mantelpiece of your home, said that you would rather believe that that statue typified the real feelings of America. It was the statue of a beautiful young girl holding a child by the hand; pointing to it, you said, "That, Tumulty, represents to me the feeling of America — a picture of America leading the way of salvation for the small nations of the world."

We then turned to a discussion of the domestic problems of America, and I recall that you used an unusual phrase in describing your feelings. You spoke of America having reached the limit of what you characterized as a "quantitative democracy," and that the business of the statesmen of the future was to discover processes to make the democracies throughout the world "qualitative." The sentence in the greeting to the National Democratic Club was not original with me. When I got into my car, immediately after leaving your home, I took an envelope out of my pocket and jotted down in shorthand the message you gave me. When I arrived at my office, a few minutes later, I called my secretary and dictated this message which, as I recall it, was as follows:

> Former President Wilson through a friend conveyed a word of greeting to the Democrats assembled at the National Democratic Club's banquet in New York in the following words, "Former President Wilson says that he will support any man who will stand for the salvation of America, and the salvation of America is justice to all classes."

So certain was I that you intended to have this message conveyed through me, and being apprised of the fact that I was to be in attendance at the banquet, it was my intention to ask the privilege of the toastmaster personally to present it. Upon considering the matter further, I drew away from this resolve, being convinced that some unkind critics of mine would say that "Tumulty was seeking to put himself forward as Woodrow Wilson's spokesman." It was then that I resolved to deliver the message to Mr. Rush. There was nothing mysterious about the way the message was handed to Mr. Rush. I frankly told him of my talk with you and of your desire that the words of greeting be delivered. There was nothing concealed or secretive about my conduct in any way. The only hypothesis upon which I could be condemned in this matter is the one that I was seeking to fabricate a message at your expense for the purpose of attaching your name to the proceedings of the banquet and to any presidential boom that might be discussed there. This, of course, is tantamount to saying that I could be guilty of an act of base treachery to you. I think you will at least give me credit for having more political sense than to propose so foolish a scheme as this of seeking at this early day, two years before a national convention, to attach your name to any move that had as its objective the advancement of the interests of a particular man. . . .

The message could not be construed, under any of the circumstances of its handling at the banquet, by any sane, sensible person as an endorsement of anybody. In the first place, it was read two hours before Governor Cox took the floor and was read in connection with telegrams from Mr. McAdoo and Senator Underwood. . . .

When I first heard of your distress at the alleged telegram, I sought an opportunity personally and frankly to lay the facts before you so that you might have from my own lips a description of the whole affair. I felt certain, from the tone of your letter to me, where you stated that you wished the incident probed to the bottom, that this meant that you would appreciate it if you could be put in possession of all the facts. Feeling that this was your desire, I sought an interview with you, but, for some reason or other, you did not feel free to grant it to me. As I have told you, I am very sorry about this whole incident. Certainly, it was no desire of mine to compromise your prestige in the least. I am sure that Governor Cox and his friends deprecate the incident as much as do I. . . .

Since the earliest days of my association with you, I have had but one thought, but one ambition, and that was to serve you and the great purposes which I know lie close to your heart. Since you left office and power, that loyalty, affection, and admiration, which I trust I gave you in unstinted fashion, have in no way been changed. No matter what the temptation may be, no matter how keenly I may feel the injustice of any public action you make take in this matter, you may rest assured that I will never engage in a controversy with you. No slight bruise nor public rebuke from you can in any way lessen my devotion to and affection for you. You will find me as a mere private in the ranks, deferring to your unselfish leadership and defending your policies at every turn of the long road which lies ahead of us. I think you know me well enough to believe that if you decide that this message of greeting, which I delivered, has embarrassed you in any way and that I must be rebuked, I shall not complain. You will find, my dear Governor, that I will not wince under the blow nor shall I grow in the least faint-hearted or dispirited.

Cordially and sincerely yours
JOSEPH P. TUMULTY

Then came the blow from Mr. Wilson, who wrote the *New York Times* as follows:

2340 S STREET, N.W.
WOODROW WILSON

WASHINGTON, D.C.
12th April, 1922

MY DEAR SIR:

I notice in the issue of the Times this morning an article headed

"DOUBT IS CAST ON WILSON 'MESSAGE'
TO THE COX DINNER."

I write to say there need be no doubt about the matter. I did not send any message whatever to that dinner nor authorize any one to convey a message.

I hope that you will be kind enough to publish this letter.

Very truly yours
WOODROW WILSON

To the Editor of
The New York Times
New York City

Mr. Tumulty's reply to the Wilson note follows:

13 *April*, 1922

If Mr. Wilson says the message was unauthorized, then I can only say I deeply regret the misunderstanding which has arisen between us. I certainly would not have given the message if I had not believed it to be authorized.

Mr. Tumulty's letter to the ex-President was courteously answered by Mrs. Wilson and Mr. Tumulty's letter to Mrs. Wilson, which follows, is most revealing:

WASHINGTON, D.C.
14 *April*, 1922

MY DEAR MRS. WILSON:

Thank you for your kind note of this morning. When one finds himself out in the cold of No Man's Land, a kind word from a real, devoted friend, like you, goes a long way to help.

It is queer how adversity brings sweet returns. Every one I met to-day, even the poor waiters at the hotel, seemed to be more kind and generous than ever to me. You see, I was brought up in a great school and have lived under the inspiration of a great leader who taught me to treat triumph and disaster as great impostors. Another thing, my dear Mrs. Wilson, I had a wonderful father and mother whose natures prepared me against the storm I am now going through. I recall a conversation with my father years ago when it appeared that I was not to be selected by the Governor as his secretary. He advised me then that in case I failed to realize what to me was a great ambition that I must show no soreness or resentment, but that I must be big and generous about it. For, he said, "Woodrow Wilson will mean much to the world and we must support him. We are as poor atoms in the great calculation." And that advice of my dear father will hold me steady now. I am, of course, hurt, but not sore. My enemies in the months to come will find that we poor Irish can smile through our tears.

The colloquy between poor Julie and Louise, in the play of "Liliom," gives a perfect picture of my feelings in this vital matter. It is as follows:

Louise: Is it possible for some one to hit you hard like that — real loud and hard — and not hurt you at all?

Julie: It is possible, dear, that some one whom you love may beat you and beat you and beat you — and not hurt you at all.

That is the way I feel toward the Governor. I want you to feel, you who have been so wonderful and generous to me in all things, that I shall always be "around the corner" when you or yours need me.

I expect no reply to this letter. I shall understand.

Cordially and sincerely yours

JOSEPH P. TUMULTY

Thus the incident closed.

D

LETTER FROM A. S. BURLESON TO NEWTON D. BAKER

Burleson Place
Austin, Texas
Nov. 29, 1924

My Dear Baker:

I was much pleased to have a line from you. . . .

During the latter part of September, 1918, it became necessary for me to visit Texas in connection with personal business matters. I informed the President of my purpose to go, and shortly thereafter he sent for me to discuss the political situation. I told him that in my opinion we were assured of success in the congressional contests then pending; that the Republicans were without an issue; the war was being prosecuted with success; every recurring action was resulting in Allied victories, and that all indications pointed to a sweeping defeat of the opposition party.

At that time many requests were in hand from candidates for Congress, for letters from the President which would be helpful in their races. These requests were so numerous that I advised the President against writing the letters, suggesting that he make one speech, preferably in the Middle West. He was loath to make the speech, as he was pressed with many matters of grave importance and did not want to give the time it would require. After considerable discussion, he finally agreed that it was the expedient thing to do — to take the time and make the speech. It was then agreed between us that the speech should be made, and Indianapolis was selected as the place for its delivery.

Also, it was understood that in this speech the President should commend, unreservedly, those Congressmen who had given him whole-hearted support, and express an earnest hope that their constituents would give them approval at the election. There were certain Congressmen who had constantly attempted obstruction tactics, and whereas they had accomplished little, their petty, nagging efforts had been quite annoying. It was further understood that in his speech the President should mention this fact and that he would name four Senators — two Democrats and two Republicans — and, in this connection, appeal to the voters to give him a Congress that would hold up his hands in the grave and responsible duties then confronting him as America's President. At the time I left for Texas all this was thoroughly understood and agreed upon as the President's policy toward the pending political contest.

I was absent eight or ten days. I returned to Washington on Cabinet day and reached the Cabinet room early. A few minutes later the President entered, and, after greeting me and making a few inquiries about my trip, started into his office. At the door he turned and said: 'Burleson, I have written a letter which I have requested Tumulty to show you. Read it and later I will discuss its contents with you.'

He did not mention the subject-matter of the letter, and of course I was in total ignorance as to its contents. A moment later the President's secretary entered the room and handed me the letter, remarking that the President had directed that it be shown to me. I commenced reading it, and before I had finished I said: 'This letter will not do. It will be charged that the President is reflecting upon the loyalty of Republicans in the prosecution of the war.'

The President's secretary replied: 'That very point was discussed during the preparation of the letter, but it was decided that in its present form the letter would not be misunderstood.'

I replied: 'I agree that no such construction should properly be given it; but I fear that it will not only be misconstrued, but that its meaning will be misrepresented if not distorted. It must be changed.'

I was then informed that my protest had come too late. The letter had already been given to the press.

When I asked what had brought about the change in the President's plan to deliver the speech at Indianapolis, I was told that he had decided he could not find time for the speech;

that the congressional chairman, Scott Ferris, and the chairman of the National Committee, Vance McCormick, had advised the letter and were consulted as to its contents.

That afternoon or the next morning, I forget which, the letter was published. Its publication was followed by screeches of denunciation in the Republican press (based largely on distortions of its contents), coming principally from an ex-President and the senior Senator from Massachusetts.

Many papers absolved the President of responsibility for the letter, and charged that I, as his 'political adviser,' had induced him to issue it.

That letter gave the Republicans an issue — something they had formerly lacked and were in need of — and you know how easy it is to mislead the voters when a partisan press resorts to deceitful propaganda. They accomplished their purpose and the election was lost.

During the remainder of the campaign I was lambasted as the person responsible for the letter. I could say nothing. To have denied responsibility by stating the facts would have given the impression not only that the letter was a mistake, but that I was willing to run from under my chief.

I did believe that within a reasonable time after the election one, at least, of the three men who had to do with that letter would make known the truth concerning it, but in this I was mistaken.

Charley Michelson, of the New York *World*, knew the facts and once said to me that he would state them at some opportune time, but I suppose he was not permitted to do so, as perhaps only the most liberal of the newspapers and magazines have entirely forgiven me for the $20,000,000 additional postage imposed upon them during my administration of postal affairs.

I have always been indifferent as to what the newspapers and magazines say about me, but I confess that sometimes I resent the injustice of charging me with the responsibility of this letter, especially when one English publication went so far as to say that upon me 'more than upon any other man rested responsibility for the defeat of the League of Nations,' as my bad advice to the President in urging this letter had resulted in the loss of the control of the Senate in the 1918 election. However, all this is a last year's bird's nest, and I apologize for imposing these details upon you.

I have heard from many who were present at the New York Convention most generous praise of your speech on the League plank. Our friend Gregory said it was the notable speech made during the convention.

With assurances of regard and esteem for yourself and Mrs. Baker, in which Mrs. Burleson joins, I am

Faithfully yours

A. S. Burleson

INDEX

Throughout the Index, W. stands for Woodrow Wilson.